Indigenous Knowledges, Development and Education

TRANSGRESSIONS: CULTURAL STUDIES AND EDUCATION

Series Editors
   Shirley Steinberg, *McGill University, Canada*
   Joe Kincheloe, *McGill University, Canada*

Editorial Board
   Heinz-Hermann Kruger, *Halle University, Germany*
   Norman Denzin, *University of Illinois, Champaign-Urbana, USA*
   Rhonda Hammer, *University of California Los Angeles, USA*
   Christine Quail, *SUNY, Oneonta*
   Ki Wan Sung, *Kyung Hee University, Seoul, Korea*

Scope
Cultural studies provides an analytical toolbox for both making sense of educational practice and extending the insights of educational professionals into their labors. In this context *Transgressions: Cultural Studies and Education* provides a collection of books in the domain that specify this assertion. Crafted for an audience of teachers, teacher educators, scholars and students of cultural studies and others interested in cultural studies and pedagogy, the series documents both the possibilities of and the controversies surrounding the intersection of cultural studies and education. The editors and the authors of this series do not assume that the interaction of cultural studies and education devalues other types of knowledge and analytical forms. Rather the intersection of these knowledge disciplines offers a rejuvenating, optimistic, and positive perspective on education and educational institutions. Some might describe its contribution as democratic, emancipatory, and transformative. The editors and authors maintain that cultural studies helps free educators from sterile, monolithic analyses that have for too long undermined efforts to think of educational practices by providing other words, new languages, and fresh metaphors. Operating in an interdisciplinary cosmos, Transgressions: Cultural Studies and Education is dedicated to exploring the ways cultural studies enhances the study and practice of education. With this in mind the series focuses in a non-exclusive way on popular culture as well as other dimensions of cultural studies including social theory, social justice and positionality, cultural dimensions of technological innovation, new media and media literacy, new forms of oppression emerging in an electronic hyperreality, and postcolonial global concerns. With these concerns in mind cultural studies scholars often argue that the realm of popular culture is the most powerful educational force in contemporary culture. Indeed, in the twenty-first century this pedagogical dynamic is sweeping through the entire world. Educators, they believe, must understand these emerging realities in order to gain an important voice in the pedagogical conversation.

   Without an understanding of cultural pedagogy's (education that takes place outside of formal schooling) role in the shaping of individual identity–youth identity in particular–the role educators play in the lives of their students will continue to fade. Why do so many of our students feel that life is incomprehensible and devoid of meaning? What does it mean, teachers wonder, when young people are unable to describe their moods, their affective affiliation to the society around them. Meanings provided young people by mainstream institutions often do little to help them deal with their affective complexity, their difficulty negotiating the rift between meaning and affect. School knowledge and educational expectations seem as anachronistic as a ditto machine, not that learning ways of rational thought and making sense of the world are unimportant.

   But school knowledge and educational expectations often have little to offer students about making sense of the way they feel, the way their affective lives are shaped. In no way do we argue that analysis of the production of youth in an electronic mediated world demands some "touchy-feely" educational superficiality. What is needed in this context is a rigorous analysis of the interrelationship between pedagogy, popular culture, meaning making, and youth subjectivity. In an era marked by youth depression, violence, and suicide such insights become extremely important, even life saving. Pessimism about the future is the common sense of many contemporary youth with its concomitant feeling that no one can make a difference.

   If affective production can be shaped to reflect these perspectives, then it can be reshaped to lay the groundwork for optimism, passionate commitment, and transformative educational and political activity. In these ways cultural studies adds a dimension to the work of education unfilled by any other sub-discipline. This is what Transgressions: Cultural Studies and Education seeks to produce—literature on these issues that makes a difference. It seeks to publish studies that help those who work with young people, those individuals involved in the disciplines that study children and youth, and young people themselves improve their lives in these bizarre times.

Indigenous Knowledges, Development and Education

Jonathan Langdon
McGill University

SENSE PUBLISHERS
ROTTERDAM / TAIPEI

A C.I.P. record for this book is available from the Library of Congress.

ISBN 978-90-8790-697-9 (paperback)
ISBN 978-90-8790-698-6 (hardback)
ISBN 978-90-8790-699-3 (e-book)

Published by: Sense Publishers,
P.O. Box 21858, 3001 AW
Rotterdam, The Netherlands
http://www.sensepublishers.com

Printed on acid-free paper

All Rights Reserved © 2009 Sense Publishers

No part of this work may be reproduced, stored in a retrieval system, or transmitted in any form or by any means, electronic, mechanical, photocopying, microfilming, recording or otherwise, without written permission from the Publisher, with the exception of any material supplied specifically for the purpose of being entered and executed on a computer system, for exclusive use by the purchaser of the work.

TABLE OF CONTENTS

Chapter 1   Indigenous Knowledges, Development and Education:
An Introduction 1
Jonathan Langdon

Chapter 2   The Indigenous as a Site of Decolonizing Knowledge for
Conventional Development and The Link with Education:
The African Case 15
George J. Sefa Dei & Marlon Simmons

Chapter 3   Reframing Development Studies: Towards an IDS Teaching
Praxis Informed by Indigenous Knowledges 37
Jonathan Langdon

Chapter 4   Indigenous Knowledges, Sustainable Development
and the Environment: Implications for Research, Education and
Capacity Building 57
Blane Harvey

Chapter 5   Indigenous Research and Decolonizing
Methodologies: Possibilities & Opportunities 73
Christine Stocek & Rodney Mark

Chapter 6   Exploring Indigenous Ways of Knowing, Being, and Doing in
Developing A Cross-Cultural Science Curriculum 97
Janine Metallic

Chapter 7   Getting into Med School or Becoming a Healer?
Western Medical Education and Indigenous Knowledges 109
Mela Sarkar

Chapter 8   Building Bridges from Broken Bones: Traditional Bonesetters and
Health Choices in Northern Ghana 135
Coleman Agyeyomah & Jonathan Langdon

List of Contributors 149

JONATHAN LANGDON

1. INDIGENOUS KNOWLEDGES, DEVELOPMENT AND EDUCATION

An Introduction

OPENING THOUGHTS

It is important when introducing a book that aims to bring different epistemic world views into dialogue with one another that there is a clear sense of who is behind the book, and where they are coming from. This is especially true when we are speaking of Indigenous knowledges, as over 400 years of colonialism and neo-colonialism have seen these knowledges alternatively appropriated and discredited, and the peoples who have produced and refined these knowledges over centuries alternatively enslaved, enclosed, infantilized and exterminated. This is a legacy of violence that requires a degree of respect and transparency from those who work with and learn from these knowledges if the legacy is to be confronted in our contemporary time. With this need in mind, it is therefore critical for me, as the editor of this collection, to speak of its inspiration.

Firstly, this book is directly inspired by ongoing work in Ghana of my colleague Coleman Agyeyomah and I[1] with Chief Isshaku Gumrana Mahamadu, the bonesetter of Loagri; his work with those who come to him for help, with broken bones of every type, has been the single biggest revelation to me of what a different epistemic world view means. He does not even see the need for a term like patient, let alone think of those who seek his help as merely a set of symptoms and ailments needing a cure. Rather than this prescriptive view, Chief Isshaku sees a person who comes to him as a whole being, which includes his/her history and future and his/her set of relations. This all-encompassing mindset is clearly revealed in the help he has asked for over the years: where governments and aid agencies are interested in building clinics, Chief Isshaku has used any support-funds that have emerged to build housing for the families of those who seek his help, so that they may be close by while their family member recovers – thereby allaying their worries while also contributing directly to the healing of their relative. As a mark of respect for the inspiration Isshaku's knowledge and approach to life has generated, the editor's royalties from this book are going to contribute to his efforts to expand these family abodes in Loagri – the community pictured on the cover of this collection.

The second inspiration behind this book is derived from the authors who have given life to the aim of the book: to bring Indigenous knowledges into dialogue with the fields of development studies and education. This aim was taken on as a project by the contributors to this book, as we first presented our ideas for the book at a conference in 2006 and then built our chapters from the collaborative and open dialogue that informed this conference space.² Throughout this process, the philosophy of the project has been one of autonomy for contributors; this autonomy gave room for the meaning and interpretation of Indigenous knowledges, education and development to be individually defined by authors, yet to contribute these individual definitions to a larger collective conversation about these terms and what they represent. For readers of this collection, it is hoped that this autonomy on the one hand and spirit of collaboration on the other leads to a multiplicity of definitions and nuanced meanings that is indicative of the open dialogue that informed our coming together to create this book. The dual nature of this coming together is in keeping with the relationships all of the contributors have with Indigenous knowledges and peoples. For each of us has a story like the one above, where the work we have been engaged in is embedded in a relationship with a particular Indigenous community – be it our own or the ones we have come to identify with; and each of us knows that these relationships are based both in collaboration and in autonomy for all those involved. The rights of communities to have autonomous ownership over their knowledges is critical, even as collaborative processes help to share their stories and knowledges in other communities, such as education and development communities. Likewise, we must all be given the room to explain our understanding of terms such as development and education if collaborative dialogue is to begin. This notion of ongoing dialogue and collaboration, taken from Mahia Maurial's (1999) work (discussed further in the Agyeyomah & Langdon chapter that concludes this collection), is the root-system that led to the growth of this book, and the community-contributor relationships are what made working on this book inspirational. Although these stories are not necessarily overtly mentioned in each chapter, authors have added some details about them in the list of contributors section below.

Thus in this introduction, I have aimed to lay out trends in ways in which each of the three key terms is individually used by contributors, and the dialogue between these uses. As is expanded upon below, development studies and education both have a long and chequered history with Indigenous knowledges and Indigenous peoples, yet the two fields and their sets of relations with Indigenous knowledges, as well as the ways in which they speak to each other through these sets of relations, has yet to be explored in the multiplicity of ways contained in this collection. In this sense, the introduction here provides brief starting points for the dialogue that continues throughout the book. It first looks at the parameters in which all of us who contributed to this book discussed the notion of Indigenous knowledges. It then situates this discussion in the convergence of the three themes amongst the various contributions, pausing briefly in this larger discussion to connect the chapters here to ongoing debates in the field of education and of development studies. Throughout the introduction there is a conscious attempt to refrain from providing set-in-stone definitions for the three key terms, but there is also an attempt to provide some background of the debates around these terms so that the reader can better situate the contributions of this collection in these ongoing dialogues and debates.

INDIGENOUS KNOWLEDGES

To speak of Indigenous knowledges is a complex undertaking for any author or editor. Not only are there a wide number of ways to interpret what is meant by Indigenous knowledges, but the term 'Indigenous' itself carries many layers of meaning. Rather than give a definitive interpretation of what is meant by Indigenous knowledge here, I want instead to briefly outline the broad parameters in which the authors in this collection are using this term, since there is some range in their usages. As mentioned briefly above, one of the fundamental organizing ideas of this collection is the autonomy of the authors to interpret the three themes of Indigenous knowledges, development and education from their experience, understanding and perspective. These are all terms with room for different meanings. Yet, the autonomy has not led to a set of definitions that do not speak to one another; instead, what follows is a synergistic set of interpretations that speak inter-textually to a similar set of meanings. Here, I will elaborate on the broad outlines of this synergistic inter-textuality in reference to Indigenous knowledges.

One key point of departure for this collection, agreed on at the outset by all authors, was a move to pluralize the notion of Indigenous knowledge. This decision was a direct result of feedback from participants in the conference presentation where the book project was introduced. For myself as the editor of the collection, and for the authors included, this pluralization represents an important point of departure for our work here for two key reasons: first, by saying Indigenous knowledges, we are acknowledging the depth, breadth and multiplicity of knowledges developed over thousands of years by Indigenous peoples the world over; second, we are muddying the waters of potential dichotomization, where Indigenous knowledge is set up as some "other" against which the drama of Western thought has emerged, or where Indigenousness is boiled down into some single set of characteristics universally determined through the gaze of Western colonization. This differentiation is important, even as the collection takes stock of those who have defined and used the term Indigenous knowledge previously. Out of these definitions, three key characteristics have emerged as being crucial to the chapters that follow.

Firstly, following Dei, Hall and Rosenburg (2000), as well as Semali and Kincheloe (1999), Indigenous knowledges are seen to be linked to the long-term everyday occupancy, knowledge production and experience of living in a particular location. Embedded in this conceptualization, and this is something many of this collection's authors echo, is a groundedness of knowledge – a resistance to and a discomfort with notions of the universal. This groundedness is also the starting point of Walter Mignolo's (2000) concept of "local histories." For Mignolo, all histories are local histories, yet some, such as Western scientific thought, have global designs – a desire to universalize their world view and impose it upon other local histories. This process of imposition, and the subsequent resulting effect on the subjugated local history, is what Mignolo has termed the "colonial difference". Mignolo's framework introduces the other two key characteristics of Indigenous knowledges that surface throughout this collection: the often-conflictual and power laden relationship Indigenous knowledges have with Western thought, and the colonial origins of these sets of relations.

As Mignolo's framework clearly illustrates, the universal aspirations of Western thought – its global designs – are the sites of its coercion of other local histories, or local ways of knowing and being; this is true not only of those local histories that have come to be identified as Indigenous, but also of the collection of local histories that make up Western thought – silenced in the name of universalization. As Semali and Kincheloe (1999) note:

> This Western modernist way of producing knowledge and constructing reality is one of a multitude of local ways of knowing – it is a local knowledge system that denies its locality, seeking to produce not local but translocal knowledge. (p. 28)

This tendency of Western thought to silence its own origins also includes its historical amnesia of the origins of many of its ideas, where the cultural origins of thoughts, and the long history of their cross-fertilized development are conveniently forgotten as they become subsumed into the universal (Rains 1999). As Francis Rains puts it:

> It is an interesting system, this "Western" knowledge production – it is self contained, self-sustaining, handy, convenient, and even tinged with a sense of righteousness ... Hermetically sealed, the closed system of "Western" knowledge production has been institutionalized, in a matter of several hundred years, to such a degree as to dismiss Indigenous knowledges based on thousands of years of experience, analysis, and reflection as primitive. (1999, p. 317)

It is precisely as a result of the power of the Western collection of local histories with global designs that this collection uses the term Indigenous knowledges: in generating a simplistic dichotomy that boils down local histories from the West and local histories not form the West into two simple categories, the richness and complexity of the epistemic origins of ideas is reified into a single different knowledge system than that of the West's whose ideas can therefore be universalized and absorbed into what Sillitoe (2007) unabashedly calls "global knowledge" – knowledge that is somehow above the local. Mignolo is quick to point out how the history of confrontation surrounding this process is precisely where this dichotomy is resisted: "if Western Cosmology is the historically unavoidable reference point, the multiple confrontations of two kinds of histories defy dichotomies" (2000, p. ix).

This then is the third point of connection in the chapters that follow: the history of colonial confrontation is the point of origin of the power relations between the Western knowledge production system and a wide array of other epistemic systems, yet it is also the site where resistance to these relations of power begin. This colonial relationship is acknowledged in some definitions of Indigenous peoples, such as that of the International Labor Organization, where a people:

Are regarded as Indigenous on account of their descent from the populations which inhabited the country, or geographical region to which the country belongs, at the time of ... colonization or the establishment of present state boundaries and who, irrespective of their legal status, retain some or all of their own social, economic, cultural, and political institutions. (Quoted in McCarty et al. 2005, p. 1)

The colonial legacy of violence is also recognized in the new UN Declaration on the Rights of Indigenous People (2007), where Article 7 states:

1. Indigenous individuals have the rights to life, physical and mental integrity, liberty and security of person.

2. Indigenous peoples have the collective right to live in freedom, peace and security as distinct peoples and shall not be subjected to any act of genocide or any other act of violence, including forcibly removing children of the group to another group. (p. 4)

And Article 8 states:

1. Indigenous peoples and individuals have the right not to be subjected to forced assimilation or destruction of their culture. (p. 4)

Both of these articles in the new UN Declaration speak to centuries of violence and forced assimilation Indigenous peoples have faced as a result of colonialism. This historical set of power relations has contributed directly to the ability of Western thought to discredit the depth, astuteness and innovation of Indigenous epistemologies. This process of hierarchization is also essential for the appropriation of ideas from Indigenous sources, the silencing of this historical root of thought, and then subsequent patenting and commercialization of these ideas/knowledges. The role of education and development in this process of knowledge hierarchization and subsequent commodification cannot be understated either – as many of the contributions that follow point out. In this sense, it is important to be reminded of the quotidian and contemporary nature of the legacy of colonialism, where the vast power differential between, say, an Indigenous community defending its knowledge of particular crops and a multi-national corporation with legions of patenting lawyers is a product of this legacy that is being played out on a daily basis around the world.

In addition to these parameters within which the chapters in this collection define Indigenous knowledges, there are also two key issues these chapters deal with in careful ways. The first of these is an overly simplistic understanding of cultural knowledge production – an understanding that positions Indigenous communities as if they exist in some isolated context without any cross-fertilization of ideas from other cultures. This is a continuation of the desire to resist facile dichotomizations of Indigenous knowledges elaborated above, and it means the chapters pay particular attention to those instances where attempts are made to essentialize what it is to be Indigenous – regardless of the strategic purpose of this essentialization. As Semali and Kincheloe state, "addressing the problem of essentialism is a complex but necessary step in the study of Indigenous knowledge[s]" (1999, p. 22). While on the one hand being cautious about essentialism means questioning essentialist pejorative portrayals of the indigene that discount Indigenous peoples contributions to certain kinds of knowledge, it also means resisting attempts at essentializing Indigenous identity in either romantic or polemical directions. This does not mean a discounting of the knowledge production processes of Indigenous peoples, and their original, dynamic and innovative ways of knowing and being, nor the intrinsic link between these knowledges and the ways of life and experiences that produced them. What it does mean is that the chapters in this collection tread cautiously on the ground of reifying indigeniety in such a way that ignores the ongoing knowledge production by Indigenous peoples in contemporary times, and how these new knowledges are grounded in a millennium of learning. Bryan Brayboy (2005) has described this tension perfectly when he notes:

> Culture is simultaneously fluid and dynamic, and fixed or stable. Like an anchor in the ocean, it is tied to a group of people and often to a physical space. For many Indigenous people, culture is rooted to lands on which they live as well as to their ancestors who lived on those lands before them. However, just as the anchor shifts and sways with the changing tides and the ebbs and flows of the ocean, culture shifts and flows with changes in contexts, situations, people, and purposes. (p. 434)

This then leads to the final issue all of the chapters that follow contend with, namely the position of the researcher with regards to the Indigenous communities and knowledges being discussed – especially important when one considers the dangers of appropriation mentioned above. As Semali and Kincheloe (1999) note, this danger is even present when scholars are attempting to develop research *with*, and not *on*, Indigenous communities. Briggs and Sharp (2004) have made a similar caution in connection with the way in which Indigenous knowledges are being used within the development industry, noting that many projects speak of the importance of local and Indigenous knowledge, yet in the end either appropriate this knowledge into larger scientific processes, or marginalize local communities after all the initial requisite symbolic gestures have been made. The position of the researcher and his or her relationship with the given Indigenous peoples is the subject of much writing, ranging from Smith's (1999) influential discussion of the ways in which to decolonize research methodologies in order for Indigenous communities to have greater say and control over the research conducted by them or with them, to Spivak's provocative questioning of the ability of subalterns, such as marginalized Indigenous communities, to actually speak (1988). The question in many ways is whether the researcher can or should speak on behalf of a marginalized community, even – following Spivak's question – if they come from that community but have become a part of different community in the process of becoming a researcher. How the authors of this collection negotiate this question is different, yet each has been very open about his or her relationship with a given community in much the way that this introduction began. It is these transparent relationships that must be the foundation of discussions of bringing Indigenous knowledges into dialogue with both the field of education and of development: it is important to know where people are positioned in commencing these dialogues (Harding 1998).

INDIGENOUS KNOWLEDGES, DEVELOPMENT AND EDUCATION

Moving on from these discussions of Indigenous knowledges, it is important to indicate where this book is going, even as we establish where this book, and those contributing to it, is coming from. For those familiar with academic writing on the subject of Indigenous knowledges, there should be an inherent question hanging in the mind, namely how is this book different than the many other collections out there. This brings us to the connection in the book's title between Indigenous knowledges, development and education. Indigenous knowledges have been an important topic in both the development and education field, yet there has been little effort to bring these two rich sets of writing into dialogue. This dialogue is important not only for purposes of enriching academic understanding in both fields of their mutual engagement with Indigenous knowledges, but also because development and education have a similar concern with practice – the way in which development and/or education is enacted – as well as a similar chequered legacy with Indigenous peoples and knowledges.

To elaborate on the first similarity, education and development studies maintain a tight-rope existence between action and reflection: both fields reflect constantly on the theory and practice emerging in their respective domains of study/work. For many within both fields, a theory that has not been tested in either the classroom or the community indicates potential problems. Most of the academic writing in each of the two areas of study is preoccupied with this tension. Both fields of study also directly connect to the world of implementation, where large amounts of money are invested in both endeavors with specific outcomes in mind. As such they also have whole bureaucracies engaged in enacting educational or developmental policies, and a vast quantum of grey literature (reports, evaluations, project proposals, policy documents, etc.) that surrounds these bureaucracies and resources. Finally, both fields have extensive writing that engages with Indigenous knowledges – writing that is discussed briefly below in reference to each field.

In terms of the chequered legacy of either education or development, both of these disciplines are also intrinsically tied to the 'global design' of Western epistemology discussed above (Mignolo 2000). There are countless historical and contemporary instances of Western knowledge being imposed on other ways of knowing within the practice of both of these disciplines. One need only think of residential schools in Canada or Australia to connect this type of imposition to education; and similarly, one need only reflect on the disastrous effect of World Bank structural adjustment policies on rural populations throughout Africa, Asia and Latin America to be able to see development practice as harmful to alternative ways of being.

In this sense, it is the similar concern with practice as well as the legacy of engagement with Indigenous populations that make both these fields of study apt for comparison and dialogue, especially through the lens of their relations with Indigenous knowledges. It is therefore ironic that this dialogue in connection with Indigenous knowledge has largely failed to materialize. It is towards a more conscious merging of these sets of writing that this book is headed. It is hoped that by beginning this dialogue here, both disciplines might learn from one another's complex set of relations with Indigenous knowledges, even as they deeply reflect on past and ongoing attempts to impose a global design on these knowledges. This is in addition to learning from Indigenous knowledges themselves.

DEVELOPMENT AND INDIGENOUS KNOWLEDGES

Since what some consider to be its beginning in 1945 – and others see as the continuation of Western colonialism – development as a practice and as a field of study has had a preoccupation with Indigenous knowledges. This history has moved from attempts to label these local ways of knowing as the obstacles to development to contemporary times where they are seen as intrinsic starting points for development (Sillitoe 2007). Recent critiques of development (Escobar 1995; Rist 2002; Briggs & Sharp 2004) and development studies (Sylvester 1999; Sumner 2006) resonate with Mignolo's framework established above. For instance, Escobar (1995) and Rist (2002) criticize the Eurocentrism of development, and the way in which it colonizes the notion of progress in particularly ethnocentric ways. Similarly, Briggs and Sharp (2004) warn of the ways in which Indigenous knowledges are being appropriated by current development practice in order to continue to force local communities to develop in ways external to their frame of reference, while superficially speaking of respect for local ways of knowing. Sylvester (1999) has labelled this as one of the blind spots of development studies: an inability to truly listen to and connect with local community voices and ways of being. Likewise, Sumner (2006) notes that a key current challenge faced by the discipline is "how it addresses heterogeneity" and "opens up space for alternative 'voices'" (p. 647).

In this sense then, the collection that follows pushes thinking in development studies about its engagement with Indigenous knowledges. Dei and Simmons contribution tackles head-on the legacy of development in engaging with Indigenous knowledges. Langdon's contribution exposes the Eurocentric frame that encloses development studies. Harvey elaborates the ways in which development expert knowledge is used to exclude local ways of knowing. Stocek and Mark's contribution presents a direct epistemic challenge to Eurocentric visions of development by beginning a discussion of an alternative iteration of development based in Cree values. Metallic thinks-through the implications of a decolonized science, grounded in a respect for Indigenous epistemics, and what it can contribute to a community's development. Sarkar presents a personalized account of her daughter's growing awareness of challenges facing Western health systems and the potential of other ways of conceiving of wellness. On the same theme, Agyeyomah and Langdon's chapter concludes the collection by asking how different epistemologies of wellness can contribute to greater community choice, health and, ultimately, self-determined development. The chapters each provide one angle through which to see Indigenous knowledges engaging with development. These engagements are not simplistic, nor are they aimed only at critique. Each has attempted to provide different avenues through which the critical engagement of development and Indigenous knowledges can lead to mutual enrichment.

EDUCATION AND INDIGENOUS KNOWLEDGES

Education as a practice has, in many ways, a much longer history of engagement with Indigenous knowledges and Indigenous peoples than the development industry. As mentioned above, this history has been until recent times, one of cultural devastation and what some call linguicide (Skutnabb-Kangas 2000). Much contemporary research has been done to document this history, both in countries colonized with settler populations (such as the United States, Canada, South Africa, New Zealand and Australia) and countries colonized, yet not settled (Hall 2000; Maurial 1999; Adams 2008). Equally so, a rich vein of research in the field of education has focused on the Eurocentric nature of education as a practice as well on as the possibilities that Indigenous knowledges provide in challenging this Eurocentrism (Battiste 2008; Bartolome 2008; Dei, Hall & Rosenburg 2000; McIssac 2000; Smith 1999; Semali & Kincheloe 1999). Similarly, educational research has challenged the ways in which research is conducted *on* Indigenous communities, rather than *with*, or *by* Indigenous communities and researchers (Cajete 2008; Lomawaima 2008; Holmes 2000; Smith 1999; Abdullah & Stringer 1999). Finally, contemporary research in education has concentrated on providing theoretical as well as empirical discussions of ongoing efforts to bring Indigenous knowledges and education into dialogue in the classroom (Liberman 2008; Kaomea 2005; Semali 1999; George 1999), in the academy (Couture 2000; Ng 2000; Wright 2000; Semali & Kincheloe 1999), in informal learning situations (Fasheh 2008; Kardos 2008; Dudziak 2000), and knowledge production in Indigenous social movements (Choudry 2007; Kapoor 2007). Like development studies, much writing in the educational field connected to Indigenous knowledges also speaks about Indigenous scientific knowledge (Awang 2000; Parrish 1999; Knijnik 1999; Prakash 1999; Jegede 1999) and health knowledge (Katz 2008; Shroff 2000; Dudziak 2000). Yet, in a different vein than development studies, education has also been preoccupied with the question of narrative, language and voice, where it comes into contact with Indigenous knowledges (Reiken & Strong-Wilson 2006; Skutnabb-Kangas 2000; Batiste 1998). Finally, it should be noted how much writing in education circles takes a critical stance and sees subjugated knowledges such as Indigenous knowledges as the starting place of social justice and social change (Brayboy 2008; Kapoor 2007; Shiva 2000; Dei, Hall & Rosenburg; Semali & Kincheloe 1999; Freire & Faundez 1989).

Many of these issues surface in the chapters that follow. While exploring the colonial legacy of education, Dei and Simmons ask how African education can be re-indigenized. Langdon offers thoughts on how the educational process at the heart of development studies can be re-framed through Indigenous epistemic inflections. Harvey suggests that incorporating Indigenous knowledges into environmental programs without also addressing the ways in which these knowledges are used or taught will not only fail to lead to sustainable development, but will also undermine the very potential this knowledge exchange contains. Stocek and Mark provide a living example where Indigenous knowledges and research approaches have led to new ways of conceiving of learning and development. Metallic elaborates an example where science education can be reconceived through Indigenous knowledges, and through the introduction of the Mi'gmaq language. Sarkar explores the implications of being confronted with different ways of knowing and being on the educational choices of a young medical student – her daughter. And, Agyeyomah and Langdon introduce conceptions of education from the perspective of Chief Isshaku Gumrana Mahamadu, a traditional bonesetter in Northern Ghana. Not only do these chapters provide a range of ways in which education is conceived, they also share a variety of examples of the ways in which education interacts with Indigenous knowledges.

CONCLUSION

As noted in the outset of this introduction, it is the hope of all the contributors that the multiplicity of experiences and articulations found in these chapters will help provide an indicative example of the ways in which Indigenous knowledges can and do influence concepts of education and development, and the ways in which both these disciplines of study can become more and more open to alternative epistemic lines of thought. Not only is there a challenge before the Western epistemic system institutionalized in the university academy to become more open to other ways of knowing and being (Battiste, Bell & Findlay 2003; Semali & Kincheloe), but there is also the greater challenge of facing the legacy of Eurocentrism's "global design." Disciplines such as education and development studies have an important role to play in decentering the universal pretensions of Western thought through the introduction of other epistemic systems, such as those derived from Indigenous knowledges. This role is important not only because of the chequered legacy of both fields of thought, but also because each discipline represents an important site of implementation, where theory meets practice. The implications for both of these disciplines should they fail to become more responsive and open to other ways of knowing and being is the potential further alienation of the populations that developed these knowledges (Battiste 2008), but also the very real risk that failure to act will facilitate the continuation of the colonial legacy.

This then is the starting point of this book. The chapters that follow speak to the interconnection of education, development and Indigenous knowledges, and examine how these different fields of knowledges co-exist in a number of specific sites. As the beginning of this introduction outlined, this book aims not to define the terrain of these sites of convergence – and thereby apply a form of global design – but rather to allow for a dialogical interplay of ideas, yet a dialogism that resists a form of synthesis. Ultimately, the book is an attempt to provide a number of varied examples of how different epistemologies can inform each other and contribute to knowledge production that reflects diverse ways of knowing and contests a singular global design.

NOTES

[1] For information about Coleman, myself or any other author in this collection, please see the List of Contributors below.
[2] Special thanks must be given here to Dr. Elizabeth Meyer who agreed to chair this session and whose comments helped all of those in the project deepen their reflections. Also, our thanks go out to those who attended this presentation and added their thoughts to our work.

REFERENCES/BIBLIOGRAPHY

Adams, D. W. (2008). Fundamental considerations: The deep meaning of Native American schooling, 1880–1900. In M. Villegas, S. R. Neugebauer, & K. R. Venegas (Eds.), *Indigenous knowledge and education: Sites of struggle, strength, and survivance*. Cambridge: Harvard Education Press.

Awang, S. S. (2000). Indigenous nations and the human genome diversity project. In G. J. S. Dei, B. L. Hall, & D. G. Rosenberg (Eds.), *Indigenous knowledges in global contexts: Multiple readings of our world*. Toronto: University of Toronto.

Bartolomé, L. I. (2008). Beyond the methods fetish: Towards a humanizing pedagogy. In M. Villegas, S. R. Neugebauer, & K. R. Venegas (Eds.), *Indigenous knowledge and education: Sites of struggle, strength, and survivance*. Cambridge: Harvard Education Press.

Battiste, M. (2008). The struggle and renaissance of Indigenous knowledge in Eurocentric education. In M. Villegas, S. R. Neugebauer, & K. R. Venegas (Eds.), *Indigenous knowledge and education: Sites of struggle, strength, and survivance*. Cambridge: Harvard Education Press.

Battiste, M., Bell, L., & Findlay, L. M. (2003). Decolonizing education in Canadian universities: An interdisciplinary, international, Indigenous research project. *Canadian Journal of Native Education, 26*(2), 82–95.

Brayboy, B. (2005). Toward a tribal critical race theory in education. *The Urban Review, 37*(5), 425–446.

Brayboy, B. M. J. (2008). "Yakkity yak" and "talking back": An examination of sites of survivance in Indigenous knowledge. In M. Villegas, S. R. Neugebauer, & K. R. Venegas (Eds.), *Indigenous knowledge and education: Sites of struggle, strength, and survivance*. Cambridge: Harvard Education Press.

Briggs, J., & Sharp, J. (2004). Indigenous knowledges and development: A postcolonial caution. *Third World Quarterly, 25*(4), 661–676.

Cajete, G. A. (2008). Sites of strength in Indigenous research. In M. Villegas, S. R. Neugebauer, & K. R. Venegas (Eds.), *Indigenous knowledge and education: Sites of struggle, strength, and survivance*. Cambridge: Harvard Education Press.

Choudry, A. (2007). Transnational activist coalition politics and the de/colonization of pedagogies of mobilization: Learning from the anti-neoliberal Indigenous movement articulation. *International Education, 37*(1), 97–112.

Couture, J. (2000). Native studies and the academy. In G. J. S. Dei, B. L. Hall, & D. G. Rosenberg (Eds.), *Indigenous knowledges in global contexts: Multiple readings of our world*. Toronto: University of Toronto Press.

Dei, G. J. S., Hall, B. L., & Rosenberg, D. G. (Eds.). (2000). *Indigenous knowledges in global contexts: Multiple readings of our world.* Toronto: University of Toronto Press.

Dudziak, S. (2000). Partnership in practice: Some reflections on the Aboriginal healing and wellness strategy. In G. J. S. Dei, B. L. Hall, & D. G. Rosenberg (Eds.), *Indigenous knowledges in global contexts: Multiple readings of our world.* Toronto: University of Toronto Press.

Escobar, A. (1995). *Encountering development: The making and unmaking of the third world.* Princeton, NJ: Princeton University Press.

Fasheh, M. (2008). Community education: To reclaim and transform what has been made invisible. In M. Villegas, S. R. Neugebauer, & K. R. Venegas (Eds.), *Indigenous knowledge and education: Sites of struggle, strength, and survivance.* Cambridge: Harvard Education Press.

Freire, P., & Faundez, A. (1989). *Learning to question: A pedagogy of liberation.* New York: Continuum.

George, J. M. (1999). Indigenous knowledge as a component of the school curriculum. In L. Semali & J. Kincheloe (Eds.), *What is Indigenous knowledge: Voices from the academy.* New York: Falmer.

Harding, S. (1998). *Is science multi-cultural? Postcolonialisms, femenisms, and epistemologies.* Bloomington, IN: Indiana University Press.

Holmes, L. (2000). Heart knowledge, blood memory, and the voice of the land: Implications of research among Hawaiian elders. In G. J. S. Dei, B. L. Hall, & D. G. Rosenberg (Eds.), *Indigenous knowledges in global contexts: Multiple readings of our world.* Toronto: University of Toronto Press.

Jegede, O. J. (1999). Science education in Nonwestern cultures: Towards a theory of collateral learning. In L. Semali & J. Kincheloe (Eds.), *What is Indigenous knowledge: Voices from the academy.* New York: Falmer.

Kaomea, J. (2005). Indigenous studies in the elementary curriculum: A cautionary Hawaiian example. *Anthropology and Education Quarterly, 36*(1), 24–42.

Kapoor, D. (2007). Subaltern social movement learning and the decolonization of space in India. *International Education, 37*(1), 10–41.

Kardos, S. M. (2008). "Not bread alone": Clandestine schooling and resistance in the Warsaw Ghetto during the Holocaust. In M. Villegas, S. R. Neugebauer, & K. R. Venegas (Eds.), *Indigenous knowledge and education: Sites of struggle, strength, and survivance.* Cambridge: Harvard Education Press.

Katz, R. (2008). Education as transformation: Becoming a healer among the !Kung and the Fijians. In M. Villegas, S. R. Neugebauer, & K. R. Venegas (Eds.), *Indigenous knowledge and education: Sites of struggle, strength, and survivance.* Cambridge: Harvard Education Press.

Knijnik, G. (1999). Indigenous knowledge and ethnomathematics approach in the Brazilian landless people education. In L. Semali & J. Kincheloe (Eds.), *What is Indigenous knowledge: Voices from the academy.* New York: Falmer.

Liberman, K. (2008). Aboriginal education: The school at Strelley, Western Australia. In M. Villegas, S. R. Neugebauer, & K. R. Venegas (Eds.), *Indigenous knowledge and education: Sites of struggle, strength, and survivance.* Cambridge: Harvard Education Press.

Lomawaima, K. T. (2008). Tribal sovereigns: Reframing research in American Indian education. In M. Villegas, S. R. Neugebauer, & K. R. Venegas (Eds.), *Indigenous knowledge and education: Sites of struggle, strength, and survivance.* Cambridge: Harvard Education Press.

Maurial, M. (1999). Indigenous knowledge in schooling: A continuum between conflict and dialogue. In L. Semali & J. Kincheloe (Eds.), *What is Indigenous knowledge: Voices from the academy.* New York: Falmer Press.

McCarty, T., Borgoiakova, T., Gilmore, P., Lomawaima, T., & Romero, M. (2005). Editors' introduction: Indigenous epistemologies and education-self-determination, anthropology, and human rights. *Anthropology and Education Quarterly, 36*(1), 1–7.

McIsaac, E. (2000). Oral narratives as a site of resistance: Indigenous knowledge, colonialism, and western discourse. In G. J. S. Dei, B. L. Hall, & D. G. Rosenberg (Eds.), *Indigenous knowledges in global contexts: Multiple readings of our world.* Toronto: University of Toronto Press.

Mignolo, W. (2000). *Local histories/global designs: Coloniality, subaltern knowledges and border thinking.* New Jersey, NJ: Princeton UP.

Parrish, A. M. (1999). Agricultural extension education and the transfer of knowledge in an Egyptian Oasis. In L. Semali & J. Kincheloe (Eds.), *What is Indigenous knowledge: Voices from the academy.* New York: Falmer.

Prakash, M. S. (1999). Indigenous knowledge systems - ecological literacy through initiation into people's science. In L. Semali & J. Kincheloe (Eds.), *What is Indigenous knowledge: Voices from the academy.* New York: Falmer.

Rains, F. (1999). Indigenous knowledge, historical amnesia and intellectual authority: Deconstructing hegemony and the social and political implications of the curricular "other". In L. Semali & J. Kincheloe (Eds.), *What is Indigenous knowledge: Voices from the academy.* New York: Falmer Press.

Riecken, T., & Strong-Wilson, T. (2006). At the edge of consent: Participatory research with First Nations student filmmakers. In B. Leadbeater, E. Banister, C. Benoit, M. Jansson, A. Marshall, & T. Riecken (Eds.), *Ethical issues in community-based research with children and youth* (pp. 42–56). Toronto: University of Toronto Press.

Rist, G. (1997). *The history of development: From western origin to global faith.* London: Zed.

Semali, L., & Kincheloe, J. (1999). Introduction: What is Indigenous knowledge and why should we study it. In L. Semali & J. Kincheloe (Eds.), *What is Indigenous knowledge: Voices from the academy.* New York: Falmer Press.

Semali, L. M. (1999). Community as classroom: (Re)Valuing Indigenous literacy. In L. Semali & J. Kincheloe (Eds.), *What is Indigenous knowledge: Voices from the academy.* New York: Falmer.

Shiva, V. (2000). Foreword. In G. J. S. Dei, B. L. Hall, & D. G. Rosenberg (Eds.), *Indigenous knowledges in global contexts: Multiple readings of our world.* Toronto: University of Toronto.

Shroff, F. (2000). Ayurveda: Mother of Indigenous health knowledge. In G. J. S. Dei, B. L. Hall, & D. G. Rosenberg (Eds.), *Indigenous knowledges in global contexts: Multiple readings of our world.* Toronto: University of Toronto Press.

Sillitoe, P. (Ed.). (2007). *Local science vs. Global science: Approaches to Indigenous knowledge in international development.* New York: Berghahn Books.

Skutnabb-Kangas, T. (2000). *Linguistic genocide in education? Or worldwide diversity and human rights?* Mahwah, NJ: Lawrence Erlbaum Associates.

Smith, L. T. (1999). *Decolonizing methodologies: Research and Indigenous people.* London: Zed Books & University of Otago Press.

Spivak, G. (1988). Can the subaltern speak? In C. Nelson & L. Grossberg (Eds.), *Marxist interpretations of culture.* Basingstoke: Macmillan Education.

Sumner, A. (2006). What is development studies. *Development in Practice, 16*(6), 644–650.

United Nations Declaration on the Rights of Indigenous Peoples, 61/295 C.F.R. (2007).

Wright, H. K. (2000). Not so strange bedfellows: Indigenous knowledge, literature studies, and African development. In G. J. S. Dei, B. L. Hall, & D. G. Rosenberg (Eds.), *Indigenous knowledges in global contexts: Multiple readings of our world.* Toronto: University of Toronto Press.

GEORGE J. SEFA DEI & MARLON SIMMONS

2. THE INDIGENOUS AS A SITE OF DECOLONIZING KNOWLEDGE FOR CONVENTIONAL DEVELOPMENT AND THE LINK WITH EDUCATION: THE AFRICAN CASE

I. INTRODUCTION

In conventional discourses the link between education and development is often simply assumed. While, no doubt, it is important to understand the connections, we believe the linkage itself needs to be theorized. In this paper, we seek to re-conceptualize 'development' by affirming the relevance of Indigenous epistemologies. Our objective is to show how reframing 'development' discourse through the lens of Indigenous knowledges and an anti-colonial paradigm, allows for a problematization of conventional understandings of 'development', as well as, to reveal pointed counter-narratives about genuine educational options for Africa. In this discursive exercise we unmask the complexities of the role of education in the search for African-centered development. Our learning objective, academic and political hope, is to diminish the lacuna between the expertise of theory/knowledge as situated in the Western text, and the epistemic immanent within the dialogicalness of Indigenity. At the foreground, the study works with local historic contexts of African colonial education, to discern ways in which Indigenous knowledges and/or local cultural knowing help to disentangle Eurocentric epistemic discursive 'truths'. The inquiry takes on the challenge of centering daily lived experiences of subjects and linking embodied knowledges to Indigenous alterities, in order to 'extricate' theory as a discourse in practice by local peoples within their communities. Further, the contemporary 'classroom' of Eurocentric education is interrogated as the imperial sacrosanct as a 'regime of truth', as constitutive of a panoptic epistemic, which brings a disciplinary modality on Indigenous and non-hegemonic ways of knowing.

II. DEFINING AND CRITIQUING 'DEVELOPMENT'

Before defining 'development' and the appropriate role for Indigenous knowledge we would like to raise five general questions which provide some context for our critique of conventional development (see also Dei, 1998). First, how do current conceptions of 'development' correspond to, or reflect on the reality of contemporary North-South relations [e.g., the history, context, and contemporary reality of South-North inequities in the global economy]? Second, we ask 'development' for whom, for what purposes and at what costs? Third, how to challenge and resist the conventional understandings of 'development' conceived in terms of what local people lack and/or what they are expected to do/become? Fourth, how does the practice of global development address the unequal power relations between expert knowledge and local Indigenous knowledge? And fifth, how do we assist local communities to sustain basic livelihoods, informed by their local cultural knowledges? We raise these questions acknowledging that development as we know it is heavily anchored in economic, technological and material constraints and possibilities, with little emphasis on the spiritual, emotional, and social-cultural dimensions. Development must be about how local peoples are using their own creativity and resourcefulness to respond to major economic and ecological stressors. Local Indigenous knowledges point to the ways communities come to share power and resources in order to address questions of difference and inequities. A failure to understand the local Indigenous knowledge base and its relevance to discussions of change is bound to present roadblocks to the possibilities of social transformation. For example, we need to look at current global developments, particularly natural and human made disasters like the Tsunami, Katrina, Wilma, and civil wars. How are local knowledges impacting on the search for rebuilding communities? Events a couple of years back in Mexico regarding the World Trade Organization (WTO) summit, and what happened in the follow up in Seattle and Atlanta, and at the Summit of the Americas, present a significant message about disregarding local knowledges in the question of 'development' at our own peril. Similarly, the recent confrontations in France, Britain, US, and elsewhere involving disenfranchised youth, bring home clearly to us the inequities that afflict approaches to 'development' that have scuttled the hopes and futures of youth and disenfranchised communities. We are witnessing 'divided communities' that pose a threat to human and social survival.

Our intellectual project is to bring the social, spiritual, and cultural dimensions front and centre to our discussions about development. There is a need to situate the social as central to discussions of development. This calls for shifting the focus away from what we term "the technologizing of development" to the "socialization of development". In other words local knowledge, the Indigenous cultural resource knowledge base, is all critical to rethinking 'conventional development.' We need to theorize development beyond the materiality of existence and social politics and seek to understand the social contexts and knowledge implications of development. But in framing 'the social' in discussions about 'development' the concern is not simply with the social, cultural, and spiritual contexts/determinants of development but also with how we address the social well-being of the knowledge systems that undergrid human understandings. A particular concern in this paper then is how the vocabulary we use for 'development' can be limiting and can constrain the possibilities for change and global transformation if we are to rethink Indigenous knowledges.

We must therefore critique the conventional discourse of 'development' and, also, bring a broad definition to the concept in ways that affirm local knowings and culture and subject agencies and resistances. Obviously 'development' is ensuring the social, cultural, spiritual, educational, income, food and shelter, peace, security, equity and social justice needs of all peoples. We know that globalization, increasing poverty, unemployment, and homelessness have all contributed to the social problems of "nations." Development requires an integrated intervention from the various sectors of the national communities that expand beyond current narrow confines to embrace health, politics, environment, education, economy, culture, knowledge and spirituality. Development is more than a material resource issue. It is about knowledge and the power of ideas to bring about social change.

In conventional development models we see the denial of local knowledge, of local peoples' aspirations. So, in rebuilding communities after natural and human made disasters such as the Tsunami, Katrina, Wilma, and civil wars we need to ask how are we using local knowledges in such undertakings? Is there a place for local knowledge in our definitions of 'development'? When it comes to the issue of national development how are Indigenous (local) models for sustainable change being developed? How is an organized resistance to agencies like the WTO, to NAFTA and to policies such as IMF/World bank inspired economic sector adjustments developing? Development must be about the satisfaction of locally defined and determined needs and aspirations. The possibilities for local (majority world) participation in the formation, implementation and transformation of dominant development models are critical. Local peoples must be involved in their own development. After all, if there is little room at the table for those whom the projects are allegedly serving, then how can such development ever truly address the task at hand? If the subjects of our work (development) cannot become the theorists informing it, how do we hope to succeed? The most remarkable feature of Western development models is not their overtly political underpinnings, but rather the fact that despite over 50 years of abysmal failure, they are still praised and undertaken. They simply do not work. Part of the problem is that there is a powerful cultural, political and intellectual currency that is traded (exported/imported) through dominant development models.

III. THEORIZING 'DEVELOPMENT' THROUGH THE LENS OF INDIGENOUS KNOWLEDGE

Of importance here, is understanding how the matter of 'development' ushered and partitioned forms of knowledging, and also how it constituted globalized "truth" systems (Foucault, 1977b, p. 131-132) onto the African geo-politic. We also need to be aware of how certain knowledges emerging from Anglo/Euro/American lands were deemed as expert, as having authority, and how this body of knowledge when reified, formed a discursive classificatory strategy, one that organized, inscribed and disseminated meaning, meaning which thereby proclaimed the project of 'development'. Vital to this discussion then, is recognizing the epistemological vanguard that guides and continues to inform the 'development' project. Immanent in the discursivity of 'development' is the dominant Eurocentric epistemological tradition, which forms a disciplinary specificity inherent in the Western text. In re-thinking development, one of the challenges is coming up with strategies that work to introduce/affirm/re-inscribe knowledges, knowledges which have been positioned outside the limits of the system of knowledge production that governs "truth regimes" (Foucault, 1977b). By no means is this a simple task. We need not remind ourselves of the way science/social sciences with their attendant governing rationale, exude overarching edicts, whereby knowledges emanating from multiple locations are continuously nullified by the Western academy. Multi-ethnic/multi-lingual African peoples have been producing local culturally rooted knowledges since long before colonialism imposed its will. These knowledges over time as passed down by generations have come to mold African identity. But part of the intellectual aggression on Africa is to make inferior those bodies of knowledge that reinvigorate African identity. But perhaps much more telling is the inferiorization of embodied knowledge, knowledge that helps revitalize one's memory of Africaness. To challenge this intellectual aggression then, conventional 'development' models must resist ways of assigning authorial and discursive control over Africa; they ought to help African learners and youth re-invent their Africaness. They ought to help African learners assert themselves in the political, psychological, cultural, artistic, and creative spheres. Regarding the on-going contest over knowledge production in the Western academy, we ask, how do we utilize an African-centered perspective to develop alternative and oppositional paradigms that can see its emancipatory potential? We must keep in mind that historically, African-centered perspectives have been located "beyond the boundary" of the authentic Eurocentric position that informed the production of knowledge designated as 'truth.' From this location, African peoples have struggled to find collective voices, African peoples have struggled to break free from Eurocentric mimicry. Instead what came from this location was a mode of thought and action, which saw African peoples taking up the logic of the colonizer as affirming and as one's own (Du Bois, 1989; Fanon, 1967). As discussed elsewhere, it is no secret that the now discredited Structural Adjustment Policies and Programmes (SAPs) have a material/discursive hold on African education (Dei, 2004). Its duplicitous nature presents existing World Bank/IMF inspired policies on educational reform as being designed to meet the need of local African peoples while simultaneously in the back room we have an ordering being dispelled which accommodates the commodification/marketisation of Western shaped knowledges. What is long overdue in conventional curricula, is a critical education that imbues a consciousness onto African peoples which allows for everyday questioning around issues of African 'development.' Questions such as, how is knowledge for 'development' imposed and controlled? And how does this imposition of knowledge stifle new imaginings, local creativity, and resourcefulness? How do the activities of the international community, those of the World Bank and the IMF as such, come to legitimize and form the dominant paradigm as to what constitutes 'development'?

In bringing fragility to the constituents of 'development', a "return to knowledge" is much needed (Foucault, 1977b, p. 81). With this "return to knowledge," the local nature of knowleging ought to be theorized, that is, "in reality, an autonomous, non-centralised kind of theoretical production, one that is to say whose validity is not dependent on the approval of the established regimes of thought" (Foucault, 1977b, p. 81). Important to this "autonomous, non-centralised kind of theoretical production" is Indigenous knowledging. As mentioned elsewhere, "to speak of 'Indigenousness' in the African context is to articulate questions about local cultures and social identities, Indigenousness highlights the importance of decolonizing the 'international development' project" (Dei, 2000b, p. 72). Indigenousness is not totalizing in claiming this homogenous African experience. Part of the process in understanding Indigenousness is recognizing the flux of the Indigene. So, in re-thinking 'development', how then do we work with the uncertainty and complexity of the Indigene as both subject and place of knowledge? How do we work with the embodied spatio-temporality of the Indigene? How do we work with the "elusiveness, the ineffability of the pedagogy," (Van Manen, 1997, p. 142-148) immanent in the Indigene? How do we work with the incommensurability of the Indigene? We do not presume to have answers for all these questions. We raise these to offer food for thought. We need to theorize African Indigenousness beyond the boundaries of Africa. The challenge here is retrieving the ontological alterity (Ladson-Billings, 2000) immanent within the African Indigene. To recall, "'Indigenousness' may be thought of as knowledge consciousness arising locally and in association with the long-term occupancy of a place" (Dei, 2000b, p. 72). The 'local' though, always exists in flux, a flux that anachronistically embodies the spatio-temporal of the Indigene. So to 'return to knowledge', the Indigene then, ought to be informed through the liminal discursive, (Bhabha, 1994) it ought to be informed by the embodied displacement of Indigenity. But utilizing this liminal consciousness to inform the Indigene in order to re-conceptualize 'development', presents numerous challenges in theorizing African Indigenousness beyond its boundaries. The project of 'development' with its governing discursive gatekeepers produced an epistemological tradition which panopticised local knowledges (Foucault, 1977a). What emerged was an epistemology which brought a form of governmentality (Foucault, 1991; Gordon, 1991; Lewis, 2000; O'Malley, 1997; Rose, 1996) onto the Indigene, that is, it regulated and simultaneously pre-conditioned the Indigene to a form of regulation imbued through self.

Indigenous knowledges of African peoples are informed by "cognitive understandings and interpretations of the social and physical/spiritual worlds, including concepts, beliefs, perceptions, and experiences of local environments, both social and natural" (Dei, 2000b, p. 72). Such knowledges undergo a materialization through a particular form of docility. This docility, when informed through the epistemological authority of 'development' discourses, gives the conditions of possibility for a disciplinary mode (Foucault, 1977a) of interpreting Indigenous knowledge systems. With this, we can think of 'Indigenousness' as consciousness, a form of embodiment, which can help us peep at the constant surveillance/subjectification immanent in the Indigene. This phrasing helps us to better understand how 'development' discourse with its organizing and inscriptive self-regulating epistemic 'truths', posits a sense of 'twoness' onto the Indigene (Du Bois, 1996, p. 5). The Indigene then is normalized in and through this prison/prisoner relationship of self (Foucault, 1977a).

The question then, is how can the Indigene be 'extricated' from self (Fanon, 1967, p. 10)? How can the Indigene be extricated from the discursive formations of 'development'? In thinking about the process of 'extrication', we ought to recognize a particular Indigenous-brittleness, that part of Indigenity which is informed through what Du Bois tells us is a "double consciousness". We need to think about Indigenity as always already existing, not in a positivistic sense though, to say having fixed universalistic values, but to theorize Indigenity beyond colonial and the so called post-colonial. We need to be guided by the dynamic social and subject location of the Indigene. Part and parcel with the 'extrication' process is understanding the bifurcation of the Indigene, that is, the subjectification of Indigenousness knowledges through the discursive formations of the Western text and also, as spoken before, the subjectification immanent to Indigenity, that Indigenousness, engendered through "epidermal levels of inferiority and the lactified consciousness" (Fanon, 1967). But these knowledges, these experiences, this Indigenousness/Indigene co-exist constitutively taking up different subject positions. To say they are entangled might be too much, but we need to understand the flux, and how they inform each other. We can think of Indigenousness in its embodied form. We can think of Indigenousness as a consciousness operating in an anachronistic spatio-temporal. We can also think of Indigenousness as knowledge base systems; to compartmentalize these subjectivities could present some difficulty for the 'extrication' process. Bringing discursive authority to the Indigene is very much a complexity. Being mindful of the Eurocentric epistemological authority which pillars 'development' discursive 'truths,' one might argue, that Indigenousness knowledge is of itself a 'truth' system, but as discussed elsewhere (Simmons, 2006), "truth systems are positioned the top, as coming from the state, with authority, as having hegemonic order, where the subject, that is, Indigenity, acquiesce, takes on the Western discursive authority as this given natural order, bringing conformity and forms of control onto self". On the counterpoint, we situate Indigenousness as a discursive practice which centers the experiences of the African body, forming counter-hegemonic relations with existing ontological discursive 'truth' formations, in that, Indigenousness (the subject) is cognizant of its designated discursive place in relation to the circulating discursive authority (Gramsci, 1971; Foucault, 1977a; 1977b).

Though Indigenous knowledges are centered through the experiences of (in this discussion) the African peoples, this does not posit a delimiting factor onto this said body of knowledge. As Roberts mentions, "Indigenous knowledge as knowledge accumulated by a group of people, not necessarily Indigenous, who by centuries of unbroken residence develop an in-depth understanding of their particular place in their particular world" (Roberts, 1998, p. 59). It is significant to reiterate that Indigenous knowledge is non-hegemonic, anti-colonial, and does not masquerade as the expert knowledge. It is not about the search for the universal 'truth' with vestige to one geographic location, with lineage to a particular ethnic group. 'Development' then, a project with a colonialistic 'historic specificity', ought to be re-thought, through the local nature of Indigenous knowledge, where different peoples, experiences, values, beliefs, and knowledges are centered in this decision making process (Dei, 2000b). Indigenousness though, is deeply embedded more so as a "positive unconscious of knowledge, as that which eludes the consciousness of the scientist" (Foucault, 2002, p. xi). Through this "positive unconscious of knowledge" local peoples can bring to the surface a critical discernment that ought to subvert Western discursive authority on 'development,' local peoples can bring discontinuities and irregularities to governing Eurocentric epistemological traditions immanent to Western discursive rules on 'development'. We can think through Indigenousness in order to locate disjunctures which are informed through long term lived experiences, and also through this "positive unconscious of the Indigene"; we can then engage in more meaningful discussions to bring alternatives to existing colonizing knowledges.

Thus far we have used the term 'we' with a certain sense of 'taken for grantedness', but to share a bit about this 'we', we understand this 'we' as those of us who have taken up the struggle against colonialistic/imperialistic forms of relations/knowledging. We recognize Indigenousness knowledges as buttressed by and as constitutive of an anti-colonial discursive framework. As mentioned elsewhere:

> The anti-colonial challenges any form of economic, cultural, political, and spiritual dominance. It is about identifying and countering all forms of colonial domination as manifested in everyday practice, including individual and collective social practices, as well as global interactions. An anti-colonial perspective is about developing an awareness/consciousness of the varied conditions under which domination and oppression operate. Such a perspective seeks to subvert the dominant relations of knowledge production that sustains hierarchies and systems of power. It challenges the colonizer's sense of reason, authority and control. (Dei, 2006, p. 5)

'We' then, includes those who have taken up the anti-colonial discursive approach to improve the quality of social justice. Much of the anti-colonial approach though, is taken up with the everyday encounter of colonizing knowledges, where these colonizing knowledges work as the legitimate vanguard to the propagation of the state (Smith, 1999). Regarding the 'everydayness' of colonizing knowledges, that which is 'developed' and dependent on socio-historic specific codetermining apparatuses of the state, we implicate classificatory systemic epistemes of familyhood, religion, spirituality, schooling, law, media and cultural representations (Althusser, 2001).

In re-thinking 'development' through the Indigene, one of the challenges is countering how colonizing knowledges are constantly imputed as a normative within these "state apparatuses" and simultaneously taken up as an idealized body of knowledge. Part and parcel of coming to know this idealized body of knowledge is the interpellatory process, which transforms the body/personhood to that of subject. In a neo-Marxist way the body/personhood is transformed, re-positioned as the 'ideologue' where the 'everydayness' of colonizing knowledges is taken up as a "ritualized practice" of one's own. Hence, one comes to understand, to interpret, to make meaning, to see their existing surroundings with a lens circumscribed with a socio-historic conjuncture specific to colonialism. With this we can understand that not every body that embodies the material discursive of the 'other' may take up the anti-colonial walk. As subject/ideologue, one as if by nature readily marshals the existing discursivity on 'development' as one's own. We can look not too far away to newspapers, magazines, and television advertisements, where society is constantly bombarded with hyper-humanitarian images of the benevolent savior in relation to the 'Othered' body. In a sense then, what emerged from Western society was this endowed interpretive framework, imbued in and through colonialism, which informed the repeatability of which body ought to be 'developed' and which body ought not to be 'developed'. 'Development' discourse with its shifting flux materialized in a myriad of ways, through science, technology, architecture, geography, religion, and other forms masquerading as modernization with which it posited itself. But within the discursive formation of 'development', there exists a specific locus point to the body. The question then, is how is 'development' embodied and practiced? And how is 'development' organized and inscribed onto the body? What knowledges are produced/reproduced through this embodied form of 'development'? And how is it legitimized as expert/truth knowledges within institutions?

Consequently, the interpellating nature of 'development' discourse cannot be overlooked, insofar as so-called 'Third World' populations readily take up these strategies governed by organizations with their self-determining limits, that is, the IMF, the World Bank and multinational corporations, in order to come to this designated space of the First World. But in doing so, in readily taking up this position which furthers the destabilization of these regions deemed 'Third World,' what emerges is the 'fixed homogenous geographic subject', that is, a transformed region circumscribed by what Fanon calls the 'epidermalization of inferiority' (Fanon, 1967). Moreover, in taking up these governing strategies, peoples from colonizing lands inculcate normalizing approaches, which exercises a gaze onto themselves, whereby lived experiences are internalized and transformed as inferior. What we are left with then, is a totalizing interpretation of a way of life, of a culture, of a body of knowledge, of a geographic region that thinks and accepts that by nature it was meant to have this perennial less-than value. 'Development' must be informed through local specific knowledging; the problem arises when these embodied knowledges are deemed inferior both by the West and by local peoples.

We ask then, to think about 'development' discourse, as a strategy of power (Foucault, 1977b), which commits a form of "epistemic violence," (Yancy, 2004, p. 132) onto the said geographic subject. Congruent with colonial master narratives, 'development' discourse signifies a colonial disguise, which re-disciplines subjugated locations into the culture of colony. This culture of colony, sedimented epistemologically into our 'everydayness,' predetermines a bifurcated consciousness with Indigenity. So the Indigenousness within is constantly not necessarily negotiating, but always looking for that space to breathe, for that space to nurture itself, for that space of insularity from which it can be re-nourished. To reiterate, Indigenousness has a spatio-temporality and multiple positions. Though at times Indigenousness might be difficult to pin down, what needs to be understood is the constitutive determinant of the pedagogic nature of Indigenity. In thinking of its many forms, we can think of Indigenousness as a body of knowledge, as a form of consciousness, having its own spirituality, as codetermining raw resources counter-hegemonic to the culture of colony. 'Development' then as a culture of colony is no "imagined community" (Anderson, 1991). 'Development' and its materiality are very much alive, duplicitous cohabitants as savior/modernizer actively producing/reproducing 'refugees'/asylum seekers/'Third Worldisms'. Dependency theorists have long fought to counter 'development' narratives. While much work has been done in de-tangling the economical, political, and Eurocentric needles that have woven 'development' discourse, dependency theorists "failed to address the cultural dimension of domination, that which is key to understanding power relations and strategies of resistance" (Tucker, 1999, p. 12). While we recognize the contribution made by dependency theorists in contesting Western hegemonic forms of knowledging, in the African context however, we feel obligated then, that as starting points, not as a by product or as a result of, to come to a form of knowledge which firstly involves thinking through the lived experiences, the interpretations, and cognitive understandings of African peoples (Asante, 1991; Dei, 2000b). But bringing Indigenousness knowledges to the classrooms/curricula is a challenging process, given the way Eurocentric knowledge systems are everyday re-normalizing and re-colonizing the Western text. In taking up this challenge we interrogate the contemporary 'classroom' of Eurocentric education as the imperial sacrosanct; as a 'regime of truth', as constitutive of a panoptic epistemic, as that which brings a disciplinary modality on Indigenous and non-hegemonic ways of knowing.

IV. THE ROLES AND IMPLICATIONS OF CONTEMPORARY [AFRICAN] EDUCATION

We position the contemporary classroom as a disciplinary 'regime of truth,' which deploys its attendant curricula as a historic specific technique of power (Foucault, 1977a; 1977b), over certain forms of knowledges. Historically these knowledges have their origins within the racialized/minoritised body, and as being produced from lands that have been colonized by Europeans. With the matter of the contemporary classroom as being disciplinary, we can think of how the everyday knowledge produced in contemporary classroom spaces has come to govern and regulate everyday societal relations, that is, as producing of an ethic, as a particular code of conduct on the said African body, which in a cryptic way works to script the lived experiences of African learners. What concerns us is the way in which knowledge being produced in the classroom is discursively constituted and populated with experience, meaning and consciousness from the monolithic voice, from particular geographic locations, and then appears as this all inclusive voice. Further, this everyday imperial process gives the way in which African peoples come to *understand* their classroom experiences, and also, it informs how African peoples make meaning of their lives. The inappropriateness of the school curriculum and how education fails to serve local needs first must be identified as a concern of African schooling. We ask then, how do we make our schools inclusive of local knowledges so as to contribute to the search for genuine development options for Africa? And how can all learners be able to develop a sense of connectedness and identification with their schools? What is needed is the capacity for schools to prepare learners for today and tomorrow by developing appropriate and effective instructional strategies to empower learners to know about themselves, their communities, and their responsibilities. Educators then must teach about the diversity of ideas and events that have shaped and continue to shape human growth and development. As a strategy of resistance, African peoples may interpret the Western text as if it were their own, as coming from their histories, as coming from their cultural milieu, inculcating in a sense an omnipresent amnesia. But in re-thinking 'development,' part of the process then, is centering the implications of which body of knowledge African peoples align themselves with and the effects on the African mind. The much-quoted Du Bois "double consciousness" and his use of "twoness" is important here. When he speaks about "this double consciousness, this sense of always looking at one's self through the eyes of others, of measuring of one's soul by the tape of a world that looks on in amused contempt and pity," (Du Bois, 1996, p. 5) we then have to seriously think of how African peoples are always under constant surveillance, and how African Indigenous knowledges are disciplined daily through 'development' discourse which presents itself with its self accorded epistemological authority.

Returning to the contemporary classroom, curricula, the site of the everyday panoptic apparatus, (Foucault, 1977a) have an attendant intentionality that works to discipline from within, insofar as contemporary curricula when internalized by African peoples allow for a form of behavior, a particular performativity, which constantly brings surveillance onto the said African body. It orders and controls thought, speech patterns, what courses are chosen, what knowledges ought to be pursued and what knowledges ought not be pursued, which for the most are those that emerged from colonized lands. So in a sense, contemporary curricula when internalized imbue an axiological embodiment onto African peoples, an ethic, a way of taking care of self which fosters this "warring ideal" (Du Bois, 1996, p. 5) onto localized knowledges. We are reminded by the way African students are duped into learning popular European languages, while local African languages which can be affirming for African spirituality and providing a much needed ancestral connection, are classified by Western experts through particular procedures, culminating in African peoples consequently coming to this form of alienating self-regulation, whereby knowledges with their origins in Africa are interpreted as being inferior. We need a spiritually-grounded approach to education in order to deal with how learners are alienated from surrounding social environments and also to counter Eurocentric cycles of knowledge production. Such education will enable youth today to deploy Africaness as *an affirming* concept, be proud of their ancestry, and become conscious of their own historical situation. African education must be about understanding what our identities mean to us and the politics required in making such identifications. Spirituality plays an important role in informing African identity and with spirituality we do not mean in a proselytisation sense. With spirituality we are more thinking of ways of knowing which brings an ethic, care, and affirmation onto the African body. Today we are told that spirituality as emanating from Africa is all but superstition. We must not forget how the minds of many Africans have been thoroughly transformed by this said spirituality, which accompanied colonial education. We ought to move beyond this cloak of superstition and find ways to revitalize/recall Indigenously informed spirituality into the classroom. What we are faced with is a contemporary classroom that instills an "epistemic community," (Dei, 2005, p. 14) which propagates "capitalist schooling" (McLaren & Farahmandpur, 2005, p. 50). However, as a "spatial community" (Parker, 1998, 3-4) Indigenous knowledges and their immanent non-archived/non-partitioned (Maurial, 1999) structure can mobilize boundaries and disrupt the fixity of Eurocentric epistemologies. We need not be reminded of the often easy, seductive slippage into Eurocentric paradigms to interpret lived realities of Africans. Materializing "community as classroom", (Semali, 1999) a process which results in spaces contrapuntal to the ordering of the Western text, is a very difficult task, given the way in which education was used as a vehicle to transport the governing ethics and morals of colonialism. Pedagogically this is quite challenging and calls for a "paying attention in the moment" (Wane, 2006, p. 102). The question here then is, as a natural raw resource, how can critical Indigenous sensitivities be recalled in order to subvert everyday societal forms of domination?

Having a similitude to anti-racism/anti-colonial discursive framework (Dei, 1996), Indigenous knowledges draw on identity, practice and experience. As mentioned elsewhere, "identity is linked with knowledge production in terms of how we can make sense of our world through individual and collective histories and experiences" (Dei, 2000a, p. 36). Part and parcel of this process then in meaning making, is to "uncover what it means to have embodied knowledge." To recall, "embodied knowledge means bringing personal feelings, emotional and spiritual connectedness, and a deep passion and commitment to seek knowledge and using this knowledge to transform existing conditions as a worthy cause that emanates from within the self" (Dei, 2005c, p. 8). With embodied knowledge and critical Indigenous sensitivities in mind, the hope is to formulate a springboard whereby Indigenous knowledges as a "spatial community" (Price, 1998, p. 3-4) can enter the conventional classroom with a revitalized sense of dialogicalness (Freire, 1970; Tucker, 1999; Maurial, 1999). Hence, to bring points of disjuncture to master narratives as deposited by conventional curricula is part of the decolonizing process, which ought to be the intentionality of Indigenousnesly imbued dialogicalness. So then, critical education must be about decolonizing research and scholarship about Africa and African peoples. It should also address the misrepresentation of identities and communities in the global contexts. In responding to this need, the challenge for curricula is to instill knowledges from 'bodies of difference'. In this way, the informing pedagogy centers the lived experiences of all learners. Curricula should encourage learners to think through local Indigenous languages, the learning objective being that we can come to know through different paths. With the interconnections of language, identity, spirituality and Indigenous faith, curricula must point learners to holistic ways of learning. In inculcating "community as classroom," lessons ought to be developed which utilize the cultural and spiritual histories of Indigenous peoples. What is experienced here is a shift in the imperious knowledge centre, and simultaneously the shaping of non-compartmentalized ways of forming knowledge. Curricula should bring learners to a sense that we form knowledge from multiple positions of knowing and that historically the expert curricula dictated what knowledge and from which body "success" was conceptualized.

On the practical side, it is important for critical African education to discuss what schools can and should do with Indigenous knowledges. Historically emerging from oral traditions through fables, folklore/folkways, proverbs, and poems, Indigenous knowledges can be used to discuss historical periods in order to understand Western prominence. Understanding human enslavement and plantation life through Indigenity and how it worked to inform and organize in a very material way our present day situation, should be at the forefront for school curricula. There should be classroom discussions about African Indigenousness in relation to how historically, specific bodies came into power and how these bodies were able to establish dominant global positions, be it knowledge production to material wealth. Also discussions about how and what spaces were opened up for bodies with a history of colonization. What ways of *interpreting* are normalized through Western institutions? For example, as a body of knowledge, how and by what means did Indigenous African spiritual beliefs as practiced in and through plantation life bring upon the African body "epidermal levels of inferiority"? How as a mode of perception these "epidermal levels of inferiority" inform everyday looking/thinking of Africaness (Fanon, 1967, p. 11). Keeping in mind these so called "epidermal levels of inferiority" continue to notify the current discursive project of 'development'. Again to reiterate, our project is more to de-centre dominant ways of knowing and finding ways to integrate different centers of knowledge into the curricula.

Understanding the detriments of "capitalist schooling" is important in re-thinking 'development'. Education, as a commodity, a good readily available for consumption, has come to populate popular legitimizing marketisation strategies of 'development' and globalization (McLaren & Farahmandpur, 2005). As a disciplinary strategy of power (Foucault, 1977a), the World Bank through educational policy organizes and inscribes a governing rational (Foucault, 1991; Gordon, 1991; Lewis, 2000; O'Malley, 1997; Rose, 1996) which simultaneously seeks the interest of 'development', and forms a constitutive mode of subjectivication onto Indigenous knowledges (Tikly, 2004). Education and the installed curricula as located in the classroom tend to disseminate a form of knowledge contrapuntal to Indigenousness. This knowledge as proliferated through specific procedures and practices in the conventional classroom is shaped, as Tettey reminds us, by the "values that emphasize individual, private opportunity, and the rationality of the market – that the form it takes in terms of knowledge standardization, and its subsequent decontextualization, may not provide African students with the knowledge that is relevant for their specific milieus" (2006, p. 100).

What ought to be noted here is the way in which the population of the conventional classroom is organized (Foucault, 1990), through discursive practices which when operationalized through Western pedagogies, install a form of alienation onto the African body. This installed form of alienation then becomes the mode of production for the said subjectivication that continuously disavows the lived experiences of Africaness (Foucault, 1977a; Butler, 1997; 2004). The contemporary classroom ought to be regarded as a panoptic apparatus whereby the installed curriculum becomes the instrument of surveillance, which organizes and inscribes relations of discipline onto Indigenity (Foucault, 1977a). More so, the contemporary classroom then becomes a space that inculcates as a pedagogic practice a "procedure of subordination" (Foucault, 1977a, p. 208) onto Indigenous knowledges. It makes certain the ordering of hegemonic pedagogical cultures, which thereby transforms the African body through specific practices and forms of behavior as exercised through discursive expressions (Goldberg, 1993) into the "lactified subject" (Fanon, 1967; Foucault, 1982; 1994a). This, an interpellating procedure (Althusser, 2001), transforms the African body into a subject, which takes up the logic of colonization as if it were one's own. Fanon's words are important here, in that he wishes to "help the black man free himself from the arsenal of complexes developed by the colonial environment". The permanent question then is "How do we extricate ourselves?" (Fanon, 1967, p. 10).

Part of this process of 'extricating' African personhood from colonially imbued discursive subjectivities involves the implementation of Indigenous/African languages within the contemporary classroom. The contemporary classroom, the imperial sacrosanct as it were, installs pedagogies as informed through idealized languages of the colonizer (Bourdieu, 1991), some of which are English, French, Spanish, and Portuguese. These installed pedagogies as it were, when practiced, ensue a thinking onto African peoples, which inculcates inferiorized ways of "coming to know" local communities. (Dei, Asgharzadeh, Bahador & Shahjahan, 2006) highlight the question of language and education in Africa and the contentions. Some of the unavoidable questions, raised by these authors include:

> How could one accept a colonial language as one's official language? What would be some educational, cultural, economic, and developmental implications of such a condition? And what would be some of the consequences of having a colonial language as the language of education, vis-à-vis Indigenous, national, and local languages? (Dei et al., 2006, p. 226)

Also arising from these authors' discussions is the need for classroom dialogue to be exercised in the language of one's local community. But in contesting the language of the colonizer and the culture of colony as indoctrinated in the classroom, and with Ghana being a multi-lingual society, what then are the decisive factors that would constitute the "language of instruction"? (Cleghorn, 2005). Some significant questions, which surfaced from the discussion, which can help us think about these constitutive factors were:

> Is multilingualism a source of strength in Ghana or is it a source of weakness, conflict, and tension? How can the Indigenous Ghanaian languages be

preserved and maintained in the face of the growing popularity and importance of English as the national and standard language in Ghana? What are some of the implications of having English as the medium of instruction in Ghanaian schools and universities? What are the prospects for having one or more Ghanaian language/s as the national and standard languages of all Ghanaians? What is the role of the state in all of this? How can the state facilitate Ghanaian multiculturalism through funding, supervision, and language policies and programs? (Dei et al., 2006, p. 227)

One of the challenges for Ghanaian/African education is coming up with the language of the classroom. For mind you, concerning the "language of instruction", today there are about seventy languages spoken in Ghana, eleven of which have been identified by the Bureau of Ghana languages as 'official' languages" (Dei et al., 2006, p. 249). We ought to remember here though, that colonial is not only foreign or alien but it can also be local. So it is not that if English as the official "language of instruction" were replaced by a Ghanaian language all would be well. Not in the least, the situation is far more complex. In fact the discussion has to move beyond this singular concept of a "language of instruction" or even this category of 'official' to asking probing questions of how Ghana as a society given the power tropes accorded to its multi-lingual historic specificities can engage in meaningful dialogue in order to build communities that simultaneously respect each others language difference. In a multi-lingual and multi-ethnic society like Ghana, conflict arises between the "standard language and the dominant regional language." As such the tension among Asante, Ewe, Fante, Boron, Dagomba, Dangme, Dagarte, Akyem, Ga, and Akuapem is real. How then can schooling as a community begin to engage the complexity of how and what language constitutes the communicative medium in a multi-lingual/multi-cultural society? How would it sound and what would it look like, that is a communicative platform which allows entry points for multiple Indigenous languages that accompanies itself with the power difference of various ethnic groups? Remembering Wa Thiong'o's words, that language is not only a means of communication but also a carrier of culture, that they are a product of each other, that culture embodies those moral, ethical and aesthetic values (Wa Thiong'o, 1986). So if then language and culture are carriers of each other, what does it mean for Indigenous peoples to have their embodied knowledges disavowed in public spaces designated for learning and at the same time the colonial imposition of English as the 'language of instruction' becomes the means for communicating Indigenous lived experiences? Of importance is the way in which the different ethnic groups take up English, as the 'neutral' language, given the historic specificity of English as a tool of the colonizer and given the 'inaccessiblity' of the language within local African communities. The concern then, is the danger in using English as the "medium of instruction" and as mentioned before, "when a people use an alien, imported language, it brings with it various symbols and expressions unfamiliar to the new community, that is, the inability of a foreign language to transmit Indigenous cultural, environmental and communal experiences" (Dei et al., 2006, p. 244). From colonial 'governmentalities' (Scott, 1999), language has become a site of contestation insofar as 'power-knowledge' points are transmitted from this medium of language in and through the different ethnic bodies. Power as operationalised through language comes to shape and form hegemonic relations within the African geopolitic. Choice of language as the official language is then that which legitimizes the body, is that which produces a mode of subjectivication within African ethnicity. The claim then that English is a neutral language, that it is a language which exercises powerless relations, must be noted as a falsity. English then as the national language on the African continent must be recognized as an omnipresent procedure of subordination. However, with this in mind it is not simply doing away with English, it is not simply as making one African language the legitimate official language, but it is a question of how do local communities work with the multiplicity of African languages given the immanent hegemonic modalities of English? (Dei, 2003; 2005b)

Thinking about what ought to be done with the English language is very important for the re-conceptualization of 'development.' In nurturing an ethic and care for self, African peoples as part of the decolonizing process ought to utilize as a raw resource their local languages, only then can the fullness of Indigenity be tapped into, only then can there be comprehensiveness regarding everyday experiences of Africaness, only then can the immanent spirit of Indigenousness tacitly inform praxis, only then can insularity be circumscribed onto the personhood of African peoples. Sustainability of Indigenous African languages has been questionable, given the imperialistic durability of the English language, given the fast moving technologization of the world in the name of 'development.' With the imposition of specific knowledges through this technologization process of 'development,' Indigenous/African knowledges as a 'technology of self,' (Foucault, 1994a; 1994b; 1994c) ought to launch their will into the everyday lives of African peoples, they ought to in relation to the imposed English language bring upon African peoples a medium which not eliminate but work with the English language in ways that do not exercise "procedures of subordination" onto African peoples. This calls for addressing the problem of a lack of curricula sophistication and working with an understanding that 'bodies matter'. What schools need is representation from different bodies of knowledge and as educators our classroom teaching must subvert the institutionalization of Western dominance and intellectual hegemony. There is also the question of responsibility to not just oneself but to our communities. When raised in the context of African education it becomes a question of how we put our education to a larger cause, ensuring it compels action and that we are not imprisoned by it? Yet, as colonized as it is, African education has found ways to resist its imperious origins, despite the fact that many Africans themselves have embraced the view that African tradition, culture, and ways of knowing are forever inferior, and the only hope Africa has lies with Western ways of doing things. As we move forward, the challenge for African education lies more so with the centering of embodied knowledges within the curricula. It lies more with utilizing Indigenous/African languages that comes from homegrown social/cultural practices, which at its heart seek in genuine ways, the interest of Africa.

V. WHERE DO WE GO FROM WHERE WE'RE AT?

In this last section we will try to make sense of our ways of thinking about the link between 'Indigenous Knowledges and Development' while also looking at the African contexts of schooling and education and what we *understand* as the possibilities of critical, anti-colonial education. Colonizing education in the African context has meant not engaging with the social environment and local knowledge. Curriculum, text and classroom instruction have all been structured with an eye towards the dictates of European education. Through an anti-colonial lens that steadfastly points to the implications for contemporary knowledge production about Africa, we can begin to rethink possibilities for African education and also find ways to contribute to the search for genuine African-centered development. Education in Africa must be about creating a political, cultural-ideological frame of thought and social action, linking notions of culture, spirituality, identity, freedom, and liberation to the political and economic goal of ensuring the sovereignty of peoples. While this goal continues to be 'unending', there are implications for rethinking contemporary ways of knowledge production, as well as schooling and education in Africa. Critical African education requires asking new questions of 'materiality' and politics beyond a preoccupation with notions of identity. While there is intellectual and discursive power in seeing identity as 'text to be interpreted' rather than as an 'essence', a critical anti-colonial reading of African education must extend the overemphasis on 'texts' to broader questions of political and social action. The concept of Indigenousness as introduced into African education is about an ideological framework upholding Africa's search for genuine social, economic, political, and spiritual transformation amidst the contingencies of globalism, corporate international capitalism, imperialism, and the dominance of Westernity. Spiritual transformation though, is very much a complexity given the way the interplay of sacred/secular/superstition is configured and inserted as a contemporary normative of education. For the most part, learners in Western academic spaces experience spirituality as an exercise of theology/divinity studies all circumscribed by the discourse of religion. The result for African students is a loss of ancestral beliefs, values, concepts, and memory of historical African communities – valuable raw resources much needed for affirming African identity.

Critical African education must utilize an approach which involves the lived experiences of local subjects; it must connect problems faced in Africa to historical issues rooted in human enslavement; it must bring a critical approach which allows diasporic peoples to connect to their past, not only to the geo-physical, but also to the spatio-temporal of Africaness. In this way what surfaces is a spirituality that reinvigorates/affirms African identity. Anti-colonial pedagogies are helpful here. What they allow for is an approach to understanding our "collectives histories and experiences" which can be used to challenge the underlying colonial assumptions that informed dominant Western epistemologies, one of which is the discourse of 'development'. With anti-colonial thinking we can contribute to the decolonizing project in concrete ways. As such, epistemologies as emerging from the colonized can challenge the institutionalized narrative that has upheld Western ordering of knowing. Anti-colonial thinking allows us to move beyond the very important identity-affirmation, in that, it brings to the discussion questions concerning the interconnections of power, difference, and resistance as entrenched in colonialism. Moreover, anti-colonial thought brings to the surface historic colonizing specificities which have informed the very said disciplines that have given Western academic institutions their 'truth' positions, some of which are sociology, anthropology, political science, and history. Being constituted through Indigenous knowledges and anti-racism discursive framework, anti-colonial framework works with embodied knowledges of local/subordinated peoples which in a very material way can be inserted into Western academic spaces as oppositional to normalizing dominant epistemologies. It gives voice to oral histories and cultures, which resides outside Western academic corridors, a voice much needed for an African resurgence. In this way African peoples can draw from their history, cultures and traditions to be self-reflexive on their experiences and be better prepared to encounter the global context. Remembering the incommensurability of the Indigene, that which may not always materialize in a tangible good, we can come to understand how spiritual knowledging is part and parcel of the decolonizing process, an important building block for African personhood. It might not be perceived as that which can be readily introduced to the curriculum, but it is that which fecunds pedagogical sensitivities, a tool much needed for countering colonial conditioned ways of knowing.

Today curricula continue to miseducate Africans. Colonizing education with its imperious intentions presents itself as seeking the interest of African peoples, the outcome being that of African peoples being equipped to participate in the global from a global position. We do not dispute the need for African peoples to be well-endowed participants for the global context. But what is concerning is when this endowed position emerges from an antithetical position to the local and it is readily taken up as one's own, resulting in the same African peoples frowning upon homegrown ways of knowing. This, needless to say, is quite troubling, to see that in the name of 'development' African peoples come to develop a way of *understanding* which classifies whatever there is from within as less than. In fact it seems as if by nature Eurocentricity is the affirming desire to bring a sense of achievement onto the African body. So in finding ways to engage decolonizing pedagogies beyond the classroom, African education has to be steeped in local communities; in this way issues concerning the political, social, history, environment, and the economical to name some can be thought of with the interest of Africa and African peoples. As a point of departure African centered 'epistemes' ought not to be readily partitioned as institutionalized Western disciplines. Instead, African centered education ought to inculcate ways of knowing that mobilize the social, the cultural, the political, and the historical as constituents of knowledge and not compartmentalized as Westernity has presented. Hierarchal classifications of education have gone out of their way to maintain African knowledges as never having been and as never worthwhile of making any valuable contribution to the future of society. As such, colonizing methods have been thoroughly disseminating deeply wedged ethics into African education. African centered pedagogical practices entail questions involving multiethnic/multilingual realities. Historically, colonizers have trivialized African languages, and for the most part, curricula that informed African education have been shaped through the colonizer's language. Instead of African centered pedagogies being embedded in homegrown languages, what we have are the histories, values and beliefs of Eurocentricism coming together to codify the realities of African education. Indeed, curricula relevance for African education faces many blockades. With hegemonic Western epistemologies well saturated into African education, the way forward brings copious stumbling blocks. Yet, in utilizing African centered pedagogical practices, the foci ought to include constitutive projects, as Smith discussed, that of, "survival, development, self-determination, recovery, healing, spirituality, transformation, mobilization and decolonization" (1999, p. 117). The much asked, "colonization exists, now what?" reminds us of the urgency for these approaches.

Capitalist media often present Africa as the sole cause of their existing social, political, and cultural problems. But Africa cannot be thought of as operating in the 'now', 'free' of a colonizing history, and that Africans should take the responsibility for their role in enslavement, and Africa should get its house in order, taking the responsibility for its present economical, social, and political epidemic problems. We are not suggesting that internal problems do not exist within Africa's infrastructure, but the role of Western stakeholders in the daily re-colonization of Africa has to be taken up. So, in paving the way for what is to come in the 'then', African education must be augered in the 'before', it must as a starting point continuously remember the knowledges that were built on local customs, values, and beliefs. The purpose here is not to promote Indigenity as an idealized way of knowing, or to present Indigenous knowledges as the all purpose cure for Africa, but instead through Indigenity we can find ways to work with difference among African peoples, we can find ways to engage the already disengaged African youth. With the imposition of an alien culture, identity, language, education and religion as such, Indigenous ways of knowing allow for a resurgence of Africaness, much of which has been lost through colonial/Western procedures of education. Here it is important to note the relevance of knowledge as implemented into African educational systems. In this fast increasing globalized world, questions concerning 'suitability and sustainability' of knowledge systems and also which knowledges qualifies, are vital. Today, knowledge is more like a product of the popularity market, with commodification/marketisation of knowledge setting the popular trend. Indigenity then, is out of style, is not trendy, but the way forward for Africa is not trying to become the trend. After all, who are the trendsetters? And what are the conditions that make this popular trend possible? Again, for clarity, we are not saying that Africa should not work with the global, but we question the terms on which this relation functions, we question the silencing of the African voice, we question the taking up of an alien/colonizing voice as one's own. Yet, as we come to the very unsettling question of, 'Can Indigenity co-exist with Western systems of understanding?', we should note that the danger here lies more with the imperious nature of Western knowledge systems in this day of globalization, that is, it is that which allows for classificatory arrangements onto ways of knowing, which when embodied produces an organized and inscribed hierarchal strata onto African knowledges. This, the tragic inheritance of colonial education, gives the thrust for the decolonization of African education.

A critical discursive lens calls for looking at African education in contemporary contexts in three inter-related aspects. First, to reclaim and affirm our past intellectual traditions, knowledge, and the contributions to world history as a necessary exercise in our decolonization. Our argument here is the relevance of teaching students about how Africa did not fall from the radar screen or from a pedestal. Africa and African peoples were pushed and pushed brutally! Where are the success stories that go with the obsession with 'crisis'? Second, to reflect on the present and the necessity to theorize Africa beyond its boundaries. Africa matters politically, culturally, and intellectually. To understand the nature of the problems and challenges facing us as a people today (e.g., education, health, development, etc.), we need to bring a critical reflection about collective consciousness of our interconnected realities and social existence. And, thirdly, by seeing Africa and African peoples setting the terms of our development agenda, we can contest and project the future. This necessitates a shift away from a politics of negotiation to a politics of transformation (e.g., setting the agenda, and rules of engagement under our own terms). In other words, African peoples strategize and rethink ways of addressing the problems and the many challenges confronting us as a people. This is only possible if we heal ourselves as a people, spiritually, mentally, and materially. This calls for an affirmation of the African sense of community, social responsibility, and spiritual re-embodiment. Consequently it requires an engagement in a new anti-colonial project that allows African learners to define their own agenda for education, freedom, and recognition while making linkages with others through understandings of community and responsibility. The search for universalism in thought and practice is Eurocentric. African learners must start with home-grown solutions first and seek to address Africa's own problems and seek its own directions. The lessons of African success can then illuminate other struggles and creative projects.

REFERENCES

Abdi, A. A. (2005). African philosophies of education: Counter-Colonial criticisms. In A. Abdi & A. Cleghorn (Eds.), *Issues in African education: Sociological perspectives* (pp. 25–42). New York: Palgrave Macmillan.

Abdi, A. A. (2006). Culture of education, social development, and globalization: Historical and current analyses of Africa. In A. A. Abdi, K. P. Puplampu, & G. J. S. Dei (Eds.), *African education and globalization: Critical perspectives* (pp. 13–30). Rowman & Littlefield Publishers.

Althusser, L. (2001). *Lenin and philosophy and other essays*. New York: Monthly Review Press.

Anderson, B. (1991). *Imagined communities: Reflections on the origin and spread of nationalism* (Rev. ed.). London: Verso.

Asante, M. (1991). The Afrocentric idea in education. *Journal of Negro Education, 60*(2), 170–180.

Asante, M. K. (2003). The Afrocentric idea. In A. Mazama (Ed.), *The Afrocentric paradigm* (pp. 37–53). Trenton, NJ: Africa World Press.

Bhabha, K. H. (1994). *The location of culture*. London: Routledge.

Bourdieu, P. (1991). *Language and symbolic power*. (G. Raymond & M. Adamson, Eds., & Introduced B. J. Thompson, Trans.). Cambridge, MA: Harvard University Press.

Butler, J. (1997). *The psychic life of power: Theories in subjection*. Stanford, CA: Stanford University Press.

Butler, J. (2004). Bodies and power revisited. In D. Taylor & K. Vintages (Eds.), *Feminism and the final Foucault* (pp. 183–194). Urbana, IL and Chicago: University of Illinois Press.

Cleghorn, A. (2005). Language issues in African school settings: Problems and prospects in attaining education for all. In A. Abdi & A. Cleghorn (Eds.), *Issues in African education: Sociological perspectives* (pp. 101–122). New York: Palgrave Macmillan.

Dei, G. J. S. (1996). *Anti-Racism education: Theory and practice*. Halifax: Fernwood Publishing.

Dei, G. J. S. (1998). Interrogating African development and the Diasporan reality. *Journal of Black Studies, 29*(2), 141–153.

Dei, G. J. S. (2000a). Towards an anti-racism discursive framework. In G. J. S. Dei & A. Calliste, (Eds.), 2000. *Power, knowledge and anti-racist education: A critical reader* (pp. 23–40). Halifax: Fernwood Publishing.

Dei, G. J. S. (2000b). African development: The relevance and implications of 'Indigenousness. In G. J. S. Dei, B. L. Hall, G. Rosenberg (Eds.), *Indigenous knowledges in global contexts: Multiple readings of our world* (pp. 70–86). University of Toronto Press.

Dei, G. J. S. (2004). *Schooling and education in Africa: The case of Ghana*. Trenton, NJ: African World Press.

Dei, G. J. S. (2005a). The challenge of inclusive schooling in Africa: A Ghanaian case study. *Comparative Education, 41*(3), 267–290.

Dei, G. J. S. (2005b). Social difference and the politics of schooling in Africa: A Ghanaian case study. *Compare, 35*(3), 227–246.

Dei, G. J. S. (2005c). Critical issues in anti-racist research methodologies: An introduction. In G. J. S. Dei & G. Johal (Eds.), 2005. *Critical issues in anti-racist research methodology* (pp. 1–27). New York: Peter Lang.

Dei, G. J. S. (2006). Introduction: Mapping the terrain – towards a new politics of resistance. In G. J. S. Dei & A. Kempf (Eds.), *Anti-Colonialism and education: The politics of resistance* (pp. 1–23). Sense Publishers.

Dei, G. J. S., & Asgharzadeh, A. (2003). Language, education and development: Case studies from the southern context. *Language and Education, 17*(6), 421–439.

Dei, G. J. S., & Asgharzadeh, A. (2006). Indigenous knowledges and globalization: An African perspective. In A. A. Abdi, K. P. Puplampu, & G. J. S. Dei, (Eds.), *African education and globalization: Critical perspectives* (pp. 53–78). Rowman & Littlefield Publishers, Inc.

Dei, G. J. S., Asgharzadeh, A., Eblghie-Bhador, S., & Shahjahan, R. (2006). *Schooling and difference in Africa: Democratic challenges in a contemporary context*. Toronto: University of Toronto Press.

Du Bois, W. E. B. (1989). *The souls of black folk*. Penguin Books.

Fanon, F. (1967). *Black skin white masks*. New York: Grover Press.

Foucault, M. (1977a). *Discipline and punish: The birth of the prison*. New York: Vintage Books.

Foucault, M. (1977b). *Power/Knowledge: Selected interviews and other writings 1972–1977*. New York: Pantheon Books.

Foucault, M. (1982). The subject and power: Afterword. In Drefus & Rabinow (Eds.), *Michel Foucault: Beyond structuralism and hermeneutics* (pp. 208–226). Chicago: University of Chicago Press.

Foucault, M. (1990). *The history of sexuality, Volume 1: An introduction*. New York: Vintage Books.

Foucault, M. (1991). Governmentality. In Burchell, Gordon, & Miller (Eds.), *The Foucault effect: Studies in governmentality* (pp. 87–104). Chicago: University of Chicago Press.

Foucault, M. (1994a). Subjectivity and truth. In J. Faubion (Ed.), *Michel Foucault: Ethics, subjectivity and truth* (Essential works of Foucault, Vol. I, P. Rabinow, Series Ed., pp. 87–92). New York: The New Press.

Foucault, M. (1994b). Technologies of the self. In J. Faubion (Ed.), *Michel Foucault: Ethics, subjectivity and truth* (Essential works of Foucault, Vol. I, P. Rabinow, Series Ed., pp. 223–251). New York: The New Press.

Foucault, M. (1994c). The political technology of individuals. In J. Faubion (Ed.), *Michel Foucault: Power* (Essential works of Foucault, Vol. III, P. Rabinow, Series Ed., pp. 403–417). New York: The New Press.

Foucault, M. (2002). *The order of things*. Routledge Classics.

Freire, P. (1970). *Pedagogy of the oppressed*. New York: Continuum.

Goldberg, D. T. (1993). *Racist culture: Philosophy and the politics of meaning*. Oxford: Blackwell.

Gordon, C. (1991). Governmental rationality: An introduction. In Burchell, Gordon, & Miller (Eds.), *The Foucault effect: Studies in governmentality* (pp. 1–52). Chicago: University of Chicago Press.

Gramsci, A. (1971). *Selections from the prison notebooks* (Q. Hoare & G. N. Smith, Trans. and Ed.). New York: International Publishers.

Ladson-Billings, G. (2000). Racialized discourses and ethnic epistemologies. In N. K. Denzin & Y. S. Lincoln (Eds.), *Handbook of qualitative research* (2nd ed., pp. 257–277). Sage Publications.

Lewis, G. (2000). Configuring the terrain: Governmentality, racialized population and social work. In *'Race,' gender, social welfare: Encounters in a postcolonial society* (pp. 23–42). Cambridge: Polity Press.

Maurial, M. (1999). Indigenous knowledge and schooling: A continuum between conflict and dialogue. In M. L. Semali & L. J. Kinchloe (Eds.), *What is Indigenous knowledge?: Voices from the academy* (pp. 59–77). Falmer Press.

McGovern, S. (1999). *Education, modern development, and Indigenous knowledge: An analysis of academic knowledge production*. Garland Publishing, Inc.

McLaren, P., & Farahmandpur, R. (2005). *Teaching against global capitalism and the new imperialism*. Rowman & Littlefield Publishers, Inc.

Mills, S. (2003). *Michel Foucault*. New York: Routledge.

Mkosi, N. (2005). Surveying Indigenous knowledge, the curriculum, and development in Africa: A critical African viewpoint. In A. Abdi & A. Cleghorn (Eds.), *Issues in African education: Sociological perspectives* (pp. 151–164). New York: Palgrave Macmillan.

Munck, R. (1999). Deconstructing development discourse: Of impasses, alternatives and politics. In R. Munck & D. O'Hearn (Eds.), *Critical development theory: Contributions to the new paradigm* (pp. 195–209). London: Zed Books.

O'Malley, P., Weir, L., & Shearing, C. (1997, November). Governmentality, criticism, politics. *Economy and Society, 26*(4), 501–517.

Prah. K. (1997). Accusing the victims-in my father's house. Review of in my father's house by Kwame Anthony Appiah. *CODESRIA Bulletin*, no. 1, 14–22.

Price, E. (1998). *First thoughts toward a thesis proposal*. Unpublished Paper, Department of Sociology and Equity Studies in Education, OISE, University of Toronto.

Rabinow, P. (1984). *The Foucault reader*. New York: Pantheon Books.

Roberts, H. (1998). Indigenous knowledges and western science: Perspectives from the pacific. In D. Hodson (Ed.), *Science and technology education and ethnicity: An Aotearoa/New Zealand perspective*. Proceedings of a conference held at the Royal Society of New Zealand, Thorndon, Wellington, May 7–8, 1996. The Royal Society of New Zealand Miscellaneous series #50.

Rose, N. (1996). Governing "advanced" liberal democracies. In A. Barry, T. Osborne, & N. Rose (Eds.), *Foucault and political reason: Liberalism, neo-liberalism and rationalities of government* (pp. 37–64). Chicago: University of Chicago Press.

Sadar, Z. (1999). Development and the location of Eurocentrism. In R. Munck & D. O'Hearn (Eds.), *Critical development theory: Contributions to the new paradigm* (pp. 44–61). London: Zed Books.

Scott, D. (1999). *Refashioning futures: Criticism after postcoloniality*. Princeton, NJ: Princeton University Press.

Semali, M. L. (1999). Community as classroom: (Re)Valuing Indigenous literacy. In M. L. Semali & L. J. Kinchloe (Eds.), *What is Indigenous knowledge?: Voices from the academy* (pp. 95–118). Falmer Press.

Semali, M. L., & Kinchloe, L. J. (1999). Introduction: What is Indigenous knowledge and why should we study it? In M. L. Semali & L. J. Kinchloe (Eds.), *What is Indigenous knowledge?: Voices from the academy* (pp. 3–57). Falmer Press.

Shiza, E. (2005). Reclaiming our memories: The education dilemma in postcolonial African school curricula. In A. Abdi & A. Cleghorn (Eds.), *Issues in African education: Sociological perspectives* (pp. 65–84). New York: Palgrave Macmillan.

Simmons, M. (2006). *Truth and hue: Critical inquiry into the discourse of blackness.* Unpublished thesis, Master of Education, Department of Sociology in Education, Ontario Institute for Studies in Education, University of Toronto.

Smith Tuhiwai, L. (1999). *Decolonizing methodologies: Research and Indigenous peoples.* London: Zed Books and University of Otago Press.

Tettey, W. (2006). Globalization, information technologies, and higher education in Africa: Implications of the market agenda. In A. Abdi, K. Puplampu, & G. Dei (Eds.), *African education and globalization: Critical perspectives* (pp. 93–116). Lanham, MD: Lexington.

Tikly, L. (2004). Education and the new imperialism. *Comparative Education, 40*(2), 171–198.

Tucker, V. (1999). The myth of development: A critique of Eurocentric discourse. In R. Munck & D. O'Hearn (Eds.), *Critical development theory: Contributions to the New Paradigm* (pp. 1–26). London: Zed Books.

Van Manen, M. (1997). *Researching lived experience: Human science for an action sensitive pedagogy.* The Althouse Press.

Wa Thiong'o, N. (1986). *Decolonising the mind: The politics of language in African literature.* Oxford: James Currey. Nairobi: EAEP. Portsmouth, NH: Heinemann.

Wane, N. N. (2006). Is decolonization possible? In G. J. S. Dei & A. Kempf (Eds.), *Anti-Colonialism and education: The politics of resistance* (pp. 87–106). Sense Publishers.

Yancy, G. (2004). A Foucauldian (genealogical) reading of whiteness: The production of the black body/self and the racial deformation of Pecola Breedlove in Toni Morrison's The Bluest Eye. In G. Yancy (Ed.), *What white looks like: African-American philosophers on the whiteness question* (pp. 107–142). New York: Routledge.

JONATHAN LANGDON

3. REFRAMING DEVELOPMENT STUDIES

Towards an IDS teaching praxis informed by indigenous knowledges

INTRODUCTION

"Gha!" said the Lone Ranger. "Higayv:ligé:i"

"That's better," said Hawkeye. "Tsane:hlanv:hi."
"Listen," said Robinson Crusoe. "Hade:lohó:sgi."
"It is beginning," said Ishmael. "Dagvyá:dhv:dv:hní."

"It is begun well," said the Lone Ranger. "Tsada:hnó:nedí niga:v duyughodv: o:sdv."

"Okay?"
"Okay."
- Thomas King, *Green Grass, Running Water*

How we frame a story is important; it sets the stage not only for how the story is received, but ultimately how the story contributes to constructing the way we understand the world; as Chamberlin (2004) notes, it is through stories and the ways they are framed that we argue for our place in the world. Thomas King (1994) aptly demonstrates an example of this in the above quote, which he uses to frame, or "begin well" his novel *Green Grass, Running Water*. What is important here is that the Lone Ranger, Robinson Crusoe, Ishmael and Hawkeye have finally "begun well" after three previous tries, and that this good beginning includes Cherokee – something not included in the other three attempted beginnings. By framing the story in such a way, King has helped to destabilize assumptions over who are the insiders and outsiders of this story and, ultimately, who can understand it best.

By extension of these thoughts, how we frame knowledge is also critically important, as it not only constructs the ways in which this knowledge can be used, but also defines what does and does not count as knowledge, and finally – most importantly – who does and does not define which knowledges – or stories – count. For scholarly disciplines such as development studies, this process of framing and adjudicating what is and is not knowledge is the way in which they legitimate their place in the world (Foucault, 1972). Analysing this framing process can help us to understand not only what the normative assumptions made by a discipline are, but also who are the discipline's insiders and outsiders. Ultimately, this knowledge can allow for a reflexive process of reframing that has the potential to reconfigure insiders and outsiders of disciplinary knowledge – a process to which this chapter intends to contribute.

The passage above is one of the key framing devices for a novel that aims to contest and disrupt much of the assumed, or dominant knowledge surrounding Native Canadians. This aim is revealed in the failure of the three previous attempts to begin the story: Lone Ranger starts with "once upon a time," then tries "A long time ago in a faraway land," followed by "In the beginning, God created the heaven and the earth" (King, 1994, p. 11-14). These clichéd beginnings may feel right to non-Cherokee readers, but they are not the beginning necessary for this story. The translation of the successful beginning, provided by Davidson, Walton & Andrews (2002), is that it represents a Cherokee divination ritual and that:

> This ritual ... becomes a way to read the future that is privy only to those familiar with Cherokee practices. The ceremony cunningly subverts the fixity of Western history in its official (meaning written) form by focusing on the possibilities yet to come, possibilities that English may not have the capacity to inscribe or explain. (p. 47)

I begin this chapter on reframing development studies with this passage in an effort to connect with the quote's desire for possibilities that cannot be inscribed by Eurocentric Western histories. Development as a praxis of interventions, and development studies as a praxis of teaching and research, have both been accused in the past two decades of being Eurocentric (Nef, 2004; Rist, 2002; Escobar, 1995). Much of the post-development school of criticism has taken development to task for being a unilateral imposition of Western beliefs and interpretations of progress on the rest of the world. In the preceding chapter, Dei and Simmons aptly outline this line of criticism, revealing the enlightenment roots of concepts of development, both current and past.

In many ways, this chapter begins where these criticisms end, as it accepts this epistemic critique of development and forcefully applies its conclusions to the act of teaching development studies. As Uma Kothari (2005) has noted, development studies is a "largely unreflective ... field of study," and this lack of reflexivity "obscure[s] a longer genealogy of development" rooted in the colonial past (p. 2). Unlike other disciplines such as literature, anthropology and geography where self-reflexivity has led to broad based critiques of each discipline's Eurocentric canon, the lack of reflexivity within development studies has left the Eurocentric biases within the development studies canon unchallenged. In this sense the canonic framing texts and theorists who establish authoritatively what development is and should be have not been sufficiently problematized. Equally problematic, the focus on development interventions by the majority of development studies academics (either in critiquing or in participating in these interventions) has led to a discipline-wide lacuna where virtually no writing and reflection has been undertaken to critically examine the way in which development studies knowledge is taught.

In light of this gap in reflexivity, this chapter first examines the way in which development studies is constituted as a discipline. Next, it looks at the way in which development studies is framed as a body of knowledge to be taught to students. Finally, and taking inspiration from King's passage above, the chapter concludes with alternative framing practices, or beginnings, informed by Indigenous articulations that reimagine the possibilities that the term "development" could represent.

DEVELOPMENT STUDIES: FROM LEGITIMACY TO LACUNA

Uma Kothari's edited collection *A Radical History of Development Studies*, along with a number of recent writings on development studies,[1] is indicative of the recent recognition the discipline's gap in reflexivity and tentative emerging attempts to address it. As Andrew Sumner notes, development studies has recently "entered a period of introspection to identify its defining characteristics" as a result of "sustained critique in recent years, with accusations that it is the source of many problems in developing countries" (2006, p. 646). In the section that follows, the characteristics of development studies will be discussed. Of primary concern in this discussion is the way in which development studies is legitimated as an area of study. This legitimation acts as the frame through which the social imaginary of development studies needs to be understood. The theoretical debates that have preoccupied the discipline, as well as the meta-forms of analysis through which these debates have been understood, provide important indications of how knowledge is constructed within the field of study. Finally, in connecting development studies to its praxis as a discipline being taught to students, this section will reflect upon the way in which the discipline's preoccupation with 'field' experience is embedded in a lacuna that ignores the implications of classroom experiences in the construction of disciplined perspectives.

A convergence in the recent reflexive literature on development studies reveals a preoccupation with legitimizing the area of study on the one hand, and a desire to define its characteristics – in the past, in the present, and wished for in the future – on the other. According to this literature, the core concern of development studies is its focus on the global south: "viewing the world from the perspective of the South" (Bowles, 2004, p. 12), a "shared interest in 'less developed countries'" (Sumner, 2006, p. 645), "through a southern lens" (CASID & NSI, 2004), or "concerned with the processes of change in so-called 'third world' or 'developing countries'" (Kothari, 2005). For Loxley (2004), Angeles (2004), Nef (2004), and Bowles (2004) it is this focus on the global south that gives the discipline its legitimacy. As John Loxley puts it, development studies is "important in its own right" as it studies how southern cultures "have been and are being affected by contact with the developed world" (2004, p. 28). Added to this, many point to the interdisciplinary nature of development studies as an important legitimating characteristic (Sumner, 2006; Kothari, 2005; Harriss, 2002; Kanbur, 2002; Loxley, 2004), something Edwards (2002) has argued needs to be maintained and deepened. Harriss (1999) has further suggested that development studies represents an attempt to break the divisive disciplinary boundaries established in the 19th century and to restore unity to the social sciences. Finally, the literature points to the tension embedded within development studies between theoretical work, policy oriented work and in-the-field development intervention work (Loxley, 2004; Parpart & Veltmeyer, 2004; Angeles, 2004; Edwards, 2002). In fact, this tension and interplay between theory and practice in development studies is one of the key characteristics that students of the discipline find attractive (Child & Mannion, 2004; Loxley, 2004; Morrison, 2004) and university administrations find worrisome (Loxley, 2004; Morrison, 2004; Harriss, 1999). It is in part because of the concerns of university administration that the discipline has felt the need to legitimate itself, despite the growth of the number of development studies programs and the students registered in these programs (Kothari, 2005; Bowles, 2004).

In Canada, for instance, the desire to defend development studies has been so pronounced that the Canadian development studies community issued a white paper that both defended the importance of the field and at the same time pointed out the way in which development studies in Canada had grown (CASID & NSI, 2004). The sense of urgency at the heart of both the white paper and the special issue of the Canadian Journal of Development Studies that accompanied it, is indicative of the crisis of reflexivity Kothari notes above. But more pointedly, this preoccupation to defend the discipline is indicative of the emerging tension within the discipline as a result of the recent critiques levelled against the notion of development itself. Below, Sumner (2006) describes the various ways in which the criticism of development has manifested itself, and their corollary effects on development studies. Before turning to this critique, however, it is important to explore recent attempts at a genealogy of development studies – most fully laid out in Kothari's (2005) collection.

The Genealogy of Development Studies

As Kothari (2005) notes in her introduction, the collection "presents a critical genealogy of development studies" that "challenge[s] the dominant, modernist narrative that posits a singular, unilinear trajectory and present[s] alternative versions of ideas, institutions, and the people that embody them" (Kothari, 2005, p. 1). Importantly, one of the key framing stories of development studies that she contests is the origin of the field and of the industry it studies:

> [T]he history often rehearsed in development research and teaching has tended towards a compartmentalization of clearly bounded, successive periods characterized by specific theoretical hegemonies that articulate a singular theoretical genealogy. Typically, the story commences with economic growth and modernization theories, moves on to discuss theories of 'underdevelopment', and culminates in neo-liberalism and the Washington Consensus ... This periodization is mapped on to particular events and processes, most notably with the reification of 1945 as the key year in which development was initiated owing to the establishment of the World Bank and other Bretton Woods institutions. (Kothari, 2005, pp. 1-2)

As opposed to this compartmentalized and sequential history (a history suggestive of a Kuhnian-like progress of ideas), Kothari describes the radical history of development studies as highlighting "how bounded classifications and epochal historicizations not only obscure a longer genealogy of development but also undermine attempts to demonstrate historical continuities and divergences in the theory and practices of development, compounding the concealment of ongoing critiques" (2005, p. 2). In this sense, a critical genealogy of development studies positions the discipline "as a multi-disciplinary subject that emerged in the post-war period of decolonization, but was also informed by antecedent interests" (Kothari, 2005, p. 2). This positioning is important, not only in light of the proposed reframing I elaborate below, but also as a critical contribution to the recent attempts at reflexivity within the discipline: development studies must be understood in relation to its colonial legacy.

In contrast to this radical reading of DS history, other recent attempts to analyse the field have fallen into the normative version of the history of development studies, with its foundation in the post World War II world. The Canadian Journal of Development Studies special issue is indicative of this normative approach. While some authors in the special issue challenged the Kuhnian notion of paradigms changing over time (Parpart & Veltmeyer, 2004) and others challenged whether there has been any significant change in paradigms at all (Nef, 2004), the framing story of development studies remains relatively the same, with a progression through the paradigms of development thought (c.f. Angeles, 2004; Morrison, 2004). In contrast to this, Kothari's radical reading of the history of development studies, along with the contributions of other authors in her collection, challenges the normative compartmentalization of development eras. This critique of the notion of a compartmentalized version of the history of development is important as a first step in reframing development studies as it makes room for alternative conceptualizations of how one can frame a discussion of development studies, and how one can build a development studies curriculum that destabilizes received norms over what development means and where it comes from.

Critiques of Development Studies

As mentioned above, the emergence of critiques of *development* has helped spark an ongoing struggle for reflexivity within the development studies discipline – a struggle that may be the foundation of an alternative curriculum informed by Indigenous and southern articulations. Sumner details three grounds upon which development has been criticized: the "delivery" critique; the "neo-colonial" or "post-development critique"; and the "depoliticization" critique (2006, p. 646). The delivery critique questions the relevance of development considering the fact that those countries that have been undergoing "development" are "no better off [today] than in [the] 1950s or even before" (Sumner, 2006, p. 646) (c.f. Rist, 2002). The post-development critique argues that the discourse of development is framed by Eurocentric enlightenment thinking that imposes a Western view of progress on the global south (Sumner, 2006) (c.f. Escobar, 1995; Esteva, 1992; Sachs, 1992). Finally, the depoliticization critique sees development as constructing social problems in such a way that they require politically neutral technical solutions – thereby removing or downplaying the political motives behind given strategies (Sumner, 2006) (c.f. Ferguson, 1994). While each of these critiques is important, it is the last two that are especially relevant to the development studies discipline, as they have provoked an emerging questioning of the development studies canon, especially as it frames and contains what can and cannot be thought of as development. When one considers how development studies programs may be contributing to the technisist staff of northern development agencies, as well as to southern government institutions (such as ministries or planning commissions), then "it matters which texts and which authors are viewed as authoritative" (Sumner, 2006, p. 647). Ironically, it is precisely at this juncture of (re)considering what texts, authors, and ideas should be authoritative in development studies classrooms that the emerging trend of disciplinary reflexivity ends.

The Lacuna of Development Studies Pedagogy

While the flurry of writing around the characteristics, legitimacy and genealogy of development studies has been mounting over the last 5 years, there is very little mention, let alone in-depth reflection, on what it means to teach development studies. The only area that has been touched on by a number of writers is the need for students to couple any theoretical knowledge with practical field experiences (Loxley, 2004; Morrison, 2004; Child & Mannion, 2004). The implication, it would seem, is that like modernist visions of education of the late 19th and early 20th century that imagine the textbook as the teacher – and their contemporary rebirth under the guise of "no child left behind" where teachers read from prepared scripts – development studies imagines field experience as the teacher. The justification for this approach, and for a more skills-based curriculum across development studies instruction in general, is a better capacity for professionalization of students. Even those reflections not arguing for skills-based or experience-based student capacity, such as Sumner's, still position development studies as being "the training ground for aspiring aid agency personnel" (Sumner, 2006, p. 647). This is important as virtually nowhere in reflexive pieces about development studies are students being imagined as a) agents with their own set of desires regarding the knowledge they are acquiring, and b) potential activists envisioning and collaborating on new paradigms of international relations that question the current era of globalization.[2] In fact, and as an ironic indication of the effect of this obvious lacuna, in a study of graduate and undergraduate development studies students across Canada, there was a marked difference in student thinking about their employment opportunities when students first entered the discipline as compared to when they were getting ready to graduate (Child & Mannion, 2004, p. 168). According to the study, "neither graduate nor undergraduate students are attracted to IDS to any significant degree because of anticipated employment opportunities in the field of development"; yet, as they near graduation students become especially concerned about acquiring practical skills and field experience that will make them more employable (Child & Mannion, 2004, p. 169). This transformation in thinking clearly reflects the ways in which students are being reorientated through development studies programs towards a particular kind of educational outcome. This outcome is something being completely overlooked in the literature. It is a lacuna that must be acknowledged, not only because it fails to show any disciplinary reflexivity on the types of students development studies is producing, but also because it overlooks how knowledge is being constructed within the classroom in the first place, and to what ends it is being used. As Michael Apple and Nancy King (1983) have noted, classroom teaching tacitly constructs a normative understanding of where students fit in the world, even as the content of what is being taught may contradict these values.

DEVELOPMENT STUDIES AS TEACHING PRAXIS: FROM DEVELOPMENT CONTAINED TO DEVELOPMENT REFRAMED

Returning to the conversation in Cherokee and English that begins this chapter, my argument in the section that follows is premised on the belief that the way we frame a story, an argument, or even a whole discipline is the critical starting point from which people situate and understand information they receive. When one considers the importance of a framing device, or perspective – such as the one used by Tom King above – it is easy to see how, from a curricular standpoint, the way a course or discipline is framed becomes the lens through which information is judged to be relevant to the discipline in question. While development studies may view itself and legitimate itself as being "southern focused" and "interdisciplinary in nature" there is still a clear Northern/Western lens that frames the boundaries of the discipline. In many ways, this is the "hidden" curriculum of development studies – the unstated set of assumptions upon which the discipline bases its understanding of its place in the world (Apple & King, 1983; Apple, 2004). Given the lacuna outlined above, it is clear the discipline is still dominated by unstated assumptions, especially as there is yet to emerge any substantive analysis of this "hidden curriculum" of development studies. Therefore, to begin to unpack these unstated assumptions and the way in which these assumptions are embedded in the discipline's framing lens, I will analyse an article by David Morrison (2004) – one of the only articles from this reflexive period that explores the dimensions of, and lays out a model of a development studies curriculum. Key to this analysis is the way in which the notion of 'development' itself is constructed, as well as the set of authoritative voices that define its meaning and limits. As Sumner (2006) notes above, it "matters which texts and which authors are authoritative" as it helps to decide whether development studies is captive to its "neo-colonial … genealogy" or is rather contributing to "decolonisation" (p. 647).

Morrison's (2004) article, entitled "Teaching and studying development: making it work," extensively explores the challenges of development studies teaching as a praxis, asking "what is the appropriate scope of the field?" and "How can a good 'fit' be achieved between … the needs and interests of students and … the pedagogical and scholarly objectives of those doing the teaching?" (2004, p. 187). In response to these and other questions, the article provides a working model of a development studies curriculum that reflects "a healthy tension between theory, academic rigour, and practice; strengthen[s] interdisciplinarity; connect[s] the lessons of development processes abroad with experience in Canada; and promote[s] a critical and interactive learning environment that enables students to deepen their understanding of other cultures as well as their own" (p. 187). While the model in its entirety warrants an exploration in its own right, it is beyond the scope of this chapter. Instead, the discussion that follows will focus on two key framing processes for the construction of disciplinary identity. The first of these is Morrison's description of the introductory development studies course, proposed to take place in an undergraduate's first year. The second is the theoretical foundation course Morrison proposes should take place in a student's second year.

According to Morrison (2004), "most introductory courses begin with a review of differing conceptions of development", and then provide "an overview of colonialism in the non-Western world and the evolution of the post-WWII global economy" (p. 191). This opening can provide "some historical context for a survey of changes in thinking and strategizing about development (including debates around modernization, dependency, neo-liberalism, state and market, globalization, development alternatives and alternatives to development)" (p. 191). In this sense, the introductory course is being positioned as a survey type overview that encapsulates the contents of the discipline. This is important as it introduces students to the frame of scope of development studies, as well as to some of its Kuhnian touchstones, or what Kothari would call its "compartmentalization"; but of equal importance is the introduction of the term 'development' with its subsequent discussion of "differing conceptions" that then serve to delimit what can legitimately be called 'development'. In fact, opening courses in development studies by discussing the term 'development' is a disciplinary ritual, one that is repeated often throughout the legion of development studies related courses a student is likely to take: interdisciplinarity leads to repetition and overlap between courses cross-listed in other disciplines. In my experience taking development studies courses at the undergraduate and graduate level, the question of "what is development?" emerged as a pneumonic device that elicited groans similar to those people may feel singing the national anthem, or reciting the pledge of allegiance in other education contexts. The question began almost every course, acting both as the explicit ice-breaker for a new semester, and as the implicit hidden curricular link that defined the discipline – its own version of the pledge of allegiance.[3] The fact that Morrison (2004) has identified this as a clear beginning to the construction of disciplinary identity serves to underscore the singular position of pneumonic power of the introductory course, uniting all those development studies courses to follow in a common quest to define development – or rather to maintain these opening legitimate definitions.

Morrison (2004) does not, however, suggest this definition is simplistic. In fact, he elaborates the way in which development for him is captive of three main perspectives: the vision of change of a given society, the historical process through which societies are transformed, and, the practice of development agencies as they enact interventions in countries throughout the global south (p. 188). In some ways, this broad approach to defining development is responsive to post-development critiques of the western domination of development as a concept. For example, the post-development critic Rist (2002) notes "in every society ... people try to improve their conditions of existence, and it is not for anyone to question the legitimacy of their striving"; yet he pushes beyond what Morrison has laid out as he goes on to say, "there is nothing to indicate, however, that 'development' is the only way of achieving them, or that every society wishes the same thing" (p. 44). The critical inflection here is that, for Rist, development represents not just a vision of future improvement, but is also "built into relationships of power" (2002, p. 44) that stretch back to colonialism. This is a perspective of development that is missing from Morrison's broad spectrum, and this missing self-reflexive perspective has far-reaching implications for the construction of disciplinary identity in Morrison's model.

For instance, when Morrison's discussion of the theoretical foundation course is examined, the same lack of self-reflection of the power relations embedded in the notion of development is evident. Like the course above, this upper-level "compulsory course of theory and methods of analysis" is envisioned as an essential component of the development studies experience (Morrison, 2004, p. 192). Indicating this course's role in instilling the hidden assumptions of the discipline, Morrison claims that students "cannot expect to become agents of change until they first achieve understanding", implying that the understanding at the heart of this course will enable them to become development change agents (2004, p. 192). Yet, when the content of the proposed course is further examined, what is revealed is an "understanding" that deepens the framing process begun in the introductory course, encouraging from the outset:

> Reflection on the scope of development studies, the roots of development thinking in the Enlightenment, and an historically-contextualized overview of some of the most important intellectual antecedents of development theorizing. (Morrison, 2004, p. 192)

The clear link between the concept of development and Eurocentric frames of analysis does little to allow for the broad definition of development Morrison describes above. This is further underscored when Morrison elaborates the key "short readings from Smith, Marx and Weber ... Keynes and Schumpeter" needed to lay a foundation for the understanding described above (2004, p. 192). Therefore, what has emerged instead of a broad definition of development is the disciplinary perspective that development is an Enlightenment concept and is intrinsically tied to Western notions of progress. This is precisely the criticism Rist and others level against the notion of development, and yet it is only later in the course that Morrison suggests bringing in these criticisms – leaving the normative understanding of development essentially unchallenged. In this sense, Morrison's model is contained from the outset by this enlightened framing process. Considering this is the second compulsory course in his model, and the way in which the first introductory course provided the delimitations in which one can legitimately speak of development, it is clear that despite claims of development studies being southern focused, this focus is still being seen through a Eurocentric lens. And, while this is only one example of curricular thinking in development studies, it is indicative of the lack of self-reflection that has gone into the way in which development studies classrooms and curriculum are being constituted.

What is also clear is that the legitimacy of development studies is also at stake when this Eurocentric bias continues to frame the discipline. As Sumner (2006) notes, one of the fundamental issues development studies needs to examine in the future is "how it addresses heterogeneity in the 'Third World(s)' and opens up space for alternative 'voices'" (p. 647). Sylvester (1999) makes a similar argument, noting that development studies has much to learn from postcolonial studies as it "tend[s] not to listen to subalterns" (p. 703). This type of criticism is especially relevant considering the discipline's self-proclaimed legitimacy claim of being southern focused. As such, starting from this criticism, I want to argue in the section that follows that development studies needs to reframe not only its conception of itself – through such radical work as Kothari's collection that breaks the Kuhnian logic of compartmentalized paradigm shifts – but also work to further reframe the process through which the discipline's boundaries and its identity are constructed in the development studies classroom.

VOICES REDEFINING THE MARGINS: INDIGENOUS INFLECTIONS ON THE DEVELOPMENT STUDIES CANON

Kothari (2005) and Harris (1999) have both made the argument that development studies needs to become grounded in a more complex understanding of the historical antecedents of development as a practice and as a field of study. For Kothari this genealogy can more clearly link development studies with its colonial roots, and for Harris, a greater historical perspective can help foster a better understanding of world development, as well as challenge the disciplinary walls that surround the field. Morrison (2004) also points at the importance of the historical in broadening development studies students' understanding of development. In light of these arguments, the section that follows suggests a reframing of key historical narratives of development studies that encourage a pedagogically more complex understanding of the concept of development and its antecedents.

However, as the title of this section suggests, the complexity of this historical perspective is not drawn from voices of authority within the development studies canon (such as Smith, Locke, Hobbes, Marx, Weber, Keynes, or Schumpeter) but rather from a different set of voices. As Nef (2004), Sylvester (1999), and Sumner (2006) have pointed out, development studies needs to incorporate, represent, and respond to the voices of subaltern groups – alternative voices such as those of Indigenous peoples. As McCarty et al. (2005) note, Indigenous peoples have been amongst the most affected by the history of western colonial domination. Dei and Simmons (this volume) further note the importance of redefining development in ways articulated by Indigenous peoples and communities. Taking a more historical perspective, Mignolo's (2000) concept of local history/global design also helps reveal the power dynamics Rist (2002) discussed in this collection's introduction, where the western concept of development is embedded in a western local history that is imposing a global design on other local histories – such as those of Indigenous peoples. This does not presuppose an essential identity for indigeniety, nor downplay the back-and-forth of cross-cultural influence, but rather focuses in on a history of privileging a particular world view that frames discussions around a concept such as development.

Therefore, this section makes a first attempt at reframing the historical construction of development as a concept, and through this reframing process begins to open up the scope of development studies as a field to more subaltern and Indigenous perspectives. To do this, the section will focus on three critical historical moments/periods from which much of the normative understanding of development is drawn: the period of colonial contact between western and non-western cultures; the founding of enlightenment thought, especially in connection with economic development thought; and, the beginning of what Escobar (1995) and Rist (2002) call the development regime at the end of the Second World War. The argument I am making here is much like the one made in English Literature as it was challenged by Post-Colonial Literature and Native Literature: that the canon of authoritative texts needs to be challenged (not replaced) with texts that emerge from other perspectives/worldviews (Lefevre, 1983; Krupat, 1989). In this way, the supposedly authoritative texts are not removed – creating a new authoritative canon – but are instead drawn into tension with other texts from a similar timeframe that reveal a very different world reality. This process of reframing will add a fourth layer of Morrison's definition of development – discussed above – by broadening this concept and thereby building a more complex understanding of the historical foundations of development studies as a discipline. This beginning, while only being suggestive of one manner in which development studies can become more representative of and responsive to Indigenous perspectives, is important, not only because it deepens Kothari and Harris' call for a more complex understanding of history in development studies, but also because it helps lay a foundation for a development studies that is not just southern focused but southern inflected.

In the beginning...

Beginnings matter, and how students are introduced to the notion of development, and its colonial legacy, matters. Development studies has a history embedded in the colonial past – a fact that must be acknowledged from the beginning of disciplinary construction. As Derrida notes, the legacy of colonialism has left us with "no language – no syntax and lexicon – which is foreign to this history" (1978, p. 280). It is the logical place to begin discussions of where development comes from and what development means. This does not mean putting aside the common held origins of development studies, but rather – following Willinsky (1998) – it means "supplementing" them "with a consideration of imperialism's influence" (p. 280). Although not speaking directly about development studies, Willinsky (1998) argues that any disciplinary knowledge can benefit pedagogically from this process of introducing an awareness of the way language and knowledge have been shaped by the legacy of colonialism. In terms of beginnings, incorporating this awareness into the framing of disciplinary knowledge – what development studies is about – helps students contextualize the current world of globalization with a colonial past that helped construct it. In this sense, just as the Lone Ranger in Thomas King's novel searches and then finds the right way to begin, this reframing process will allow development studies to "begin well" in its efforts to increase southern inflections.

So, according to this new framework, a development studies curriculum would, from the outset, focus on the impact of the colonial legacy on the global south, as well as on the relationships that have emerged between the north and the south as a result of this legacy. And, as this framework proposes a new beginning to development studies, it also proposes focusing this new start on the beginning of the colonial era. As Willinsky (1998) notes, it was Columbus' voyage and contact with what is now called America that began the colonial era. Not only did the unaccounted-for presence of this new land-mass fuel western expansionism, it also generated the mental need to understand it, to locate it, to describe it, and ultimately to possess it. The resulting outpouring of writing around this unaccounted-for space established the need for:

> The historical distinctions that imperial powers used to establish colonies, divide races, distinguish cultures ... and transform [them] into universals of nature. (Willinsky, 1998, p. 246)

This process of labelling and categorizing the world is inherent to the colonial enterprise, and is the subject of volumes of writing. One of the key foundational stories of dividing up the world into those who had the potential to develop – or to become Christian and civilized – and those who didn't is the in famous mid-sixteenth-century argument between Bartolomé de Las Casas and Sepulva. In his argument, called the "Defence of the Indians", Las Casas makes the successful case for the souls of the 'Indians' of America – suggesting they are a singular race of people who could be civilized and saved through peaceful Christian conversion rather than through coercion and slavery. This last point was important, for the recognition that the Indians had souls meant they could not be used as slave labour, and therefore slaves needed to be brought from elsewhere, i.e. Africa. The resulting trans-Atlantic slave trade not only decimated Africa's own self-determined trajectory of development, but also enabled the massive generation of wealth in Europe that was necessary to begin the Industrial Revolution (Rodney, 1982). These critical historical points aside, the argument used by Las Casas also provides a perfect example of the distinctions made between people and their use-value that is at the heart of the colonial legacy – a legacy that still lingers. For instance, this way of categorizing societies is at the root of every international development index, where the productive capacities of countries are placed side by side as their economic growth is tracked over time to determine their potential in the future. These ideas are fundamental to development as a discipline, even as they receive much contemporary criticism. Yet, it is only recently that this criticism has recognized the colonial legacy behind these constructed, value-laden categorizations (Rist, 2002).

In this sense, making student's aware of Las Casas' argument provides an important opportunity to challenge contemporary modes of classification and division within the global south. But it can only truly be challenged if its attempts to provide a Eurocentric notion of the "universal of nature" is brought into dialogue with alternative understandings of the relationships betweens peoples. It may seem strange, but Las Casas' "Defence of the Indians" was written based on very little experience actually interacting with Indigenous peoples of the Americas, and all of the interactions he had were mediated by translators (Castro, 2007). In this way, his arguments for the defence of a huge number of different peoples under the banner 'Indian' needs to be understood as the myopic application of his own idealized visions. What is incredible is the way in which Indigenous voices are silenced in this period, not just in his text, but in virtually all European writing from this era (Castro, 2007). And the occasional Indigenous voices that are heard in the writing of Las Casas and other members of the "Indianist movement" are framed and mediated by them to serve the writer's particular ends (Castro, 2007). Nonetheless, through the processes of oral histories of Indigenous peoples across the Americas that dealt, and continue to deal with the legacy of colonialism, it is possible to present development studies students with an alternative understanding of the relationship between Indigenous societies and European societies. As Ali Abdi (2007) notes, the storytelling traditions of Indigenous peoples represent a different form of historical voice, one that contests not only European versions of historical relationships but also the de facto power of the written word.

The Okanagan storyteller Harry Robinson (1989), relates a creation myth that sees all the peoples of the world once being brethren, and that the first 'whites' and 'Okanagans' were brothers who god decided to divide; but upon their division god foretold of them coming back together and the importance of what each would teach the other. This tale of unity, coming from generations of storytellers, does not forget the reality of contact for the Okanagan people, who have lost lives, land and much of their way of life to western expansionism, yet it still holds to the belief that there is a brotherly bond between these two groups that should be the foundation for mutual respect and learning. In this understanding of relationships between peoples, the Okanagan approach would be to look for the ties that bind, and the learning that each people could teach each other. For development studies students just entering the discipline, this type of alternative voice would represent an important model of development through co-existence rather than the one derived from Las Casas where some people (such as development experts) speak for others, and then decide where everyone belongs in the world and their predetermined roles in 'developing' it according to the vision of these experts (please see Harvey's chapter in this volume for a discussion of voice appropriation by development experts).

Homo Economicus

One of the clear sources of disciplinary unity for development studies is its link to economics. As Sumner notes, the "dominance of economic thinking in the early years of DS is virtually beyond question" (2006, p. 645). While this dominance has been tempered in recent decades, Morrison's (2004) description of the authoritative texts and thinkers connected to development studies is certainly indicative of its continued influence as a framing set of knowledge. The importance of economics is not just part of development studies' past, as it continues to be echoed in current reflexive writing as well (Child and Manion, 2004; Loxley, 2004). Given the continue predominance of economic thinking in development studies, past and present, it is a necessary starting point in the process of reframing the discipline. As Morrison (2004) notes in his description of a theoretical foundations course, the concept of development and its link with economics finds its origin in the enlightenment thought of such thinkers as Adam Smith, therefore it makes sense that any destabilization of the power of economics as a framing set of knowledge should begin with Smith.

Smith's treatise on the wealth of nations (1776), commonly held to be the foundation of economics as a discipline, postulates how rational self-interested individuals and the notion of competition can lead to prosperity and economic growth in society. This vision has informed much contemporary economic thought, including current versions of neo-classical economics, often referred to as neo-liberalism. Smith's vision of self-interested rational individuals operating in economic tandem is also clearly linked to the satirical evolutionary category of Homo Economicus some use to describe our current stage of global development (Sumner 2006). Reading Smith and other enlightenment thinkers' writing is an integral part of development studies disciplinary identity, even as taking economics is a requirement most development studies programs still cling to. Child and Mannion's (2004) study further shows how this foundational perspective informs later conceptions of identity in development studies students who are found to place achieving "economic literacy" high on their disciplinary priority list (p. 170).

Given these realities, the privileged position Smith and his work occupies in most development studies classrooms is clearly canonical. Even when his ideas are critiqued, the vision of the rational individual operating in a self-interested way and its link with prosperity is still exceedingly influential. In essence, it is the starting place of conversations about growth and development. As such, its privileged status makes it a perfect candidate for a challenge from an author situated in the same time frame, yet in a vastly different reality.

Olaudah Equiano's 1789 autobiography has had a great impact in English Literature circles as it represents the first published slave narrative in English language history. Equiano and his text also played a critical role in the abolitionist movement that led to the end of the transatlantic slave trade (Hochschild, 2006). Briefly, the autobiography describes Equiano's story of being abducted from his home with his sister as a child, his subsequent experience in the slave trade, and his self-purchased freedom later in life. The emotive power of the text rests on the set of relationships that help Equiano arrive at his freedom, as well as on his consistent concern with the wellbeing of his missing sister. This complex set of relations, along with Equiano's integral part in the abolitionist movement, suggests a very different world from that of rational self-interested individuals as it underscores the power of collective action over individualist self-interest. Likewise, his experiences as a slave underscore the 18th century gap between those who have the privilege of playing at being rationally self-interested, and others who have virtually no agency at all – a gap many post-development thinkers would argue still exists today with the help of the 'development regime' (Rist, 2002; Escobar, 1995).

Equiano's experiences and his contribution to the abolitionist movement both help to inflect Smith's vision with a different reality from this same period - one grounded in a story of being kidnapped from an Indigenous lifestyle in West Africa and being made to suffer the indignity and hardships of the slave trade first hand. Equiano's voice helps introduce to development studies students the realities of the slave trade and links its existence to the same timeframe that Homo Economicus was being founded. Reading Smith and Equiano side by side not only gives students of development studies a more complex understanding of the global conditions of life during the enlightenment period, but also helps reveal the hierarchy in place that determines who can conceive of economic models and who is subject to their reality upon implementation. This differentiation can lead to a clearer understanding of the power dynamics at play in the modern era that led to development being framed in terms of the individual rather than the collective, and progress being seen as a national rather than a local or global phenomenon, and the consequences this type of priority setting has on those who end up losers in this economic model. It is towards the foundation of this era that we now turn.

Let the development begin

The above two alternative sets of voices help bring development studies into contact with its colonial heritage, and also help reframe this legacy along the lines Sylvester (1999) discusses: bringing development studies into dialogue with Indigenous and subaltern voices that contest its normative values. The final proposed destabilization of the development studies canon takes as its moment of intervention the supposed beginning of the development era at the end of the Second World War. Kothari (2005) is right to point out that development did not begin with Truman's famous Point Four[4], and to critique Escobar and Rist for focusing on it and ignoring the links between the colonial past and the new development present. Nonetheless, the seminal moment of Truman's speech needs to be the focus of attention, if only because it has become a canonic emblem of the birth of a new era in international relations. In it, Truman suggests a new age where a promise of decolonization comes hand in hand with a responsibility in the West to bring "the benefits of our scientific advances" to "underdeveloped areas" (as quoted in Rist 2002, p. 71). Yet, rather than merely focus on this textual creation of the developed/underdeveloped binary, and the speech's link to the foundation of the Bretton Woods institutions, as well as the contemporary post-development critiques of the new era levelled by Escobar (1995) and Rist (2002), the intervention being proposed here is to provide students with an inflection of this time-frame that re-interprets the world from the emerging 'post-colonial' perspective. At the close of the Second World War, was it really towards the universal/western ideals of the enlightenment and progress that many subaltern and Indigenous peoples were turning, or was it rather towards a desire to imagine their independence in a manner grounded in a different epistemic world view, with different sets of values and ideals as to the function of society and existence? In essence here, one must ask if development studies is supposed to be southern focused, why is the view point that frames this era embedded in a declaration of a US President and not the opinions, hopes, and dreams of a decolonizing world?

Therefore, this intervention proposes contesting and reconfiguring Truman's appeal to a Eurocentric universal notion of development, and its corollary underdeveloped binary, by inflecting it with a selection of post-colonial literature from various different locations and positions. This selection could include: reading Fanon's (1963) *Wretched of the Earth* to re-conceive of what the anti-colonial liberation struggle means, and how the foundation of the post-colonial nation betrays many of the alternative hopes of those who fought for freedom; likewise, reading snippets of Armah's (1968) *The Beautiful Ones Are Not Yet Born* to see how the promises of a modernized independent post-colonial Ghanaian nation failed to materialize; or, acquainting students with Ngugi Wa 'Thiongo's *Petals of Blood* (1977), a severe critique of homegrown comprador bourgeois who have sacrificed the potential of an independent Kenya for access to the Western materialism promised by Truman's Point Four – a critique that landed Ngugi in jail; or, giving students Momaday's (1968) *House Made of Dawn* or Silko's (1977) *Ceremony* where Native Americans returning home from the Second World War with promises of entrance into the American dream are bitterly disappointed and instead turn inwards into their own epistemic past to find some answers as to the way to live well.

All of these post-colonial voices are emanating out of lives lived in the very places Truman's point Four proposes to "develop." These voices underscore a different understanding of reality in the end of the formal colonial era, where there were hopes and dreams for new possibilities determined by people themselves, rather than supplied by external modalities. This is a very different vision of the world than that of Truman's where the decolonized world awaits the new saviour, America. Reading these multiple interpretations of the era side-by-side will inevitably lead students to gain a more complex and richer appreciation for the contradictions at the heart of the notion of development, and of the contemporary industry that enacts it. As Sylvester (1999) suggests, this type of complexity should also inflect the post-development critique of Truman's text and of this time would be well served, to focus on the voices and realities of those living in subordinated positions, and ground their critique in these realities rather than simply resorting to discursive deconstruction. This then would push Kothari (2005) and Harriss' (1999) agenda to make development studies more historically grounded as the reframing of the beginning of the development era would allow students to develop a line of critique embedded in a complex multifaceted understanding of the historical space rather than a simple analysis of the faults of logic and hegemonic predispositions of Truman's project for the global south.

CONCLUSION

The framing process that constitutes development studies as a discipline needs not only to be critically examined for the ways in which it constructs a certain knowledge/power nexus, but also the ways in which it predicts how development studies students come to understand what does and does not count as development as well as who does and does not get to decide. This chapter has attempted to illustrate the problematic nature of this practice, as well as argue for the timeliness of a reframing process in development studies given the ongoing reflexivity the discipline is exhibiting. Taking cues from other disciplines that have embarked on similar processes of canon-questioning, the chapter has elaborated three potential areas where current canonic power within development studies can be destabilized. What is crucial in these destabilizing processes is the way in which they introduce Indigenous articulations alongside normative Eurocentric views and analyses of the world. Bringing these different articulations into tension and dialogue is seen as a productive pedagogical process here, as it encourages students to maintain a complex stance towards development concepts as well as grounding their emerging understanding of the discipline in historically rich layer of multiple perspectives. Given development studies current post-development climate, this is an important stance for students to inhabit as it avoids the facile positivistic determinism of either market-based or state-based models, but also avoids overlooking the flip-side of what Sylvester (1999) points out in terms of the lacuna of post-colonial studies: the real hardship of people's – especially Indigenous people's – lives. In this sense, this chapter proposes "beginning well," as Tom King's Lone Ranger would say, so that the story of development that follows is determined by its main southern protagonists, and not by the development experts who flutter around this reality, attempting to package and rename it to fit their most recent marketing/intervention plans.

NOTES

[1] See for instance special issues of *World Development* (30(3), 2002) and the *Canadian Journal of Development Studies* (25(1), 2004), as well as Harris (1999), Edwards (2002), and Sumner (2006).
[2] Morrison (2004) and Loxley (2004) are the two exceptions to this, which is not surprising as both pieces reveal a deep connection with the make-up and needs of development studies students. Morrison's article is explored more in depth below.
[3] I even experienced this ritual in my first days taking a development studies course in graduate school.
[4] Truman's Point Four is reproduced in its entirety in Rist (2002).

REFERENCES/BIBLIOGRAPHY

Abdi, A. A. (2007). Oral societies and colonial experiences: Sub-Saharan Africa and the de-facto power of the written word. *International Education*, *37*(1), 42–59.

Angeles, L. (2004). New issues, new perspectives: Implications for international development studies. *Canadian Journal of Development Studies*, *25*(1), 61–80.

Apple, M. (2004). *Ideology and curriculum* (3rd ed.). New York: Routledge.

Apple, M., & King, N. (1983). What schools teach. In H. Giroux & D. Purpel (Eds.), *The hidden curriculum and moral education* (pp. 82–99). Berkeley, CA: McCutchan Publishing Corporation.

Armah, A. K. (1969). *The beautiful ones are not yet born*. London: Heinemann.

Bowles, P. (2004). International development studies in Canada. *Canadian Journal of Development Studies*, *25*(1), 9–16.

CASID, & North-South Institute. (2003). *White paper on international development studies in Canada*. Ottawa: CASID.

Castro, D. (2007). *Another face of empire: Bartholome de Las Casas, Indigenous rights, and ecclesiastical imperialism*. Durham: Duke University Press.

Chamberlin, J. E. (2003). *If this is your land, then where are your stories: Finding common ground*. Toronto: Alfred A. Knopf Canada.

Child, K., & Manion, C. (2004). A survey of upper-year students in international development studies. *Canadian Journal of Development Studies*, *25*(1), 167–186.

Davidson, A. E., Walton, P. L., & Andrews, J. (2003). *Border crossings: Thomas King's cultural inversions*. Toronto: University of Toronto Press.

Derrida, J. (1978). *Writing and difference*. Chicago: University of Chicago Press.

Edwards, M. (2002). Is there a "future positive" for development studies? *Journal of International Development*, *14*(6), 737–741.

Equiano, O. (1967). The interesting narrative of the life of Olaudah Equiano or Gustavus Vassa the African. In P. Edwards (Ed.), *Equiano's travels*. London: Heinemann.

Escobar, A. (1995). *Encountering development: The making and unmaking of the third world*. Princeton, NJ: Princeton University Press.

Esteva, G. (1992). Development. In W. Sachs (Ed.), *The development dictionary: A guide to knowledge and power*. London: Zed Books.

Ferguson, J. (1994). *The anti-politics machine: "Development", depoliticization, and bureaucratic power in Lesotho*. Minneapolis, MN: University of Minnesota Press.

Fanon, F. (1963). *The wretched of the earth*. Paris: Presence Africaine.

Foucault, M. (1972). *Archaeology of knowledge*. New York: Routledge.

Harriss, J. (1999). The DSA at twenty-one: A critical celebration of development studies. *Journal of International Development*, *11*(4).

Harriss, J. (2002). The case for cross-disciplinary approaches in international development. *World Development*, *30*(3), 487–496.

Hochschild, A. (2006). *Bury the chains: Prophets and rebels in the fight to free an empire's slaves*. New York: Mariner Books.

Kanbur, R. (2002). Economics, social science and development. *World Development*, *30*(3), 477–487.

King, T. (1993). *Green grass, running water*. Toronto: HarperCollins.

Kothari, U. (Ed.). (2005). *A radical history of development studies: Individuals, institutions and ideologies*. London: Zed Books.

Krupat, A. (1989). *The voice in the margin: Native American Literature and the canon*. Berkeley, CA: University of California Press.

Lefevre, A. (1983). Interface: Some thoughts on the historiography of African Literature written in English. In D. Riemenschneider (Ed.), *The history and historiography of Commonwealth Literature*. Tubingen: Gunter Narr Verlag.

Loxley, J. (2004). What is distinctive about international development studies? *Canadian Journal of Development Studies, 25*(1), 25–38.

McCarty, T., Borgoiakova, T., Gilmore, P., Lomawaima, T., & Romero, M. (2005). Editors' introduction: Indigenous epistemologies and education—self-determination, anthropology, and human rights. *Anthropology and Education Quarterly, 36*(1), 1–7.

Mignolo, W. (2000). *Local histories/global designs: Coloniality, subaltern knowledges and border thinking.* New Jersey, NJ: Princeton UP.

Mixon, N. (2007). Exploring critical theory and critical ethnography in the context of the production and reproduction of social class. In J. L. K. S. R. Steinberg (Ed.), *Cutting class: Socioeconomic status and education.* Lanham, MD: Rowman & Littlefield Publishing Group.

Momaday, N. S. (1968). *House made of dawn.* New York: HarperCollins Publishers.

Morrison, D. (2004). Teaching and studying development: Making it work. *Canadian Journal of Development Studies, 25*(1), 187–200.

Nef, J. (2004). International development studies and ethical dilemmas in academia. *Canadian Journal of Development Studies, 25*(1), 81–100.

Ngugi wa Thiongo. (1978). *Petals of blood.* New York: E.P. Dutton.

Parpart, J., & Veltmeyer, H. (2004). The development project in theory and practice: A review of its shifting dynamics. *Canadian Journal of Development Studies, 25*(1), 39–60.

Readings, B. (1997). *The university in ruins.* Boston: Harvard University Press

Rist, G. (1997). *The history of development: From western origin to global faith.* London: Zed.

Robinson, H. (1989). *Write it on your heart: The epic world of an Okanagan storyteller.* Vancouver: Tallonbooks.

Rodney, W. (1982). *How Europe underdeveloped Africa.* Washington, DC: Howard University Press.

Sachs, W. (Ed.). (1992). *The development dictionary: A guide to knowledge and power.* London: Zed Books.

Silko, L. M. (1977). *Ceremony.* New York: Viking Penguin.

Smith, A. (1776). *An inquiry into the nature and causes of the wealth of nations* (5th ed.). London: Methuen.

Sumner, A. (2006). What is development studies. *Development in Practice, 16*(6), 644–650.

Syllvester, C. (1999). Development studies and postcolonial studies: Disparate tales of the 'Third World'. *Third World Quarterly, 20*(4), 703–721.

Willinsky, J. (1998). *Learning to divide the world: Education at Empire's end.* Minneapolis, MN: University of Minnesota Press.

BLANE HARVEY

4. INDIGENOUS KNOWLEDGES, SUSTAINABLE DEVELOPMENT AND THE ENVIRONMENT

Implications for research, education and capacity building

INTRODUCTION

In this chapter I wish to contrast the long-established and mutually supportive relationship which often exists between Indigenous peoples and the ecosystems with which they cohabitate with hegemonic Western/Modernist relationships with nature, even those that are deemed sustainable. I consider what these contrasts imply in light of current calls for the integration/coupling of Indigenous and Traditional Ecological Knowledge (TEK)[1] with climate and environmental sciences to address the increasing threats to traditional Indigenous livelihoods and the ecosystems within which they are embedded. In examining the ways that ecological knowledge is conceived, valued, and transmitted in these two different approaches, I make the case that simply "collecting" Indigenous Knowledge as data for research, teaching, and learning represents a grave undervaluing and misrepresentation of the depth and complexity of Traditional and Indigenous Ecological Knowledge and its relationship with nature. Rather, I wish to shift this argument and make the case for a different form of learning imperative that Traditional and Indigenous Ecological Knowledges present to Western science and philosophy as a prerequisite to deeper collaboration. This learning imperative is to re-situate the human in ecological terms, and to re-situate the non-human in ethical terms (Plumwood, 2002, p. 8), in a move toward "ecological consciousness."

BACKGROUND:
INDIGENOUS PEOPLES AND MAINSTREAM ENVIROMENTAL DISCOURSE

Mainstream news and media have recently captured a great deal of public attention around the current state of the environment and, particularly, the potentially dire impacts of climate change and global warming. A common feature shared among media aimed at sensitizing a mass-market is that they have largely focused upon climate impact scenarios for social majority populations in the global North, such as flooding and extreme weather patterns in Europe and the United States and increases in vector-borne insects and illnesses in North America. What has spurred significantly less discussion within mainstream media is the fact that the impacts of climate change and environmental degradation are already causing massive impacts to populations throughout the global South, particularly those whose lives are inextricably tied to the earth and the ecosystem services[2] it provides. Poor,

J. Langdon (ed.), Indigenous Knowledges, Development and Education, 57–71.
© *2009 Sense Publishers. All rights reserved.*

marginalized, and Indigenous peoples have been shown to be especially vulnerable to climatic and environmental shocks and stresses related to health, livelihood, and access to services, and human security (McCarthy & IPCC, 2001; Huq, Rahman, et al., 2003; Salick & Byg, 2007). This is due to a number of contributing factors which can include their close relationship to the earth and its ecosystem resources, limited or non-availability of social safety nets, and limited social, political or financial capital at national and international levels.

Historically, Indigenous peoples have used a range of evolving adaptive processes to manage and respond to stresses and shocks to their livelihoods, which they have handed down from generation to generation through apprenticeship, ethical and cultural values and through ritual, among other forms of transmission (Berkes, Colding & Folke, 2000). However, the erosion of traditional practices, social cohesion and cultural transmission in many Indigenous communities as well as the unprecedented environmental change and unpredictability now attributed to climate change and environmental degradation threaten this historical harmony and thus Indigenous peoples' ability to both continue to fulfill their role as ecological "caretakers" or "custodians" and to sustain their own livelihoods (Salick & Byg, 2007; McGregor, 2004). This has prompted significant interest within the international scientific and development community about the types of support that can be lent to Indigenous peoples to help strengthen their resilience to increasingly severe and frequent threats.

Alongside this interest in lending assistance to Indigenous peoples with the threats they face, non-Indigenous research communities, particularly those working with concepts such as sustainable development and ecosystems management, have also grown increasingly interested in the way that Indigenous – or Traditional – ecological knowledge (IK/TEK) and practice can inform issues that they themselves are dealing with, such as biodiversity and species loss, sustainable resource management, and medical and pharmaceutical innovation (Berkes, et al., 2000; Whiteman & Cooper, 2000). Definitions of TEK vary, but most tend to share a number of key features, namely that it is drawn from local observation and experience in adapting to change over a span of many generations; is embedded within the popular culture, spirituality and language; and that it establishes a standard of conduct for self-management and respectful use of natural resources (Johnson, 1992; Berkes et al., 2000; McGregor, 2004).

As such, these two calls for knowledge sharing, typically initiated in both instances by Western actors, have created significant pressure for a *rapprochement* of Western and Indigenous systems of knowledge. To note one such example, the proceedings of a recent symposium on Indigenous peoples and climate change at the University of Oxford conclude that:

> [I]ndigenous knowledge and perceptions must be incorporated into the Climate Change forum. Indigenous Peoples offer local observations and techniques for adapting to and mitigating climate change. Indigenous Peoples must exercise self-determination and be empowered to deal with climate change which threatens their traditional livelihoods, indeed their very existence. Integration and feedback loops between climate change science and Indigenous

peoples must be established and employed. Both parties can gain knowledge from the other and support each other in action. ... We propose conjoined research and action with Indigenous peoples to afford them more prominence in international climate change discussion and action. (Salick & Byg, 2007, p. 25)

While this interest – and its implicit admission that dominant Western practices in environmental management and conservation are flawed or insufficient and in need of reconsideration – is initially quite encouraging, a closer reading of a great deal of the literature begs the question of exactly how Indigenous and traditional ecological knowledges have been interpreted and situated by those working within dominant scientific or environmental paradigms. As Deborah McGregor notes, TEK is a holistic and deeply integrative *way of life* put into action through the actual *living* of that life, and not simply a body of knowledge of *how* to live. As such, "Aboriginal views tend to move in the opposite direction to Western-trained researchers, scientists and scholars; that is, towards wholeness" (2004, p. 80). Attempting to capture or catalogue the "living of life" into scientific data, reducing it to its ecological aspects, or using it as an *add-on* to existing dominant frameworks risks undermining this holistic worldview, instead re-presenting it from a dominant-culture perspective, effectively colonizing an essential part of Indigenous peoples' knowledge systems.

This line of critique against the approaches to collaboration between Indigenous and non-Indigenous communities currently being used need not, however, be seen as a call for complete disengagement. Rather, I would argue, it presents both a caution against assuming that all collaboration or integration is necessarily good, as well as a call for non-Indigenous actors to reflect upon the positions from which they seek to enter into such collaboration. Taking these two notes of caution as points of departure, I wish to contrast the nature of Indigenous and non-Indigenous relationships with the land and ecology in greater detail, and make the case that non-Indigenous researchers and actors must strive to fully appreciate and better understand the spiritual, epistemological and historical foundations upon which Indigenous relationships rest – effectively re-situating themselves – as a prerequisite to entering into non-dominant forms of collaboration. I also wish to make the case that one of the starting points in fostering this appreciation of different worldviews and historicities – as opposed to knowledge sets – can be found in critical and anti-colonial approaches to education.

INDIGENOUS PEOPLES, NATURE, AND AGENCY

The powerful relationship between Indigenous peoples and the lands they inhabit has been studied from a host of perspectives and revealed a wide range of mostly positive impacts they have had on their natural environments. While some authors have noted maladaptive or unsustainable behaviour within certain communities or peoples (cf. Berkes et al., 2000), much more frequently studied and cited have been the positive impacts that Indigenous peoples have had, notably in preserving both species variety and habitat in global biodiversity "hotspots" (Toledo, 2000), resisting unsustainable development of their lands and resources (Coon Come, 2004; Shiva, 1991), and resilience and adaptation to environmental change (Nyong, Adesina & Osman Elasha, 2007) among others.

This has led to a growing acknowledgement of the contributions, claims and rights of Indigenous peoples, highlighted for example, in the texts of the Convention on Biodiversity, the Arctic Circumpolar Council, and the recently-ratified (despite the resistance of the Canadian and US governments) UN Declaration on the Rights of Indigenous Peoples. However, it has not necessarily led to a widespread reflection upon the philosophical and epistemological foundations at the root of these practices, nor informed a subsequent reconsideration of the logic and reasoning behind non-Indigenous environmental and development practice. Notions as fundamental as the nature and forms that knowledge takes, and how land and nature are understood and related to humans are central to the Indigenous approaches to environmental "management" applauded by the international research community, yet they tend to be glossed over in favour of detailed explications of the methods and tools that are products of TEK. McGregor notes this failure to adequately acknowledge the divergent worldviews between Indigenous and non-Indigenous actors and suggests that "non-native scholars and resource managers may object and claim that indeed they understand and appreciate the differences. If this is the case, then one can justifiably ask 'Why, then, do decision-makers continue to attempt to integrate TEK into dominant society?'" (2004, p. 82).

Deborah Rose provides some important reflections on several key points of departure between Indigenous philosophical ecology – defined as "our conceptions of our place and task in this world" (2005, p. 294) – and the hegemonic anthropocentrism of Western relationships with nature. In Rose's account of the locally contingent, multiple and recursive character of Indigenous relationships with the land, the Indigenous notion of subjectivity (characterized by sentience and agency) is not limited to humans. As such, ecological systems are seen as actively drawing humans into relationship and activity, as opposed to being activated or made meaningful by human activity. This account is in contrast to the historically held Western notion of *terra nullius* (or wilderness) where nature is seen as devoid of intentionality until it has been acted upon and put into use by humans. Closely related to this point is the assertion in much of Indigenous philosophical ecology that life processes do not prioritize human needs but rather that humans are entangled in a complex relationship of mutual dependence and sustenance with the other species of the earth, a relationship defined by reciprocal responsibilities. The recursive patterns and sequences in nature communicate vital information to humans and non-humans alike, informing them of coming changes and events and providing the means to adapt to these changes. Rose cites, for example, an Aboriginal elder, to whom information about the changing seasons is communicated by the flight patterns of swifts (a bird species): "And when the wet season begins he flies low, but when the wet season is over he flies really high now. [...] When that winter coming, go back low again and start to make that camp in the side [of the cliff] there" (Billy Bunda, in Rose, 2005, p. 298).

This situating of humans within a vast, locally contingent and ever-evolving web of life and kinship – with other humans and non-humans alike – is perhaps best evidenced by the dialogical character of creation stories shared by many Indigenous peoples, wherein humans are borne of the Earth or the universe (or, in numerous cases, of the Earth's animals), and the land is "a field of multiple interacting and collaborating agencies which can include humans but is never exhausted by them" (Plumwood, 2006, p. 125). These could be contrasted with dominant interpretations of Judeo-Christian creation accounts which see nature (or Eden) as God's gift to Man (sic.), who was made in God's image. Davis' (2000) work with the Menominee Tribe of Wisconsin evidences many of these same philosophical foundations of agency, dialogism, and co-dependence, noting:

> Both animate and inanimate objects possess spirits that need protection if the Menominee and earth are to remain healthy and whole. [...] [T]he forest is the basis of a culture. It weaves a bond between humans and the earth in a manner that protects the forest [...] If the forest is destroyed, then the culture – the very body, soul, and blood of the people – is also destroyed" (p. 54-56).

Within such a rich and inextricable dynamic, the separation of Indigenous or Traditional Ecological Knowledge from the spiritual, cultural and moral climate from which it originates seems both misguided and futile.

The contrast of Indigenous and Western – or Newtonian/Enlightenment – conceptions of agency and nature is particularly important to consider in discussing the use of TEK outside of an Indigenous discursive framework. The concept of "knowing" nature, in the Newtonian sense, implies the ability to master nature, treating it as external and controllable. In this sense nature is understood to consist of interchangeable and replaceable units (or 'resources') which can be organized and managed, rather than as infinitely diverse and exceeding the grasp of our systems of knowledge and classification. In this way, human dependency upon nature is denied and, by extension, so are the limits that nature places upon growth and the modernist enterprise. Plumwood (2006) describes this relationship with nature as hegemonic and colonizing, simultaneously reliant upon but discounting of – or "backgrounding" – subordinated Others. She also connects the discounted agency of nature by Western culture with the subordination of the lives and work of groups historically associated with the body and the animal – such as Indigenous peoples, nomads, women, and manual labourers – arguing that popular acceptance of the latter is dependant upon normalization of the former.

> The basic motivation for such denials is clear … it opens the way ethically for appropriation by the more powerful or prestigious of what the Others have helped create. … [T]his strategy relies on discounting the agency of the nonhuman sphere, that is, nature itself. It has been possible to discount the agency of subordinated groups of human by counting them or their agency as nature only because nature's agency is itself normally denied and backgrounded in western culture. (ibid, p. 133)

Thus, groups deemed pre-modern or primitive by virtue of their close and spiritual connection with the land are likely to have their knowledge and its products subordinated, or treated as less "formal." A well-documented example is the current Indigenous struggle against biopiracy in the form of pharmaceutical and agribusiness intellectual property claims to seed, crop, and plant varieties that were developed over centuries by peoples to whom claims of having "invented" or patented the life around them have traditionally been unthinkable (Shiva, 1999; Parajuli, 2004). Following this logic, the appropriation of TEK – which constitutes an important part of Indigenous peoples' cultural, spiritual and intellectual heritage – may not only imply a misuse of the knowledge, but also a continuation of a long history of physical, intellectual and spiritual colonization.

SUSTAINABLE DEVELOPMENT AND TEK: TOWARDS EQUITABLE COLLABORATION?

It would be wrong to assert that blatant agribusiness-style appropriation and "piracy" of Indigenous Knowledge is the only form of interface that has existed between Western scientific and research communities and Indigenous peoples. Increasingly, the concept of sustainable development – defined by its pioneers as "development meeting contemporary needs without jeopardizing those of future generations" (Brundtland, WCED, 1987) – has served as a rallying point for those interested in pursuing a different and more socially and ecologically "just" approach to development. With respect to the environment and ecology, this has meant accepting, among other things, that there are external limits to growth which must be understood and balanced against economic gains to ensure that humankind can maintain its current quality of life. A commonly held belief is that sustainable development represents a significant paradigm shift, one which better approximates the holistic priorities and concerns of Indigenous and some other subaltern peoples. Thus, there is an assumption among many researchers and social change actors that "Indigenous knowledge systems share the same guiding principles with sustainable development frameworks" (Nyong et al., 2007, p. 794), and that it is mutually beneficial to bring the "added value" of TEK to sustainable development initiatives (e.g. ICSU, 2002; Davies & Ebb, 1995).

However, the altruism of sustainable development frameworks and their supposed close affinity with Indigenous ways of knowing, being, and doing, has been called into question by a number of Indigenous authors who argue that while the sustainable development paradigm may shift some of the focus of the mainstream development model, it nonetheless represents a continuation of, rather than a departure from the dominant Western development paradigms of the past. They note that concepts such as conservationism, environmentalism and sustainable development, though they may decry the hegemonic and disempowering instrumentalism of corporate and neoliberal accumulation models, are nonetheless the products of Western ideology and worldviews and view solutions through a Western lens. For example, sustainable development is still understood by many of its proponents as a "hard" anthropocentric science which seeks to master or manage the obstacles and limitations presented by nature – albeit more cautiously and in different ways – so as to ensure that economic and industrial development can continue, leaving the question of agency within the land largely unchallenged. This approach continues to call primarily upon the technical expertise of scientific or managerial authorities design responses to environmental challenges such as climate change, loss of biodiversity, and threatened livelihoods; experts who, as I have noted, tend to break down or deconstruct these issues rather than seeking wholeness. The belief that technological innovation and sound environmental management offer the keys to solving our environmental crises is, in turn, reinforced by mainstream media and commerce, who offer us hybrid SUVs fuelled by gasoline with mandatory ethanol content as a means to envisioning a greener future.

As a further example of how sustainable development practices can be incongruous with Indigenous knowledge or value systems, "officially designated wilderness" such as reserves and sanctuaries, established to promote sustainable natural resource management, tend to further marginalize (sometimes through outright physical relocation) Indigenous peoples from lands they have helped to sustain for generations. Neumann provides a detailed analysis of how governmental bounding and reordering of the landscape as a part of conservation management, both in Africa and in the North, extends the colonial logic of a modernist, "rational ordering of the territorial space of the colonies" (2004, p. 202). He notes four themes consistently found in the establishment of parks and reserves both in North America and Africa, namely: the denial or failure to recognize historic human occupation and its contributions to ecology and landscapes in areas targeted for preservation; a lack of sound justification for evicting resident populations; a link with colonial and post-colonial state policies of social and territorial control; and a limiting of access to local commons (c.f. Griffiths, 2005; WRM, 2005).

Sustainable development discourse rarely seeks to disrupt the notion of development as a linear process of catching up with more "developed" societies, wherein the ends of development tend to present scant difference from the models that it was intended to critique. Thus, while there is an element of criticality at the root of the sustainable development discourse, this criticality rarely goes so far as to seriously challenge dominant Western ideology regarding science, capital, knowledge, and economic, environmental and social development – an ideology which has historically had disastrous effects on Indigenous peoples and their land. This point is brought out clearly by Deborah McGregor, who states that:

> [t]hroughout the history of colonialism, Indigenous people have been dispossessed of their lands and subjected to policies aimed at 'developing' them, often with devastating effects. Sustaining this kind of development may indeed be counterproductive as far as Indigenous people are concerned. The way sustainable development is currently conceptualized, Indigenous knowledge is required to fit the existing framework designed to fulfil the needs of Western ideals. We have been down that road before! (2004, p. 74)

McGregor's observation that Indigenous knowledge and TEK are required to complement or add to the existing Western canon is supported by numerous publications and policy papers which appear to advocate this approach. Authors have, for example, called for the integration of Indigenous knowledge into "formal" climate change mitigation and adaptation studies (Nyong et al., 2007), or "ecologically embedded" management systems (Whiteman & Cooper, 2000) and downplayed the merit of differentiating between sources of knowledge. Berkes *et al.* argue that "whether a practice is traditional or contemporary is not the key issue. The important aspect is whether or not there exists local knowledge that helps monitor, interpret and respond to dynamic changes in ecosystems and the resources and services that they generate" (2000, p. 1252). As a result, Indigenous knowledge is disembedded from its historical, spiritual, and epistemological locality, collated, formalized, and subsequently re-presented as "science" bearing the approval of those recognized authorities, ultimately to the benefit of these authorities. This process closely resembles what Linda Tuhiwai Smith terms 'trading the Other'; a process which exploits the positional superiority and authority of dominant groups to justify the expropriation of "ideas, language, knowledge, images, beliefs and fantasies" with "no concern for the peoples who originally produced the ideas or images, or who, how and why they produced those ways of knowing" (1999, p. 89-90).

This ongoing appropriation/hybridization of knowledge and culture in colonial and neo-colonial relations represents a key and frequently discussed site for debate and struggle against subversion and hegemony. Overlap and complementarity can be found between elements within the concept of sustainable development and particular Indigenous worldviews, and Indigenous knowledges have undoubtedly adopted elements from Western influence over time, leading many to claim, perhaps rightly, that through the impacts of globalization, all knowledge is now heterogeneous. No knowledge form or tradition can be neatly essentialized into binary opposition with another (be it local/global, Indigenous/Western, or otherwise). This may lead to the conclusion that making claims to the "indigeneity" of particular forms of knowledge or deliberation is misled, seeking some idealized essential form of knowledge. However, I would counter that it is nonetheless imperative that Indigenous peoples continue to contest and explore the spaces and places that they identify with and their own sense of historicity or "story", not in the aim of arriving at a neat essentialism, but as a fundamental part of resisting colonization and reclaiming identity. Dei and Asgharzadeh provide a detailed account of how this "knowledge consciousness" is denied and subverted through colonial power relations and make a case for the value of its reclamation. This consciousness, they contend, "emerges from an awareness of the intellectual agency of local subjects as well as from their capacity to articulate their condition in terms of their own geography, history, culture, language, and spirituality. The knowledge so produced can then be used to challenge, rupture, and resist colonial and imperial relations of domination" (2001, p. 302).

RE-SITUATING THE HUMAN; RE-SITUATING THE NON-HUMAN

The debate over using and compiling Indigenous and traditional ecological knowledge is not only central to the struggle against colonization and misappropriation, as

I have just discussed; it also calls into question the willingness of dominant Western ideologies to face the challenge to learn and evolve beyond the shortcomings of their own paradigms. The belief that TEK can simply be wed to the scientific traditions that have fostered Western "progress" – and the environmental impacts that have accompanied it – to produce a mutually beneficial "sum-of-all-parts" effectively frees Western traditions from the challenge to re-situate themselves, as positive change is cast as an *additive* rather than *transformative* process. As such, the expansive body of official knowledge, technical and professional expertise and authority, and the institutions that sustain it remain unthreatened, issued only with the challenge to progress and continue innovating.

A greater challenge, one aimed at more profound and meaningful change, is for Western scientific and philosophical discourses to endeavour to *re-situate the human in ecological terms, and to re-situate the non-human in ethical terms* (Plumwood, 2002). Central to re-situating the human within Western philosophy, as I have already noted, is the task of transforming the "long-term hegemonic anthropocentrism" that creates a hyper-separated, instrumentalist, master-slave dialectic between humans and other living things. Re-situating the non-human, by extension, implies shifting Western/anthropocentric conceptions of nature, and "the land", acknowledging the complex and dynamic ways that they sustain human life and act according to an inner order that exists independent of human inputs, yet is intrinsically tied to human activity. Stated another way, we are first challenged to re-consider the assumptions that underlie our sense of "place" in and with the world around us; assumptions that have historically shaped, for example our sense of "manifest destiny" in taming and transforming nature, and which today shape our societal understanding and valuation of progress, innovation and development. We are secondly and similarly challenged to reconsider the position and value we have historically granted to the non-human and natural world in which our lives are embedded – the distance we imagine between it and our selves, the priority and value we assign it, and the range of roles we imagine it playing. Together these types of re-situation form the basis of what Plumwood terms "ecological rationality," a form of reason where "ecological providers are, at a minimum, reliably sustained and strengthened, and not subject to the forms of minimization, denial and forgetting of creativity, agency and contributions characteristic of hegemonic relationships and monological rationality" (2006, 116).

Both Plumwood and Rose note the value of Indigenous collaborative – as opposed to hegemonic – frameworks for conceptualizing nature as a worldview which is reflective of the re-situated human-earth relationships that they advocate, and make the case that, as such a framework allows the space for multiple narratives and agents of change, it may serve as a starting point for a longer-term project aimed at decentring the human. Plumwood also makes the important observation that such a project serves to not only reshape and scale back our colonial relationships with nature, but with Indigenous peoples as well. "To recognize that both nature and Indigenous peoples have been colonized", she writes, "we need to rethink, relocate, and redefine our protective concepts for nature within a larger anti-colonial critique" (2006, p. 135). The final sections of this paper consider how we might begin engaging in such a rethinking (particularly as researchers and educators), the challenges it presents, and how anti-colonial education might help foster this rethinking, relocation and redefinition in dominant societies.

RESITUATING THE RESEARCHER/RESESARCHED: CHALLENGES AND REFLECTIONS

> As objects of study, Indigenous communities have been under the microscope for hundreds of years as western researchers have sought to frame the 'Indigenous problem' and apply solutions. It is now time to reverse the lens and focus on who is looking through the microscope to see if different kinds of questions can be asked. – Banerjee & Linstead, 2004: 242

Meaningfully engaging with the challenge to "rethink, relocate, and redefine" described above demands critical reflection on practices used by those, such as myself, who engage in research both with Indigenous peoples and on the environment. The challenge is further complicated when we find ourselves conducting this research from within or alongside institutions or organizations that themselves perpetuate hegemonic and colonizing approaches to engagement. As a new researcher finding himself in such a situation, I am inclined to ask myself, "where do I begin?" What does it mean to "reverse the lens" and what does research that does so look like? In what ways have I already benefited from the positional superiority of the knowledge I produce and distribute (by virtue of my formal education, language, wealth, etc.) (Said, 1979) and at whose expense has it come?

Moving beyond these initial questions, Banerjee and Linstead offer a number of more detailed considerations for researchers who engage in study with/of Indigenous communities, their practices and their knowledge, asking "in the process of 'identifying the Other', who is doing the identifying and who is being identified? Why does the Other need to be identified? For what purpose? How are the parameters of otherness defined? What kinds of subjectivities are being formed in the process?" (2004, p. 242). These questions point to the need to unpack the historical relationship that Western researchers have developed with the Other – the "object" of their study – as some critical ethnographers and anthropologists have slowly begun to do in recent years. S.H. Alatas rightly observed that "you do not find Japanese and Indian scholars roaming all over the United States and Europe collecting data, publishing them at home, in their language, and then bombarding Europe and the United States with their published results on Europe and the United States" (2000, p. 30).

Stocek and Mark (this volume) provide a detailed consideration of this issue in the context of engaging in collaborative or participatory research with Indigenous communities. To these reflections I would simply add that research seeking to engage Traditional Ecological Knowledge in the service of environmental stewardship may be best served by a critical examination of the socio-political and ideological paths and conditions that have led to subversion of ways of being, knowing and doing that we clearly have much to gain from, and reconceptualising the structures that have served to maintain and legitimize this subversion. This could contribute to a scaling-back of the unequal relations of power/knowledge that have effectively silenced marginal voices and worldviews such as those of Indigenous peoples, and open new spaces for equitable collaboration. I would further propose that an important first step in this process is a critical examination of the role our systems of education and training have played in this subversion.

DE-COLONIZING EDUCATION: AN ENTRY-POINT FOR RESITUATING AND COLLABORATION?

> If colonialism's influence had been merely the control of land that would have required only one form of resistance, but when information is also colonized, it is essential that the resistance must interrogate issues related to education, information and intellectual transformations. -Asante, in Dei and Kempf, 2004

In considering how human-nature relationships are established and legitimized within particular cultures or societies, a natural starting point is the educational practices used – be they institutional or informal – and the knowledge and worldviews they serve to transmit. As the citation from Asante above reminds us, colonization of the mind – through information, knowledge and education – and the spirit have had at least as profound and lasting an impact upon subjugated peoples as the colonization of their lands. Reflecting upon the role that education played in this process – as evidenced, for example, in Canadian residential schools' "civilizing" and assimilation policies – has prompted calls from critical educators and social change actors to develop new approaches to education which help resist and deconstruct these colonizing practices, not only toward Indigenous peoples, but also more broadly. Along these lines, Barnhardt and Kawagley suggest that:

> By documenting the integrity of locally situated cultural knowledge and skills and critiquing the learning processes by which such knowledge is transmitted, acquired, and utilized, […] Indigenous people engage in a form of self-determination that will not only benefit themselves but will also open opportunities to better understand learning in all its manifestations, thereby informing educational practices for the benefit of all. (2005, p. 20)

By using educational approaches which serve to make visible usually normalized privileging of Eurocentric and anthropocentric frameworks, and endeavouring to reclaim and re-historize marginalized and subjugated perspectives, anti-colonial education seeks to engage in such a critique with an aim of not only restoring the integrity of locally-situated knowledge and skills (knowledge consciousness), but also of prompting social, institutional and political change within dominant society. Anti-colonial education is therefore set within a discursive framework that aims to "question, interrogate, and challenge the foundations of institutionalized power and privilege, and the accompanying rationale for dominance in social relations" (Dei & Asgharzadeh, 2001, p. 300).

More specifically, anti-colonial education, as the starting point for unpacking Eurocentric ways of knowing the world, grounds its critique of Eurocentrism in alternative, non-Western knowledge traditions and positions. It engages in this critique through the analysis of material and everyday lived reality – especially that of those most affected by the reality of colonial domination – and it connects this critique with a commitment to praxis (or putting theory into action) (Langdon & Harvey, forthcoming). This process, moving from critical analysis through to praxis aimed at engaging dialogically with an other to affect collective transformation could serve as a starting point to a more honest engagement between Western and Indigenous philosophy and science. By a priori making visible and unpacking the assumptions about knowledge, human-nature relationships and development upon which calls for collaboration have so often been grounded in the past, the anti-colonial framework serves to recast the shape of the discourse that can emerge.

The potential impact of anti-colonial education within formal (particularly academic) educational settings has been explored in a number of recent publications and is addressed elsewhere in this collection (see Dei and Simmons, this volume). Elsewhere Dei has noted how, in an academic context, anti-colonial education can serve to "rupture the sense of comfort and complacency in conventional approaches to knowledge production, validation and dissemination in Euro-American educational settings" (2000a, p. 111). Similar discussions have also explored the value of such educational approaches in elementary and secondary education. What has been less frequently discussed is the potential for the use of anti-colonial approaches to reshape technical or skills-based forms of training and education, such as human capacity building, within the context of international development assistance.

Capacity building is commonly described as the "process of developing and strengthening the skills, instincts, abilities, processes and resources that organizations and communities need to survive, adapt, and thrive in the fast-changing world" (Philbin, 1996). The use of anti-colonial pedagogies in such contexts could represent an important new site of engagement, one where unquestioning faith has tended to be placed in the techno-scientific approaches of those designated as experts (generally coming from the global North, or working within Northern-based institutions) despite the commonly-cited importance of ensuring it be locally driven and responsive to the specific needs of local needs and priorities. Here, particularly in the context of environmental management where discussion from all corners focuses on the urgent and immediate need for action, time is seldom set aside for any critical reflection on the rightness of fit between proposed capacity building approaches for sustainable livelihoods or resource use and the holistic worldviews and traditions of the Indigenous peoples these initiatives are so often touted to help. Mention is invariably made of integrating traditional knowledge and the perspectives of Indigenous peoples into capacity building in multilateral environmental agreements such as the UN Framework Convention on Climate

Change, the Kyoto Protocol and the Convention on Biodiversity, but again these peoples tend to only have peripheral involvement in establishing the modalities of these agreements or in their implementation (Griffiths, 2005). Indigenous activists have expressed their frustration at being forced to work within a framework that they have had so little opportunity to help develop, and some have wondered whether it wouldn't simply be easier to disengage from the processes altogether. On this point, D. Roy Laifungbam argues that:

> We are now, whether we like it or want it or not, forced to play this game in the field we have agreed upon, by the rules we have acquiesced to, so we have to play it well or never show up. With this belief, we shall continue to attempt and support any activity that can enhance the usefulness and effectiveness of the Forum. [...] We must prise our way into these difficult negotiations, not leave it to NGOs, claim our legitimate places and work our role if we believe that these can serve our collective aspirations and agenda. We must also have the courage to reject them outright and claim no part to these negotiations if they are proven to be destructive to us, devoid of morality and political commitment. (Laifungbam, in WRM, 2005).

More specifically, in negotiations on articulating specific approaches of capacity building in developing and least developing countries (LDCs), debate over whether these initiatives actually strengthen, or instead further "mine" Indigenous communities and their knowledge is altogether absent. Thus, while there is now a growing exploration of the potential of critical and anti-colonial educative approaches to expose and shift commonly held positions on Western knowledge while opening space for Indigenous peoples to re-assert the value of their worldviews, its effect has thus far failed to penetrate the orthodoxy of dominant development institutions and their initiatives aimed at strengthening human capacity in the global South. This could represent a site for future exploration and struggle.

NOTES

[1] The terms *Indigenous* and *traditional* appear throughout this chapter in the context of ecological knowledge. It is important to note that not all groups who might be understood to be using "Indigenous" forms of knowledge fall under what are officially defined as Indigenous peoples. Drawing on the work of Dei (1993; 2000) among others, the shared commonality between these two terms refers to societies with historical continuity in occupancy of a place and resource use practice and which are generally non-industrial, and are accumulated through current and historical experience, though the peoples themselves may or may not be *officially* Indigenous. One such example may be nomadic Fula (or Peul) peoples in West Africa.

[2] The conditions and processes through which natural ecosystems, and the species that make them up, sustain and fulfil human life. Examples include provision of clean water, maintenance of liveable climates (carbon sequestration), pollination of crops and native vegetation, and fulfilment of people's cultural, spiritual, intellectual needs (FAO, 2005).

REFERENCES/BIBLIOGRAPHY

Alatas, S. H. (2000). "Intellectual imperialism: Definitions, traits, and problems. *Southeast Asian Journal of Social Sciences*, *28*(1).

Banerjee, S. B., & Linstead, S. (2004). Masking subversion: Neocolonial embeddedness in anthropological accounts of indigenous management. *Human Relations*, *57*(2), 221–247.

Barnhardt, R., & Kawagley, A. O. (2005). Indigenous Knowledge Systems and Alaska Native Ways of Knowing. *Anthropology and Education Quarterly*, *36*(1), 8–23.

Berkes, F., Colding, J., et al. (2000). "Rediscovery of traditional ecological knowledge as adaptive management. *Ecological Applications*, *10*(5), 1251–1262.

Brundtland, G. H., & World Commission on Environment and Development. (1987). *Our common future*. Oxford; New York: Oxford University Press.

Coon Come, M. (2004). Survival in the context of mega-resource development: Experiences of the James Bay Crees and the First Nations of Canada. In M. Blaser, H. Feit, & G. McRae (Eds.), *In the way of development: Indigenous peoples, life projects and globalization* (pp. 153–165). London: Zed Books.

Davies, S., & Ebbe, K. (1995). *Traditional knowledge and sustainable development*. Environmentally Sustainable Development Proceedings Series No. 4, held at the World Bank in September 1993, World Bank, Washington, DC.

Davis, T. (2000). *Sustaining the forest, the people, and the spirit*. Albany, NY: SUNY Press.

Dei G. J. S. (1993). Indigenous African knowledge systems: Local traditions of sustainable forestry. *Singapore Journal of Tropical Geography*, *14*, 28–41.

Dei, G. J. S. (2000). "Rethinking the role of Indigenous knowledges in the academy." *International Journal of Inclusive Education*, *4*(2), 111–132.

Dei, G. J. S., & Asgharzadeh, A. (2001). "The power of social theory: The anti-colonial discursive framework." *Journal of Educational Thought*, *35*(3), 297–323.

Dei, G. J. S., Hall, B., et al. (Eds.). (2000). *Indigenous knowledges in the global contexts: Multiple readings of the world*. Toronto: University of Toronto Press.

FAO. (2005). *Water for food and ecosystems glossary*. Retrieved April 27, 2008, from http://www.fao.org/ag/wfe2005/glossary_en.htm

Griffiths, T. (2005). *Indigenous peoples and the Global Environment Facility (GEF): Indigenous peoples' experiences of GEF - funded biodiversity conservation*. Moreton-in-Marsh, UK, Forest Peoples Programme.

Huq, S., Rahman, A., et al. (2003). *Mainstreaming adaptation to climate change in Least Developed Countries (LDCs)*. London: IIED.

International Council for Science. (2002). *Science, traditional knowledge and sustainable development*. ICSU Series on Science for Sustainable Development No. 4.

Johnson, M. (Ed.). (1992). *Lore: Capturing traditional environmental knowledge*. Ottawa: Dene Cultural Institute and the International Development Research Centre.

Langdon, J., & Harvey, B. (accepted, 2007). Building Anti-Colonial spaces for global education: Challenges and reflections. In A. Kempf (Ed.), *In Breach of the colonial contract: Anti-Colonialism in the US and Canada*. SENSE Publishers.

McCarthy, J. J., & Intergovernmental Panel on Climate Change. Working Group II. (2001). *Climate change 2001: Impacts, adaptation, and vulnerability: Contribution of Working Group II to the third assessment report of the Intergovernmental Panel on Climate Change*. Cambridge, UK; New York: Cambridge University Press.

McGregor, D. (2004). Traditional ecological knowledge and Sustainable development: Towards coexistence. In M. Blaser, H. Feit, & G. McRae (Eds.), *In the way of development: Indigenous peoples, life projects and globalization* (pp. 72–91). London: Zed Books.

Neumann, R. P. (2004). Nature-State-Territory. In R. Peet & M. Watts (Eds.), *Liberation ecologies: Environment, development, social movements* (2nd ed.). London: Routledge.

Nyong, A., Adesina, F., et al. (2007). The value of Indigenous knowledge in climate change mitigation and adaptation strategies in the African Sahel. *Mitigation and Adaptation Strategies for Global Change, 12*(5), 787–797.

Parajuli, P. (2004). Revisiting Gandhi and Zapata: Motion of global capital, geographies of difference and the formation of ecological ethnicities. In M. Blaser, H. Feit, & G. McRae (Eds.), *In the way of development* (pp. 235–255). London: Zed Books.

Philbin, A. (1996). *Capacity building in social justice organizations.* New York: Ford Foundation.

Plumwood, V. (2002). *Environmental culture: The ecological crisis of reason.* London: Routledge.

Plumwood, V. (2003). Decolonizing relationships with nature. In W. Adams & M. Mulligan (Eds.), *Decolonizing nature: Strategies for conservation in a post-colonial era.* London: Earthscan.

Plumwood, V. (2006). The concept of a cultural landscape: Nature, culture and agency in the land. *Ethics & the Environment, 11*(2), 115–150.

Rose, D. (2005). An indigenous philosophical ecology: Situating the human. *The Australian Journal of Anthropology, 16*(3), 294–305.

Said, E. (1979). *Orientalism.* New York: Vintage.

Salick, J., & Byg, A. (2007). *Indigenous peoples and climate change.* Symposium, April 12–13, 2007, Environmental Change Institute, Tyndall Centre for Climate Change Research, Oxford, UK.

Shiva, V. (1991). *Ecology and the politics of survival: Conflicts over natural resources in India.* Thousand Oaks, CA: Sage Publications.

Shiva, V. (1999). *Stopping biopiracy.* Retrieved November 2, 2007, from http://www.zmag.org/sustainers/content/1999-09/6shiva.htm

Smith, L. T. (1999). *Decolonising methodologies: Research and indigenous peoples.* New York: St. Martin's Press.

Toledo, V. (2000). Indigenous peoples and biodiversity. In S. A. Levin (Eds.), *Encyclopedia of biodiversity* (pp. 451–463). Princeton, NJ: Princeton University Press.

Whiteman, G., & Cooper, W. H. (2000). Ecological embeddedness. *Academy of Management Journal, 43*, 1265–1282.

WRM. (2005). *Indigenous peoples, their forests, struggles and rights.* Montevideo, Uruguay: World Rainforest Movement.

CHRISTINE STOCEK & RODNEY MARK

5. INDIGENOUS RESEARCH AND DECOLONIZING METHODOLOGIES: POSSIBILITIES & OPPORTUNITIES

In the words of Eddie Cook, "It doesn't have to be this way, it could be otherwise".[1]

INTRODUCTION

This chapter is a story of collaboration between the co-authors as it has evolved over 10 years of working together in the Cree Nation of Wemindji. Wemindji is a community located at the mouth of the Maquatua River along the east coast of James Bay, Quebec. Rodney Mark began to work for the Cree Nation of Wemindji as Youth Chief, then became Deputy Chief and is now the Chief of Wemindji's Band Council. Christine Stocek has been involved living and working in Wemindji on a number of culturally sensitive projects as a non-native employee, volunteer, and now as a PhD candidate and researcher. What distinguishes this story is how our collaboration based in hope has emerged in reaction to a long history of colonization, exploitation, and patronizing relationships. This legacy forged in the past lives on, together with a legacy of resilience and faith in beliefs that Cree ancestors and the power of their traditional knowledge and values continues to contribute to future generations and defines their distinct culture in a manner that creates quality of life through self-determining means. These events resonate with Grande's (2004) description of 'red pedagogy':

> It is as much about belief and acquiescence as it is about questioning and empowerment, about respecting the space of tradition as it intersects with the linear time frames of the (post) modern world. Most of all, it is a hope that believes in the strength and resiliency of Indigenous peoples and communities, recognizing that their struggles are not about inclusion and enfranchisement to the "new world order." (p. 28)

We begin by introducing in the following section *How To Approach Collaborations*[2], which includes 12 points that Rodney wrote after being challenged by Christine to come up with practical suggestions to help improve the evolution of collaborative projects in a locally controlled, culturally appropriate manner.[3] This text features the description of a participatory action research project that aspires to de-colonize collaborations[4] between native and non-native partners by implementing Indigenous research protocols. Battiste (2000), discussing Indigenous protection and research states:

> The main principle for research practice must be that Indigenous peoples should control their own knowledge. They should do their own research and, if they should choose to enter into any collaborative relationship with others, the research should empower and benefit their communities and cultures not merely the researchers. (p. 41)

What follows in this chapter is a renewed emphasis on local research and implementation of *The Wemindji Eeyouch Core Values*,[5] as they apply to the work of a Cree traditional artists group. This is the focus of Stocek's doctoral research. It exemplifies possible shifts in research and economic paradigms, opening paths to opportunities that Indigenous leaders and scholars are calling for, supporting local control over adult education and development.

HOW TO APPROACH COLLABORATIONS

Aboriginal people must be constantly vigilant concerning political, cultural, and educational questions that go directly to the core of who they are and the type of future they want their children to inherit. Native people throughout history have been questioning the colonizing role of education, asking for what reason, by whom, and for whom. Only in the past 20 years have they begun to answer some questions to their satisfaction. Holt, Christie, and Fry (1997) raise some interesting questions for native people to consider when working in collaboration with non-native colleagues. How do you combat inherent institutional racism? What is education? What can it offer? Is it just about mere schooling or skills, rather than life-long learning and life-affirming education, that includes learning from one another and from one's Elders, through culturally rich and supportive means? Is it about assimilation, adaptability, and accountability? Given the historical loss of control suffered by native people regarding education and development on native territory, it is integral to ask ourselves whose vision is this and who should be leading the way to learning our way out.[6] Native people are beginning to highlight the deficits of education and development that have led to identity loss at the cost of accreditation. Native people are questioning more often aspects of success that have conspired against their identity (Holt, Christie, and Fry, 1997, pp. 188-195).

Foley (1999) writes, "learning can be emancipatory, producing recognition, 'critical consciousness', a movement towards more equitable and just social relationships. Or the learning can be dominative, reproducing oppressive and exploitative relationships and ideologies" (p. 74). Aboriginal people have historically had to struggle to get an education that maintains culturally appropriate curriculum and forms of delivery through layers of abuse or indifference. The inherent experience of colonization seems in many ways to be reflected in the overwhelming feeling Mark felt in a variety of adult education or training for community development projects. Mark describes this as an evolution of an unidentifiable form of governance that has infiltrated from some space outside the community. It is felt as an all-powerful force, the sensation of its inevitability and one's inability to check its progress, as the power of economics to enforce itself beyond local influence. Mark further described the experience evolving as one of:

Feeling an ominous threat that things could just change, despite our efforts to get things going. Money often comes late, and we have to spend it for equipment and services that we are unable to deliver. In the beginning we started out excited, confident even if we were not competent, but as projects come to realization, we lost our confidence and seriously doubted our capabilities. In the end we didn't take full ownership of projects because the project would have happened anyway. The reality is even if we didn't do anything I honestly believe things can still get done. In some ways I have felt that I don't need to work hard at all; that really has an impact on motivation. Our involvement becomes tokenistic. No matter what effort is made, we know the region will do the work anyway. The excitement of doing a totally new project dissipates. There often is not any need for us to work - we just had to ask the regional administration. I find it completely frustrating. (Fieldnotes: September 3, 2003, verified by Chief Mark July 2007)

These experiences reflect the reality that, despite the strength and perseverance of native people to re-claim their institutions and the process of institutionalization itself, the process is far from satisfactory. The possibilities offered in working alongside native people are rich. Indifference, and even well meant intentions, continues to patronize or override these lessons. Scott, (2001) in reference to autonomy and development in Cree territory writes:

Political survival demands a dual, seemingly contradictory, strategy. On the one hand, First Nations are impelled to enlighten and persuade outsiders about the character and meaning, in Aboriginal cultural terms, of their relationship to homelands and waters. On the other hand, in order to create legal and constitutional space for the defence and autonomous development of their territories, they are forced to negotiate Aboriginal cultural and political landscapes in relation to Euro-Canadian concepts of property and jurisdiction. (p. 7)

It is true that through the persistence of colonizing symptoms – in their efforts to struggle for self-governance – their own polity can become colonizing; native people risk becoming both the colonizing and the colonized.

Mark has offered the following 12 points that have become a guiding source for discussion on subsequent projects, including the focus on the Cree artists group in the rest of this text. These point to issues of self-determination and the ways in which native people have chosen to courageously challenge colonization within their own institutions, raising key questions for non-native collaboration and the theory, changing implementation, and practice of adult education and development on native territory.

How To Approach Collaborations

– Work using a collaborative team concept approach. Identify values, vision, and specific objectives. How is this project meaningful to the community and the individuals involved? Both parties need to develop a sense of ownership.

- Decide together the rules of engagement, what are the roles, responsibilities, and accountabilities; once the agenda is set, the main principles supporting the work should not change. The expectations of each party need to be clarified in order to best deliver the project in a process that engages all.
- Decide what to do if things are not going as planned, especially if they are evolving too fast or too slow for one partner.
- Demonstrate respect for key individuals involved at the local level who are committed to many projects. Limited human resources are a reality in small communities; very often you are working with individuals who are responsible for many files.
- Plan a schedule or action plan together, specifically what needs to be accomplished, with target dates. Going with 'the flow' of the community is hard to do.
- Plan how to integrate fiscal relationships into the partnerships. Often the funding source limits the project to a strict schedule. There should be some understanding by both parties regarding these impacts. Funding sources rarely consider local capacity building and can be detrimental and threatening to both the project and the work being carried out.
- Define passive roles, advisory roles, and leading roles. Who ultimately has the authority to make decisions? Financial reasons should not be used to create pressure when decisions are jointly made. Disregard for local values, human resources, and capacity building fosters a lack of accountability and a breakdown in local ownership. Often the threat of losing a project, or missing out on a potential funding opportunity, forces the community to agree to decisions they are not ready for. Decisions should not be made before all partners understand the implications and feel ready or capable of beginning a new development.
- Consider seriously when starting and ending a project whether you are creating the need for a perpetual advisory role. This is a crucial factor. How will the project develop local capacity and how will the partnership conclude?
- Set the agenda for independence and local ownership as an end result. Local ownership builds capacity and increases the chances of achieving ongoing development and the quality of the project or services being offered. Real ownership may lead key local people to long-term interest and commitment, remaining with the project or services.
- Plan activities and allow time for getting to know the people you are working with, as well as the people they are serving. This is vital to the work at hand. Establish a mutual, meaningful relationship.
- Collaborate and work to build confidence within the community and with the people involved. How can this be built into the process?
- Ask yourself, if you are not involved in this project will it succeed and if the answer is no, then you should seriously evaluate how to ensure the success of the project when you are no longer involved.

Indigenous people working in partnership with their non-native colleagues are calling for the recognition of Indigenous research protocols and methodologies that increasingly expect their partners to decolonize their ideology and methodology. Understanding how dominant structures diminish one's ability to manoeuvre is key to decolonizing one's imposition. One method to achieve this is to extend the boundaries of participatory action research to include Indigenous research protocols. Non-native partners must consider in what ways it is possible to decolonize their practice. Key to these PAR objectives are concepts of procedural justice and relational accountability, (definitions by Wilson follow in the proceeding section) which characterize the nature of this cross-fertilization of PAR with Indigenous research protocols. PAR is an intentional example of how recent developments in Indigenous research protocols can be provided space and actively implemented in education, development, and research projects. Table 1, below, outlines the basic relationships between Hall's (1981, pp. 6-7) founding criteria for participatory research and the principles common to the intent found in numerous Indigenous research protocols. How they relate to Mark's suggestions for improved collaborative projects follows.

Table 1: Participatory Research: A Response to Indigenous Protocols

Hall's Criteria for Participatory Research:	*Principles Common to the Intent Found in Indigenous Research Protocols:*
Participatory research involves the people in the workplace or the community in control of the entire process of the research. Research is a dialectic process, a dialogue over time, involving interaction between both the community and researchers and the gathering and interpretation process in an ongoing manner.	Indigenous researchers, individuals, and communities must be involved as research collaborators in each step and stage of the research program, including opportunities to react and respond to research reports. Participants have control over results of the research process, including restricting access or withdrawing information.
Focus of PR is on work with a wide range of exploited or oppressed groups - immigrants, labour, Indigenous peoples, women.	The ownership, use of, and access to research results should be agreed. Clear and accessible language should be used.
The problem originates in the community or workplace itself. PR is of immediate local benefit.	Negotiation of outcomes should include results specific to the needs of the researched community.
Central to PR is its role of strengthening the awareness in people of their own abilities and resources and its support to mobilizing/ organizing.	Trust should develop and serve as the basis for a partnership that does not privilege any one partner.
Participatory research involves the people in the workplace or the community in the control of the entire process of the research.	Indigenous values must be acknowledged by incorporation within the research design and methodology of a project.

The ultimate goal of the research is fundamental structural transformation and the improvement of the lives of those involved. The beneficiaries are workers or people concerned. Research is integral to education and broader community planning.	As a negotiated partnership, control issues must be clarified, shared, and continually monitored; the community's interests should also be taken into account. Communities should benefit from, not be disadvantaged by, research.
The term 'researcher' can refer to both the community or workplace persons involved, as well as those with specialized training.	All scholars shall assume responsibility to learn protocols and local traditions, ensuring sensitivity to cultural practices and issues that ensure respect and researchers' accommodations to local norms. All research partners should attempt to impart new skills into the community and include mutual sharing of research skills and outcomes.
Although those with specialized knowledge often come from outside the situation, they are committed participants and learners in a process that leads to militancy rather than detachment.	Participants must be recognized and treated as equals in the research done, instead of as "informants" or "subjects".
A priori theories are not developed beforehand to be tested. The community describes reality as it develops its own theories about itself. Research objectives should be the liberation/mobilization of human creative resources/potential for the solution of social problems.	Approaches should be consistent with Indigenous self-determination. All scholars should consider research processes that move beyond the dominant quantitative methods and empower Indigenous voice and skills.

Mark's elaboration of the points *How To Approach Collaborations* exemplifies the need for collaborative projects to construct their working relationships to reflect the objectives and ethics of PAR and Indigenous research protocols. Given Mark's deep comprehension and ability to pin-point the difficulties native communities experience directing the development of their own institutions and policy, Mark's work demonstrates how local leadership needs to be accorded more authority and autonomy. A willingness to work with many people is evident; Mark repeatedly emphasizes a collaborative approach and the need for all partners to have a clear sense of ownership. How people negotiate their work must be transparent. Consideration for the needs of all partners and their manner of carrying out objectives should be culturally appropriate and taken into account. Fiscal relationships should not dictate sensitive cultural projects where cultural values and ethics must take priority. Building local capacity – obtaining the education and training one wants – is central to ownership, autonomy, and the ongoing success of projects. These ought to be considered throughout the process. In Mark's vision the pace of the project is controlled so the people involved are informed and active throughout the entire process as their roles are clearly defined and understood. This increased understanding is motivating, fostering the quality of the work, ownership, and sustainability of projects.[7] The regional government should support, not dictate, community projects, especially when compromises made perpetuate the need for regional control negating local objectives, the pace of participation, and capacity building that leads to sustained commitment.

Castellano (2004) believes that developing ethical codes of conduct for research with aboriginal communities or with external partnerships helps to "place the discussion of research ethics in the context of cultural worldviews and the struggle for self-determination as peoples and nations" (p. 98):

> Just as colonial policies have denied aboriginal peoples access to their traditional lands, so also colonial definitions of truth and value have denied aboriginal peoples the tools to assert and implement their knowledge. Research under the control of outsiders to the aboriginal community has been instrumental in rationalizing colonialist perceptions of aboriginal incapacity and the need for paternalistic control. (p. 107)

Mark concludes by saying:

> As a result of these types of experiences, when the opportunity for local accountability is taken away, so too is the people's sense of responsibility creating the need for perpetual dependency ... Being involved opens the door for the opportunity to be empowered. If you take away local responsibility and accountability, you shut the door on empowerment. As an end result, how we value the quality of life and work depends on our self-determination. (Fieldnotes: September 3, 2003, verified and elaborated on by Chief Mark July 2007)

Indigenous peoples share many common approaches in how they conduct their day-to-day lives with mainstream Canadians. However, individual First Nations and communities do demonstrate local beliefs and goals concerning community development and the ways and means to determine this development. These methods are based on particular histories informed by how Cree people have lived in relation to the land, fostering the development of distinct cultural world views. Wemindji has a population of approximately 1,300. Wemindji comes from the Cree word *wiiminuchii* meaning "red ochre mountain". The Cree people living here call themselves *Eeyouch* in the Cree language, meaning "the people". Cree people have a deep attachment to the past and to keeping their traditions alive. The *Eeyouch* continue to practice the ancient hunting, fishing, and trapping way of life that has sustained Cree ancestors for many generations. Today a third of the community's population continues to live year-round in the bush.[8]

In the next section we offer an example of this community's particular set of beliefs and values. The community is working to bring this knowledge to the forefront of their collaborative education and development practices, creating their own institutions and policy.

WEMINDJI EEYOUCH CORE VALUES: RESPECT & RELATIONSHIP

In the opening to *Indigenous Knowledges in Global Contexts* (2000), editors Sefa Dei, Hall, and Rosenberg offer a definition of Indigenous knowledges that is useful and inclusive:

> Indigenous knowledges are understood as the common sense ideas and cultural knowledges of local peoples concerning the everyday realities of living. They encompass the cultural traditions, values, belief systems, and world views that, in any Indigenous society, are imparted to the younger generation by community elders. They also refer to world views that are products of a direct experience of nature and its relationship with the social world. (p. 3)

Indigenous knowledges address issues of location, politics, identity, culture, and the history of people in relation to the lands they inhabit. As a dynamic form of living knowledge, they are not static but rather woven from inherited knowledges in relationship with new experiences. Knowledge is also passed on orally by trusted Elders and, for the most part, is learned within informal settings and related to the earth and its people. The process of research and learning about Indigenous history and its culture is an act of political resistance to the processes of colonization and hierarchical ways of knowing. Indigenous knowledges are not fixed categories; commonalities addressed for the purpose of perpetuating subjugation of complex experiences and social practices serve to rethink what has constituted valid or legitimate forms of knowledge.

In the forward to the same text, Shiva (2000) writes cultural diversity has suffered from the politics of knowledge:

> Colonialism has from the very beginning been a contest over the mind and the intellect. What will count as knowledge? And who will count as expert or innovator? Such questions have been central to the project of colonizing knowledge systems. Indigenous knowledges have been systemically usurped and then destroyed in their own cultures by the colonizing West ... The priorities of scientific development and R & D efforts, guided by a Western bias, transformed the plurality of knowledge systems into an *hierarchy* of knowledge systems. When knowledge plurality mutated into knowledge *hierarchy*, the *horizontal* ordering of diverse but equally valid systems was converted into a vertical ordering of *unequal* systems, and the epistemological foundations of Western knowledge were imposed on non-Western knowledge systems with the result that the latter were invalidated. (p. vii)

This section provides an example of how one community is restoring the horizontal ordering of its value system and reclaiming its authority to guide education, development, and governance.

Cree beliefs and sacred stories originating from pre-contact heritage continue to inform and construct contemporary expressions of Cree knowledge and culture. For instance, Cree beliefs traditionally "recognize the balance of nature and how people fit into this spiritual and physical world. Their traditional laws of nature and spirituality reveal their deep respect for maintaining a harmonious relationship with nature" (Gnarowski, 2002, p. 11).

Chief Mark and the Council wanted to draw on the cultural heritage of the community and its Elders to develop a new vision statement for the community, including principles to govern the Band Council. The project became known as "Revitalizing and Strengthening Our Traditional Philosophies and Principles Towards Building Strong Governance, Administration and Accountability Systems".[9] The purpose was to develop a transparent process for local government that originated from Cree knowledge within the community, to guide the Council and its administration. The intention was to ensure quality services for the entire community. To be successful the process had to fully involve the community's members.

Focus groups were identified including youth, men, women, trappers, Cree teachers, as well as former leaders from within the community, and most importantly the Elders. Two questions framed the workshops: What do you want to see 25 years from now? and What is good Government? Many issues were discussed to inform the Governance project. However, Mark felt that something key was missing and decided to hold four additional Elders sessions. Specifically, Elders were asked to describe what leaders were like and how a leader was identified in the past. It became apparent that a list of qualities that could be credited to one leader or person would not be forthcoming. Instead the Elders shared stories and events in keeping with Cree views of shared leadership. Events elicited leadership; when a situation demanded particular skills or action, an opportunity was provided for people involved to demonstrate their individual leadership abilities, as they stepped forward to address the situation at hand.[10]

Out of this rich process Elders discussed what leadership traditionally meant and how one exemplified qualities of leadership as necessary. Mark identified a consistent set of values revealed within the stories that were specifically discussed with the Elders in their last meeting; they have become known as *The Wemindji Eeyouch Core Values*. Respect and relationship are the main principles identified as integral to all the stories told.

Diagram 1 below depicts these values, with a discussion of how they operate to follow.[11] It was described by Mark and visually conceptualized by Stocek. The process evolved over time. Mark, recognizing the significance of the knowledge the Elders were sharing, did not rush the process. He understands these core values as the principles required to guide the Chief, Council and the administration. The content of the "Revitalizing and Strengthening Our Traditional Philosophies and Principles Towards Building Strong Governance, Administration and Accountability Systems" project may be adapted under different leadership. *The Wemindji Eeyouch Core Values*, however, are understood as an overall guiding set of principles that over time have remained and will remain constant.

Respect and relationship form *The Wemindji Eeyouch Core Values*. Respect and relationship connect our physical and spiritual being. Intellectual and emotional being are also are integral to the connection between the physical and spiritual self.

They are needed to achieve equilibrium in life represented by the horizontal band. The horizontal band depicts this balance representing how the core values combine to work together according to Mark. These values and their relationship to one another were derived from Cree heritage and concepts of leadership as told through stories and events by Wemindji's Elders.

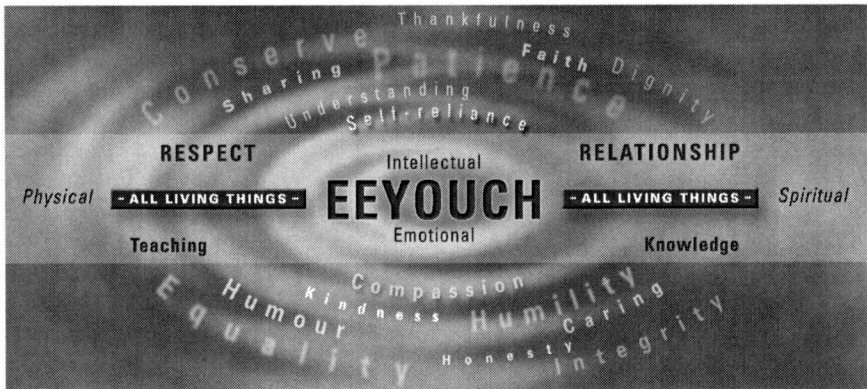

Diagram 1: The Wemindji Eeyouch Core Values Diagram Eeyouch in the local Cree dialect means "people of the land". In the Cree Nation of Wemindji Eeyouch is commonly used to refer to the Cree people themselves. In this diagram the use of the word Eeyouch both specifically locates these Cree people geographically and at the same time illustrates how the values identified from the stories told by community Elders are local and land-based in origin.

In our day-to-day lives we need to work to try to achieve and maintain a healthy balance between our physical and spiritual being. This is manifested by establishing a healthy sense of self, balancing both our intellectual and emotional lives exhibited through our interconnectedness and active engagement in respectful relationships. Teaching and knowledge are gained through this process. We must be taught these values. As your life becomes a reflection of this, by the way we live on a day-to-day basis, we become in turn a mentor or a teacher. Teaching and knowledge are engaged through reciprocal and reoccurring relationships, as are respect and relationship. Once the rapport between these values becomes a living manifestation in our life, our intellectual and emotional states are balanced, and our physical and spiritual well-being is achieved. At that moment the ability to think clearly and express wisdom is manifested.

Our intellectual, emotional, physical, and spiritual well-being is demonstrated through the expression and combination of many values. According to Wemindji's Elders, these values are key to Cree culture, and include kindness, humility, humour, honesty, ability to conserve, thankfulness, compassion, sharing, caring, dignity, integrity, faith, understanding, patience, equality, and self-reliance. These values are all interconnected and interdependent. When a value is not active, the balance at our core shifts; in an infinite, never-ending variety, these values all work hand-in-hand. Life is understood as challenging; how we respond to the events in our life provides ample opportunity to achieve this balance.

Maintaining this balance is not only a reflection of our relationship with our internal self but, just as important, it is a reflection of our relationship to our environment, to everything outside of us. Therefore our values are depicted curving into the ripples of water within the environment. The interactive exchange between human kind's values, our impact on the environment and all living things, as well as how the environment has an impact of its own, in turn shaping man's values, is represented. The distinction between inner and outer borders of being is deceptive. If we are balanced and have achieved interconnectedness, these divisions become immaterial. The animals and everything the environment contains is imbued with life, humanized with feeling. Our relationship to the environment, to the animals, or to other people is a reflection of who we are.

Equally important is the relationship the environment, the animals, and other people have with us; it is both a reflection of who we are and how the environment is. The balance (also represented by the horizontal band) we achieve within ourselves is a reflection of how our values manifest in our life and how the environment, manifesting in an infinite variety, relates and interacts with our lives. The band is transparent in order to illustrate the shifting and reciprocal exchange between human kind and the environment, both of which are represented by the expression 'all living things'. This phrase pierces the band where humankind is represented, depicting this profound interactive exchange. The pervasive strength of the environment to support life and its vulnerable fragility co-exist simultaneously.

Mark's research with Wemindji Elders and his description of *The Wemindji Eeyouch Core Values* relates to many aspects of Indigenous knowledge written by academic scholars. For example Mark's research describes one's relationship to the environment, as well as the environment's relationship to the individual, as a central part of one's experience. Castellano (2000) considers Couture (1991, p. 61), who describes the relationship between inner and outer reality:

> Reality is experienced by entering deeply into the inner being of the mind, and not by attempting to break through the outer world to a beyond. This positions the native person in 'communion' with the living reality of things. His 'communion' is his experience of the ideas within, concentric with reality without. Thus, to 'know,' to cognize, is experiential, direct knowing. (p. 28)

Mark has described the 'communion' Couture refers to when he points out the profound depth of our relationship to life's events and the environment. He seamlessly takes it one step further, describing this relationship from an environmental position or perspective. Scott (2006) has written specifically how Cree people understand the humanization of animals. In the case Scott offers he refers to the significance of the bear to Cree life and the Cree to bear life. Shawn Wilson (2001) believes that Indigenous epistemology is connected to Indigenous methodology. He believes that Indigenous researchers need to "move beyond an 'Indigenous perspective' in research" to "researching from an Indigenous paradigm" (p. 175). Examples such as *The Wemindji Eeyouch Core Values* and the case cited by Scott illustrate the need to recognize the importance Indigenous knowledge has in collaborations that strive to not only accommodate an Indigenous perspective but to work from it. Wilson defines paradigm as a "label for a set of beliefs that go together that guide my actions. So a research paradigm is a set of beliefs about the world and about gaining knowledge that go together to guide your actions as to how you're going to go about doing your research" (p. 175). Wilson states that an Indigenous paradigm is based on the foundational concept of relational knowledge:

> Knowledge is shared with all creation. It is not just interpersonal relationships, not just with the research subjects I may be working with, but it is a relationship with all creation. It is with the cosmos, it is with the animals, with the plants, with the earth that we share this knowledge. It goes beyond the idea of individual knowledge to the concept of relational knowledge …You can extend this to say that ideas and concepts, like objects, are not as important as my relationship to an idea or concept. This language speaks from an epistemology that is totally foreign to the other research paradigms, an epistemology where relationships are more important than reality. (pp. 176-177)

For Wilson (2001), an Indigenous methodology "means talking about relational accountability … you are not answering questions of validity or reliability or making judgments of better or worse. Instead you should be fulfilling your relationships with the world around you" (p. 177). Wilson is asking himself, as a researcher, how to meet his obligations to the relationships in which he is engaged. Building knowledge must be carried out not as an abstract goal but also as a process integral to meeting all the relationships forged through the research process. "This becomes my methodology, an Indigenous methodology, by looking at relational accountability or being accountable to all my relations" (p. 177). Steinhauer (2003) agrees with Wilson's emphasis on relational accountability, stating that as Indigenous researchers "we are dependent on everyone and everything around us – all our relations, be it in the air, water, rocks, trees, animals, insects, humans, and so forth" (p. 72).

Like Wilson and Steinhauer, Mark and Wemindji's Elders have articulated their concern for fulfilling relationships, relationships that permeate one's existence, interconnected with the environment. Being accountable to all one's relations means maintaining a balance by living one's values and, therefore by extension, expressing wisdom. Indigenous scholars have written that Indigenous research, like one's life, should be a function of one's values. Mark, as Chief, like Indigenous academic scholars, is advocating that on behalf of the community, governance, leadership, and local development should also be guided by and reflect these values, maintaining balance in all decisions and in all their relations. In essence to think through and work from *The Wemindji Eeyouch Core Values* is to work from a local Cree paradigm. It is Mark's hope that these values will also serve to guide all entities within the community that run independently from the Council.

In the next section of this text we illustrate this by showing how the Cree artists' group, *Investing in Traditional Skills* strives to live up to the 12 points *How To Approach Collaborations*, whereby PAR became an extension of Indigenous protocols. Stocek, working with the group and other community volunteers, in an attempt to decolonize her presence, introduces *The Elements of Development* (Salway Black, 1994) into their research process. The choice of *The Elements of Development* was explicitly made based on how the model respects and responds to Cree perspectives and world views identified in *The Wemindji Eeyouch Core Values*. It serves as one means to collaborate and approach Cree world views and beliefs that are threatened by capitalism and its ever-growing impact on economic development opportunities for Cree traditional artists.

INVESTING IN TRADITIONAL SKILLS

In 2001, Cree traditional artists in Wemindji formed the non-profit group *Investing In Traditional Skills* or 'Skills'. 'Skills' is known for its expertise in working with traditionally handcrafted moose hide making moccasins, mukluks, gloves, mittens, and walking out ceremony outfits, as well as weaving snowshoes. They produce quality beadwork and are recognized for their embroidering on hide. 'Skills' uses traditional patterns, creates contemporary images and has begun to research historic Cree work such as folded spruce bark baskets. The group currently consists of 5 women of diverse ages. A committee selected the members of 'Skills' based on their knowledge and ability to share and to teach one-another in a given area. 'Skills' is concerned with revitalizing and practicing Cree traditions. They make conscientious efforts to consult the Elders and to pursue the ideas of their younger members in order that Cree traditions maintain a living presence in today's society.

In Wemindji, due to a determined investment in the mixed economy and perhaps also to its isolation, modifications in craft production have served the local population, not a tourist trade. Historically, the range and quality of 'educational opportunities' has been extreme; some members learned skills through traditional observation in the bush, others were taught in residential schools. Residential schools taught the 'home' crafts of the colonizing population; the materials were of poor quality, manufactured and often so limited that miniatures became popular. In the late 1970's and early 1980's some members took craft courses funded by Indian Affairs. These courses were better suited to production line skills, often emphasizing business trends and ideas that did not originate from local values or material resources.[12]

Native self-determination is engaged when people insist on the freedom to access the means to maintain and determine their own concepts and cultural policy. Former Grand Chief Dr. Ted Moses has stated "creativity has been an important part of Eeyou lifestyle since time immemorial ...The Eeyou know-how has been transmitted through countless generations ... it is our duty and responsibility to ensure that this heritage is maintained and that creative expression is allowed to grow and find contemporary means of expression."[13]

The artistic mandate of *Investing in Traditional Skills* provides a strong foundation for the living culture of today's Cree by serving the community in several ways. 'Skills' maintains the highest possible standards of quality craftsmanship and celebrates the learning process necessary in acquiring these standards. 'Skills' practices both popular forms of Cree craft and those craft skills that are in danger of being lost. The work carried out by 'Skills' ensures that Cree cultural practices and values form part of the community's daily life. 'Skills' produces a variety of crafts from handcrafted local resources that serve today's contemporary life within the community and out in the bush, just as these same skills and values served traditional practices that grew from the people's special connection to the land.

The group has incorporated officially as a non-profit organization and is developing its activities in partnership with community and regional cultural programs. 'Skills' began as a short-term band initiative whose objective was to use its resources to create employment based on existing skills within the community. The group will continue to be eligible for funding administered by the band, as well as other sources of funding, but will also be self-employing. 'Skills' is proud that their products are accessible and that they sell all their art within the community. They have recently decided that recognition of Cree culture is increasingly important to both the community's youth and to the larger public and have decided to hold back a percentage of items for sale exclusively outside of Wemindji. The group has successfully experimented with sales outside of the community. They are collaborating with the newly formed Cree Native Arts & Crafts Association in promoting their work as well as in developing the means to meet the demands for their work.

THE ELEMENTS OF DEVELOPMENT: THE PATH OF A MOOSE HIDE

Wuttunee (2004) cites the First Nations Development Institute's (FNDI)[14] definition of Indigenous economics as the "science of dealing with production, distribution, and consumption of wealth in a naturally holistic, reciprocal manner that respects humankind, fellow species, and eco-balance of life" (p. 3). Like Indigenous scholars who are calling for a paradigm shift in Indigenous research, so too are Indigenous entrepreneurs, community development organizations, and business people. Wuttunee writes (2004) that the FNDI's definition is responding to more then a supply and demand capitalist program common to Western objectives. They are calling for a "shift of perspective in the heart. It requires a connection to spirit that goes beyond the scientific analysis of numbers of jobs created and revenues generated" (p. 3). The Western mind-set uses indicators for success that do not account for cultural assets and broader objectives integral to Wemindji values. The *Investing in Traditional Skills* research process is an example of how a small group initiative can have larger implications. Wuttunee (2004) understands it as a:

> Move instead towards an economic development approach that includes these costs but also attempts to quantify all costs of development decisions on environment, people, communities, and future generations. Profit is important

as a measure of success, but it is not the only measure. "Reasonable" profit that honours the limits of the planet's resources must replace the idea of "maximum" profit. (p. 7)

Drawing on *The Wemindji Eeyouch Core Values* as a set of principles guiding development of new projects also requires this change in perspective. When implemented, a remarkably new economic reality cannot help but emerge in a system that has historically been infiltrated and surrounded by a continuous colonizing, capitalist assault that has marginalized it.

The example of implementing PAR to combine processes such as How To Approach Collaborations, *The Wemindji Eeyouch Core Values*, and adopting holistic forms of analyses like The Elements of Development, described below, entails changing research, education and economic paradigms. Finger and Asún (2001) discuss how the "instrumentalisation of adult education theory and practice by the business literature and management schools was precisely at the price of evacuating the issues of power and institutionalization" (p. 179). Indigenous adult education has to be vigilant not to become a tool for furthering colonizing processes of institutionalization nor can it rest as a tool for "helping business learn how to compete better and faster" (Finger and Asún, 2001, p. 180). PAR as a research methodology combined with Indigenous world views supports native adult education in its capacity for social action and self-determination. Finger and Asún (2001) write how PAR allows for "communes of resistance to reappropriate their destiny and become more sustainable communities, thus uncoupling, to a certain extent, from the industrial development process" (p. 179). They do, however, perceive gaps in PAR's ability to address institutions and deinstitutionalization in heavily industrialized areas.

While it is true that Wemindji is far from industrialized and is an isolated Northern community, Mark and Stocek believe that PAR processes stemming from native world views have much to offer these questions as they relate to issues of the proliferation of colonizing institutions on native territory. Wuttunee quoting Salway Black (2004, p. 24) reminds us, "that most programs for aboriginal peoples encourage them to enter the very market-based, capitalist system that has marginalized many of them". This need not be the case when "relationships between people, communities, and environment with a spiritual underpinning are honoured and are the focus for economic development within the context of values, culture and tradition" (p. 24). Indigenous communities are struggling with the process of decolonizing the construction of developing their new institutions. These same challenges helped 'Skills' conceptually rethink the relationship between learning and organizations and better understand the power and dynamics of economics to organize institutions. They discovered how success, in limited economic terms, can conceal the fact that institutionalization governed by economics can be counterproductive and ultimately destructive to Cree ways of being and knowing, to Cree livelihood.

Sherry Salway Black (1994), through *The Elements of Development*, has proposed a model used by FNDI that encourages Indigenous communities to evaluate their economic projects on their own terms. The model can be adjusted to suit individual and community beliefs, demographics, and cultural assets. It places decisions in the hands of local Indigenous people to identify the impact of their projects through a collaborative process. Of interest for *Investing in Traditional Skills* were the issues and needs that arose throughout the process, generating projects that sought solutions to problems they had highlighted - solutions that were drawn from the community's capabilities and strengths. The importance of maintaining the balance the model suggests depends on the emphasis each group places on their values, what shifts are acceptable, and what trade offs demand too high a sacrifice. *The Wemindji Eeyouch Core Values* provided guidance crucial to this decision making process.

The model working from the centre outwards begins with a focus on the individual, the project, the community, and the nation. Salway Black's model is divided into four equal sections; each section features an additional three reference points. If you want to evaluate and analyze a new project holistically, from an Indigenous perspective, FNDI, Salway Black & Wuttunee propose you consider how it functions as a reflection of the 16 elements.

The four main points of axis, reflecting economic development factors, are *Control of Assets, Spirituality, Kinship,* and *Personal Efficacy*. *Control of Assets* is situated at the northern axis of the model. Circling to the right, to the eastern axis between *Control of Assets* and *Spirituality*, are environmental balance, hope & future orientation, and choice/vision. Between *Spirituality* and the southern axis point, *Kinship*, are cultural integrity, social respect, and political & civic participation. Moving from *Kinship* around to the western axis point is *Personal Efficacy*, which comprises vibrant initiative, responsibilities & consequences, and health & safety. From *Personal Efficacy* back up to *Control of Assets* are productivity skills, income, and trade & exchange. For an in-depth description of each element Salway Black (1994) and Wuttunee (2004) offer thorough descriptions of each and possible indicators of success in each quadrant.

The Elements of Development revealed information that supported *Investing in Traditional Skills* as a PAR project, respecting Indigenous research protocols and most importantly *The Wemindji Eeyouch Core Values*. The process was collaborative and was guided by Mark's 12 points *'How To Approach Collaborations'* – a set of principles that improved our work. These principles served as a review of the group's vision, setting new objectives towards its achievement. The agenda called on a variety of local people and regional organizations to help contribute to the project. Working with the recommended FNDI model, *The Elements of Development*, served to guide the group through a decision making process which clarified the scope and importance of their work for the group, the community, and to Cree cultural issues currently impacting all Cree communities in Québec. It also illustrated how as an in-depth process it engaged native and non-native people in collaborative conversations, expanding many themes in a positive manner. It proved to be the catalyst needed to take the *Investing in Traditional Skills* group in new directions, revealing their abilities, required skills, and encouraging initiatives, as well as formulating new goals. Stocek wrote these goals into a grant request, with the collaboration of 'Skills'. The Cree Native Arts & Crafts Association or CNACA awarded the grant. The group then shared their progress and concerns at CNACA's regional general assembly. The assembly was held in Wemindji, due in part to the group's research initiatives. They shared their research and plans with their colleagues, obtaining valuable feedback. Some interesting points involved the differences between commercialism and exploitation, safe-guarding the interests of artists, updating prices charged for products, maintaining quality in the face of production, and the use of natural resources. The group will return to report a summary of the research results and a feasibility study at the next general assembly.[15]

The group collaborated with the Director of Wemindji's Tawich (in the bay) Development Corporation, who volunteered to plan a process that maximized the model's use. The Director suggested that the group learn how to use *The Elements of Development* by focusing on one moose hide project and offered to invite local Cree experts from different specialized areas to participate in the discussion and analyses. He suggested we call the consultation *The Path of a Moose Hide*.

The Path of a Moose Hide invited experts in hunting, tanning, producing crafts, and marketing products to participate in a discussion that followed the moose hide within its habitat, from its seasonal movements to the moment the moose was hunted, tanned, sewn into a product, and sold. Local experts shared their knowledge describing each step the work demanded. "Kinship acknowledges the system of giving, sharing, and reciprocity ... By acknowledging and building on the kinship system, a strategy builds on local strengths" (Wuttunee quoting Black 2004, p. 22). These distinct Cree skills vary from community to community. They are significant as they recognize considerable cultural assets that "salute empowerment through ownership and control, enabling wealth creation" (Wuttunee, 2004, p. 23). Cree cultural assets value heritage and traditions, skills, hunting rights, kinship, Cree institutions such as the Cree Trappers Association, CNACA, access to funds and credit, and natural and human resources.

The artists were not all aware of key hunting processes that ensured obtaining quality meat and the best hide while respecting the *ouchimaw's* (tallyman's)[16] understanding of seasonal factors and environmental balance. Capitalist economics are not based on nature's seasons and cycles, which are living systems of renewal. Economics are increasingly based on cycles of consumption, the creation of waste as consumer products are used up and the need to make continual purchases becomes necessary. Cree spirituality is intricately related to its relationship and understanding of nature and the land, which the Cree have occupied for millennia. Urban, industrialized, colonizing capitalism has no boundaries and recognizes no habitat (Wuttunee, 2004, p. 9). Making cultural and spiritually led decisions, instead of token factoring, is necessary if one wants to pay more than lip service to *The Wemindji Eeyouch Core Values*, which call for respecting both human relationships to the environment and supporting the environment's relationship with mankind, all things being interrelated and interconnected. Detailing *The Path of the Moose Hide* project helped the group communicate its needs to the Cree Trappers Association, which supports the project, and the Cree Regional Authority, which, after having reviewed the environmental impact of the pilot project, has approved it. Cree spirituality may also reflect one's contribution to Cree life, teaching, mentoring language and traditional skills, creating a vision of the future built on Cree foundations that foster a vision for the future maintenance of a healthy and respectful balance of Cree beliefs, practices, and values.

Wemindji is known for the quality of its handcrafted smoke tanned hide. The moose hide once tanned, using Cree processes, is so soft and supple that the artists can embroider intricate designs. The group determined that approximately only 12 people in the community were physically able and experienced enough to carry out the traditional process. Traditionally skills were taught and shared through extended kinship relations. The group also realized that many homes with freezers contained raw hides because people living in the community did not have the time required to spend with those who could carry out the process. As people's freezers became full, some hides were not being used, which does not reflect Cree values. While traditional forms of learning through observation and practice on the land continue, for many the time required to become sufficient practitioners of these cultural skills is no longer possible. Today the majority of people live in the village of Wemindji itself. 'Skills' acknowledges that school and work increasingly structure the community's time; therefore, 'Skills' strives to provide alternatives within community life. By carrying out their daily work in the workshop, the living practice of cultural traditions can continue, fostering a sense of well being by providing important opportunities for observation and learning in the daily life of the community.

A special benefit from the process was the translation of the local tanning process, with its specific practices and tips, into Cree syllabics for the local school's Cree cultural education. Some tools, names, and processes could not be explained adequately in English. Maintaining the language helps to maintain highly specialized local skills.

Investing in Traditional Skills knew through its research that the cost of purchasing handcrafted smoke tanned moose hide was creating a deficit. Yet the labour and time engaged in tanning hide themselves did not offer financial relief, although they could control the level of quality required by their artistic standards. Also the time and labour engaged in embroidery and hand sewing moose hide products was clearly an artistic choice based on the group's high standards but did not improve the financial picture. How to understand the economic impact in the bigger picture and come up with possible solutions had not been evident.

Within the group itself one member volunteered information about specialized skills using a hand operated fleshing machine which she had learnt how to use when Wemindji once operated a silver fox farm. She found, properly used, the quality of this normally labour intensive step (removing flesh from the hide), which many Elders have been finding increasingly beyond their abilities, could be maintained. The group wants to study the impact on both the quality of the product and the experience of tanning hide itself when integrating this labour saving step into the traditional process. 'Skills' wants to see if they can reduce the cost of purchasing moose hide by tanning hides themselves and offering this service to the community. Self-confidence and personal efficacy celebrate individual achievements and honour accomplishments "when they benefit the extended family and the community" (Wuttunee, 2004, p. 22).

The analysis was completed using *The Wemindji Eeyouch Core Values* to guide the process and decisions taken. Investing in Traditional Skills has recognized an urgent need to revitalize and research its local moose hide tanning processes. Equally important is the need to develop the means to support this work. The group acknowledges the need to teach youth to pass on their skills, as well as, realizing the rich cultural heritage that fostered these skills. Consequently the group wants to integrate five youth into the project. They wish to extend their community presence to include the tanning of hide. Purchasing tanned hides from other communities does not foster an environment that supports the local transmission of these cultural skills.

Effectively implementing the points *How To Approach Collaborations* discussed previously in the text has not always been successful. A time line and agenda has been coordinated with the objectives to be carried out once they were clearly identified. Reaching that point was challenging and time consuming. The group's objectives evolved over time, changing significantly, shifting the group's orientation. The group experimented and negotiated what it meant to function in a variety of roles including entrepreneurial or business person, craftsperson, historian and keeper of traditions, as well as the role of Cree traditional artist, which they seemed to have settled into. At different points in the group's experience the objectives required by these different roles seemed relevant, containing the answers they required. At other times they conflicted with local Cree values and ways of being and doing. Answers that functioned in narrow or singular ways were seductive but always seemed to fall short when the group considered broader Cree views.

Different key individuals within the group, including the authors and other members of the band administration, have agreed on their roles, although several key people have left the project or their roles have changed, thus interrupting and delaying the process. Funding has been set up but remains an issue; as funds are often held up and distributed late, this has caused lay-offs and at one time a pay reduction. The group has identified and made all its decisions collectively. The process for Stocek to become an integral member of the group took several years of really getting to know and to be known by the 'Skills' group despite her number of years living and working in the community. As an outsider Stocek was a dedicated participant but not the expert. Risks, challenges, and successes were engaged and shared by all. Observing, participating, sewing, tanning hide, interviewing Elders, traveling with the group to research historic Native work, and selling their work did establish the trust required for Stocek to become an integral and functioning member of the group.

The *Investing in Traditional Skills* group has developed a strong sense of ownership as a new organisation, in part due to its growing sense of accomplishment from the realization that as traditional artists they can address economic concerns that reflect contemporary fiscal issues and respect their cultural heritage at the forefront and as the foundation of their work. The recognition Investing in Traditional Skills has received from a variety of Cree media sources reporting on their work, and the financial support and grants they have been awarded for research, has served to build the group's esteem and confidence. Financial independence remains an unresolved issue. However, the group is currently engaged in developing a folded spruce bark basket fund-raising project to support pursuing the practice of more costly moose hide work in addition to research into offering the community a fleshing or tanning service. 'Skills' has recognized, at heart, that it has an educational and service oriented mission, which the community increasingly appreciates. Recognition has encouraged the group to continue to courageously address problems relating to their work, sharing its relevance with artists from all the Québec Cree communities. This has brought positive attention to the community as a whole and to those Cree traditional artists who continue to persevere, working from their homes to produce both innovative and traditionally rich artwork.

CONCLUSION: EACH NEW BEGINNING BRINGS AN END TO SOMETHING ELSE

The authors' earlier experiences collaborating on Wemindji projects were not always successful at putting into service local decisions or obtaining, in their view, a satisfactory response to local questions and concerns. Both Mark and Stocek feel that through these types of experiences community institutions risk becoming increasingly dependent on the Cree Regional Administration, therefore implementing services that create a perpetual need for support. This diminishes local ownership, furthermore constructing services that do not provide the objectives the community had originally envisaged.

Through the *Investing in Traditional Skills* project, we have tried to address how these failings occur, collaborating in a manner that respects local values, beliefs, and the pace of decision-making. We have worked to share and exchange our experiences and questions with the community and regional entities in ways that are consultative and supportive. The project is strong due to a foundation based on broader Cree interests that seeks to be accountable to all one's relations and that aspires to live up to shifts in research, adult education, and economic perspectives that engage what it means to be Cree.

'Skills' is a good example of how native people can strengthen and build the capacity of their people, organizations, and communities by assuming the authority of local values and world views. Thereby the group has challenged the colonial mindset of paternalistic programs that offer opportunity, provide security, but do so by fostering dependency. 'Skills' has assumed some risks along with the challenges it has taken on for the benefit of the community and their children's heritage. Working with dynamic leadership who respect and collaborate with their Elders exemplifies Newhouse's (2005) description of the new aboriginal leadership who are gathering the knowledge and creating opportunities and the wealth necessary to effect changes in Canada and within its own governing bodies for our collective well-being. Newhouse describes this leadership as:

> Well-educated, and courageous, determined to achieve a better world for themselves and for their children ... this highly educated group have a different understanding of the world than those who came before them. They are now imbued with a sense of the fundamental condition of modern Aboriginal society; that is, they have developed a post-colonial consciousness.

It is a society that understands that it has been colonized in many ways; a society that is aware of the implications of its colonization and that is choosing deliberately, consciously, and systematically to deal with that colonization; a society that is coming to terms with its colonial past. (p. 4)

Collaborating with Elders, volunteers, and the *Investing in Traditional Skills* group served to demystify cultural and economic processes by understanding them through local Cree perspectives. This raised local critical consciousness, motivating solutions to problems identified and establishing a more socially just and equitable decision-making process, which drew on cultural beliefs, local values, strengths, and abilities. Placing the development of a culturally sensitive project in local hands promotes a people-centred approach to development. This encourages the possibility, through contemporary projects, for many more shared learning opportunities, enriching the emergence of a proliferation of knowledge based on cultural heritage. These efforts serve to decolonize non-native collaboration, helping Cree people to accept where they have been colonized and choosing to address it on their own terms. These experiences were not always positive. Disappointments are a testament to the resilience and courage of Cree people, motivating them to work harder to bring about new opportunities where possibility was denied. Working to meet the criteria and indicators for success raised by *The Elements of Development* through *The Path of a Moose Hide* consultation process, which was guided by local experts and *The Wemindji Eeyouch Core Values*, fostered a sense of ownership and self-reliance. These approaches are a departure from Western reductionist points of view supporting local efforts to decolonize the process of institutionalization within their own administrative processes. The holistic, balanced approach fostered the emergence of research objectives suited to participatory action research and demonstrated the importance of implementing Indigenous research protocols. This community project responds to the shifts in research and economic paradigms that Indigenous leaders and scholars are calling for.

Elders consulted at the time were living in the Cree Nation of Wemindji: [17]

Winnie Asquabaneskum	Billy Gilpin
▢▢ ▢▢▢▢ (Daisy Atsynia Sr.)	Ellen Gilpin
Daisy Atsynia Jr.	Sarah Gilpin
Florrie Atsynia	Emily Hughboy
▢▢▢ ▢▢▢▢ (Raymond Atsynia)	Harry Hughboy
Rupert Atsynia	▢▢ ▢▢▢ (John Matches)
Sally Atsynia	Angus Mayappo Sr.
Richard Blackned	Isabel Mayappo
Alfred Georgekish	Margaret Mistacheesick
▢▢▢ ▢▢▢▢▢▢ (Beulah Georgekish)	Annie Shashaweskum Sr.
▢▢▢▢▢ ▢▢▢▢▢▢ (Clifford Georgekish)	Annie Shashaweskum Jr.
Emily Georgekish	Clifford Shashaweskum
▢▢▢▢ ▢▢▢▢▢▢ (Johnnish Georgekish)	ElizabethShashaweskum Sr.
Mary R. Georgekish	Lloyd Shashaweskum
Roderick Georgekish	Minnie Shashaweskum
▢▢▢ ▢▢▢▢▢▢ (Simeon Georgekish)	Harry Stewart
▢▢ ▢▢▢▢▢▢ (Sophie Georgekish)	▢▢ ▢▢▢▢ (Charlie Tomatuk)
	Nellie Tomatuk
	Frank Visitor

NOTES

1. Eddie Cook testified before the MacKenzie Valley Pipeline Inquiry in 1975: Dr. C. Chamber's rhetorical analysis is in the 1992, (Other) Ways of Speaking: Lessons from the Dene of Northern Canada.
2. Fieldnotes: *'How To Approach Collaborations'* was originally written by Mark for Stocek on January 9th, 2004.
3. Stocek, C., (2003). *Leading the way to 'learning our way out' Aboriginal education, possibility & vulnerability*. Unpublished paper that describes in depth an adult education and development project that, while successful, was not to the degree Mark or Stocek had envisaged.
4. Tuhiwai Smith, L. (2001) has offered in her seminal text *Decolonizing Methodologies Research and Indigenous Peoples* the means to counter practices of western thought and research reclaiming control over Indigenous ways of knowing and being.
5. *Eeyouch* in the local Cree dialect means "people of the land" and is in common use in Wemindji.
6. Finger & Asún (2001) discuss the dual meanings of 'Learning Our Way Out' framed in the introduction to their text of the same name, Adult Education At The Crossroads 'Learning Our Way Out'. The authors raise current challenges inherent in adult education's rise to success to its commodification and its consequential demise as an intellectual discipline.
7. Fieldnotes drawn from a March, 2005 interview conducted evaluating the authors' progress implementing the 12 points, *How To Approach Collaborations* and from an audio recording Mark made on the same subject June, 2005.
8. Wemindji is one of nine Cree communities located in northern Québec. For a description of the community visit the website: http://www.wemindji-nation.qc.ca/history.html
9. See the website for the Cree Nation of Wemindji where the "Revitalizing and Strengthening Our Traditional Philosophies and Principles Towards Building Strong Governance, Administration and Accountability Systems" is posted at: http://www.wemindji-nation.qc.ca/
10. Chief Mark told four stories for the 2007 keynote delivered by Stocek and Mark at the 12th Annual International Wanapitei Aboriginal History and Politics Colloquium: Sharing the resources? Examining, exploring, and discussing the changing dynamics of Aboriginal use practices – past, present, and future. Examples of the Elders stories told by Chief Mark include: A Dream From Lake Sakami, Supply Trip to Old Factory Post, Leadership Qualities, A Dog Incident.
11. Graphic support work donated by Stuckey-Design, www.STUCKEY-DESIGN.COM.
12. Fieldwork observations, participants no. 1, 3, summer 2003.
13. Cree Regional Authority (2001, May) Draft report on the feasibility of forming a Cree Native arts and crafts association and an arts and crafts marketing program for Eeyou Astchee, quoting former Grand Chief Dr. Ted Moses.
14. See the First Nations Development Institute (FNDI) website, http://www.firstnations.org/
15. Matthews, L. (2007). Minutes of the Annual General Assembly of the CREE NATIVE ARTS & CRAFTS ASSOCIATION (CNACA) Wemindji, *Grow and diversify sustainable Cree Arts & Crafts*, Oujé-Bougoumou, Québec. 1-22.
16. *Ouchimaw is the Cree term for* a tallyman who holds a respected position within the community; the responsibilities involve stewardship of the land related to the trap lines and Cree territory.
17. The Cree Nation has standardized the written form of Cree syllabics. These Elders learnt to write Cree before this time and when signing their names many do not use modern standardized Cree.

REFERENCES

Akwesasne Task Force on the Environment. (1996). *Protocol for review of environment and scientific research proposals*. Retrieved July 8, 2003, from http://www/slic.com/atfe/Prot.htm

Alaska Federation of Natives. (1993). *Alaska native knowledge network. Alaska federation of natives guidelines for research*. Retrieved July 8, 2003. from http://www.ankn.uaf.edu/afnguide.html

Battiste, M. (2002). Decolonising university research: Ethical guidelines for research involving Indigenous populations. In G. Alfredsson & M. Stavropoulou (Eds.), *Justice pending: Indigenous peoples and other good causes essays in honour of Erica-Irene A. Daes* (pp. 33–44). The Hague: Martinus Nijhoff Publishers.

Association of Canadian Universities for Northern Studies. ACUNS. (1997, November). *Ethical principles for the conduct of research in the north*. Revised Document. Retrieved June 10, 2003, from Yukon College Access: http://www.yukoncollege.yk.ca/~agraham/ethics.htm

Asún, J. M., & Finger, M. (2001). *Adult education at the crossroads learning our way out*. London: Zed Books.

Australian AIATSIS The Australian Institute of Aboriginal and Torres Strait Islander Studies. (2000, May). *Guidelines for ethical research in Indigenous studies*. Retrieved June 10, 2003, from The Australian Institute of Aboriginal and Torres Strait Islander Studies Access: http://www.aiatsis.gov.au/corp/docs/ethicsGuideA4.pdf

Canadian Royal Commission on Aboriginal Peoples. *Appendix E: Ethical guidelines for research*. Retrieved June 10, 2003, from the Department of Indian and Northern Affairs Canada Access: http://www.ainc-inac.gc.ca/ch/rcap/sg/ska5e_e.html

Canadian Tri-Council Policy Statement. (1998, August). *Ethical conduct for research involving humans*. Retrieved June 10, 2003, from Social Sciences and Humanities Research Council of Canada Access: http://www..sshrc.ca

Castellano, M. (2004). Ethics of aboriginal research. *Journal of Aboriginal Health, 1*(1), 98–114.

Foley, G. (1999). *Learning in social action: A contribution to understanding informal education*. London: Zed Books.

Gnarowski, M. (Ed.). (2002). *I dream of yesterday and tomorrow a celebration of the James Bay Crees*. Ottawa: The Golden Dog Press.

Grande, S. (2004). *Red pedagogy native American social and political thought*. Toronto: Rowman & Littlefield Publishers.

Hall, B. L. (1981). Participatory research, popular knowledge and power: A personal reflection. *Convergence, 14*(3), 6–19.

Matthews, L. (2007). Minutes of the annual general assembly of the CREE NATIVE ARTS & CRAFTS ASSOCIATION (CNACA) Wemindji. *Grow and diversify sustainable Cree Arts & Crafts*, Oujé-Bougoumou, Québec. 1–22.

Mi'kmaq College Institute. (1999). *Mi'kmaq research principles and protocols*. Retrieved July 8, 2003, from http://mrc.uccb.ns./prinprohtml

Salway Black, S. (1994). *Redefining success in community development a new approach for determining and measuring the impact of development* (The Lincoln Filene Centre Education for Action, Ridhard Schramm Paper on Community Development). Tufts University.

Scott, C. H. (2001). On autonomy and development. In C. H. Scott (Ed.), *Aboriginal autonomy and development in Northern Quebec and Labrador* (pp. 3–20). BC: UBC Press.

Scott, C. H. (2006). Spirit and practical knowledge in the person of the bear among Wemindji cree hunters. *Ethos, 7*, 51–66.

Sefa Dei, G., Hall, B., & Rosenberg, D. G. (Eds.). (2000). *Indigenous knowledges in global: Multiple readings of our world*. Toronto, ON: University of Toronto Press.

Steinhauer, E. (2003). Thoughts on an Indigenous research methodology. *Canadian Journal of Native Education, 26*(2), 69–81.

Tuhiwai Smith, L. (2001). *Decolonizing methodologies research and Indigenous peoples*. New York: Zed Books.

University of Victoria. (February 2003). *Protocols & Principles for conducting research in an Indigenous context*. Retrieved July 8, 2003, from http://web.uvic.ca/igov/programs/masters/igov_598/protocol.pdf

Wilson, S. (2001). What is an Indigenous research methodology? [Electronic version]. *Canadian Journal of Native Education, 25*(2), 175–180.
Wuttunee, W. (2004). Living rhythms lessons in aboriginal economic resilience and vision. Montreal: McGill Queens University Press.

JANINE METALLIC

6. EXPLORING INDIGENOUS WAYS OF KNOWING, BEING, AND DOING IN DEVELOPING A CROSS-CULTURAL SCIENCE CURRICULUM

INTRODUCTION

In this chapter, I will explore how the concept of "Indigenous ways of knowing, being, and doing" (Martin, 2003) can be used to inform the development of cross-cultural science curriculum, particularly for Indigenous students. Specifically, I will show how this concept can be used as a theoretical framework for incorporating Indigenous epistemologies and ontologies within cross-cultural science education. I will begin with a brief overview about Western science and Indigenous science and the need for culturally relevant curriculum. Next, I will discuss existing colonial thoughts about science and efforts to decolonize education through the use of Indigenous languages, stories, and cultural values. Finally, I will consider how educators and students can begin thinking differently (perhaps even critically) about Western science and Indigenous science so as to better understand differences and similarities.

DISTINGUISHING BETWEEN WESTERN SCIENCE AND INDIGENOUS SCIENCE

Snively and Corsiglia (2001) "distinguish between 'Western modern science' [WMS] which is the most dominant science in the world and 'Indigenous science' which interprets how the world works from a particular cultural perspective" (p. 8). Snively and Corsiglia (2001) argue that the definition of science should be broadened; they explain that the "intention is not to demean WMS, but instead to point out a body of scientific literature that provides great potential for enhancing our ability to develop more relevant science education programs" (p. 8).

Culturally relevant science programs are required since "Aboriginal knowledge about the natural world contrasts with Western scientific knowledge in a number of ways" (Aikenhead, 1997, p. 220). Aboriginal and scientific knowledge differ in their social goals, in intellectual goals, and in their association with human action. "They even differ in their basic concepts of time: circular for Aboriginals, rectilinear for scientists" (Aikenhead, 1997, p. 220).

As a Mi'gmaq person trained in Western science, I have experienced first hand the tensions between these different worldviews in science knowledge. I first perceived differences in the different ways of knowing during my undergraduate studies in science, but could not explain them. Yet, I knew there were other worldviews about science besides the Western model taught in schools and universities. Later in my studies, as a Master of Science student, I started to question (and sometimes challenge) the Western ways of "doing" science, particularly when it came time for me to carry out research on diabetes in an Eeyou (Cree) community in Northern Quebec. Outside of my readings for my graduate courses, I started reading books and journal articles written by Indigenous authors and learned more about various Indigenous philosophies about science. Indigenous research methodologies would begin to guide my research. In doing research on diabetes, I was interested in hearing stories about people's lived experiences, so I decided to learn more about qualitative research methodologies as well. At the time, I was pushing the boundaries of what was deemed acceptable by my department. However, I felt it was worth exploring research methods that were culturally relevant, both for me as well as for the research participants. Like Snively and Corsiglia (2001), I feel that a culture-based curriculum needed to be explored since "each culture has a science, a system for adapting in an environment. The solutions are different from those of Western science, but they are by no means inferior. (Snively & Corsiglia, 2001, p. 21).

CHALLENGING COLONIAL EPISTEMOLOGIES

Hermes (2000) has noted that "the culture-based curriculum movement in Native American education seems ... to be 'stuck,' and although this is certainly due to externally imposed restrictions, it can also be traced to internally accepted ideas about what *culture is* and what *schools are*" (p. 388, italics in the original). Internalized colonial epistemologies are evident – sometimes even among Indigenous students themselves. One teacher explains:

> When I teach kids nowadays, they think that science and culture are isolated, that they can't be merged and that you can only learn one without the other. But I try to point out that science and culture are interconnected, no matter how much people want to separate them. And I want to show them that science has always existed within the Mi'kmaq community; it wasn't introduced by Europeans or the white man. I try to point out that science has always been with us in different forms, in medicine, fishing or in terms of navigation using star charts. It's always been there in terms of the ocean, the forest and the atmosphere. Science is culturally relevant, and vice versa: you can't separate the two. (Orr, Paul & Paul, 2002, p. 340).

Even if we can show how science and culture are interconnected, there are still perceptions that studying Western science is more scholarly and academic, while studying Indigenous science is not. Among Indigenous educators and students, it seems that we "have internalized our own version of segregation and students respond by resisting what they perceive as assimilation. In this way, the false distinction between academics and culture promotes student failure" (Hermes, 2000, p. 391). Indigenous students, in other words, are choosing not to pursue a formal academic education, for fear having to choose between a mainly White society and their own cultural identity. This situation echoes Munro's (1996) "complexities of resistance" (p. 432), especially when resistance has the effect of reproducing the dominant order (i.e., Indigenous students struggle academically and remain oppressed).

This notion of having to choose between Western and Indigenous ways of knowing in education is not surprising given that "in many educational settings where Western modern science is taught, it is taught at the expense of Indigenous science, which may precipitate charges of epistemological hegemony and cultural imperialism" (Snively & Corsiglia, 2001, p. 7). Perhaps, then, the road to success in education requires that Indigenous students and educators value and trust their own ways of knowing. Hermes (2000) insists that,

> In order to construct categories that come from an Indigenous epistemology, we must begin by challenging the colonial ones. The position of students as actively engaged in the creation of what they are learning shifts the culture of the classroom. (p. 396)

Having had the experience of learning only Western science and research methodologies in academic settings, I am now interested in questioning those grand narratives and shifting the culture of the classroom to find possible strategies for decolonizing education and making science education more culturally relevant, particularly for the next generation of Indigenous students studying in science.

DECOLONIZING EDUCATION

Teachers can play a key role in working toward decolonizing education in the classroom. Their efforts to understand different ways of knowing, being, and doing can provide students with options throughout their educational journeys. For instance, Orr et al. (2002) "believe that Mi'kmaq teachers who are bringing their Aboriginal cultural practical knowledge onto the school landscape through pedagogy and relationality are a necessary part of the decolonization of Mi'kmaw education" (p. 333). The teachers Orr et al. (2002) interviewed in their study were "successfully living out the decolonization process in the classroom" (p. 333) by infusing "their cultural knowledge onto the school landscape" (p. 333). By sharing their personal experiences, these teachers also connected with students by addressing "the inadequacies and pains of their own schooling" (p. 337), and addressing "their students' needs in the face of poverty, identity dislocation, and colonialism" (p. 337).

In my current research as a doctoral student in education, I am interested in studying the interconnectedness of Indigenous knowledge, language, and science. Again, as with my Master's research, I am interested in sharing stories and experiences with research participants. This time, however, I will be doing research in my home community where there is a renewed interested in revitalizing our heritage language and our ways of knowing, being, and doing. In particular, I am inspired by the work of my mother, Mary Ann Metallic, and my aunt, Janice Vicaire. Both have always been important in my own learning of the Mi'gmaq language, but now I see them sharing their knowledge in particularly innovative ways, teaching language to community members that are learning Mi'gmaq as a second (or sometimes third) language. Neither one of them is formally certified as a teacher, yet they have a wealth of traditional and cultural knowledge, particularly regarding language, as a result of their lived experiences.

SHARING STORIES

Part of the cultural knowledge that teachers bring into their practice in schools is in the form of "powerful narrative life histories" (Orr et al., 2002, p. 349). Stories are also an important way of showing "how the land, the language, and we are linked together" (Gardner, 2000, p. 10). Traditionally, this "remembered sensory information" (p. 10) – is transmitted orally through descriptive names, stories, and metaphor. According to Snively and Corsiglia (2001),

> Metaphor and stories can be used to encapsulate and compress oral wisdom and even make it entertaining. Such stories can be decoded in relation to specific circumstances upon appropriate reflection or contemplation. (pp. 12-13)

In turn, these ways of knowing can be transmitted to the next generation. Orr et al. (2002) provide an example of a Mi'gmaq school where intergenerational transmission of cultural knowledge is connected to cultural stories that "teachers and their students construct and re-construct together in classrooms in honor of home, community, and Mi'kmaq National knowledge" (pp. 334-335).

Through stories, teachers can also pass on cultural values to their students. One teacher recounts how, in teaching, she tries to remember what she was taught in her youth. "I tell my students stories about when we were small and how we were told to respect our elders" (Orr et al., 2002, p. 337). The lessons learned from these cultural values further reinforce other lessons since a "fundamental principle taught by Indigenous elders is that subject matter is properly examined and interpreted contextually" (Snively & Corsiglia, 2001, p. 11). When students participate in culturally relevant activities in the classroom, they also learn culturally appropriate ways of being. Orr et al. (2002) provide an example of one teacher's use of a talking circle as a regular classroom activity:

> On Fridays we do a circle and I tell them about the past. If one person is talking, then we show respect and listen to that person. Whatever they say, you listen to them and you don't interrupt. We talk about our parents, our homes and how we should respect. (p. 343)

As a result, classroom environments become places where "students find it possible to give expression to their own emerging cultural knowledge" (Orr et al., 2002, p. 348) and their own relationships. Stories are also used to locate the self in relation to others. For example, science researchers and students can

> learn from both the practices and the narrative stories of Native Americans. Languages, myth, and ritual generally articulate culturally and ecologically located conceptions of self in relation to others and communicate a sense of the connections which bind their communities together and to the land. (Snively & Corsiglia, 2001, p. 16)

RESPECTING "ALL MY RELATIONS"

Fostering cultural knowledge in the classroom needs to be done in a much deeper and respectful way than most people realize. Like Hermes (2000), I would also propose "that we begin to view culture as a complex web of relationships, not just material practices, and enact this in our schools in a way that is central to the curriculum" (p. 389). The expression "all my relations" is "a phrase many Aboriginal people use to acknowledge that we are in relationship with one another in this world, and to remind ourselves of this in whatever activities we are engaged in" (Brown, 2003, n.p.). Martin (2003) describes such relationships between entities as

> a truly relational ontology. All things are recognised and respected for their place in the overall system. Whilst they are differentiated, these relations are not oppositional, nor binary, but are inclusive and accepting of diversity. These relations serve to define and unite, not to oppose or alienate. (p. 207)

What is missing from most formal school settings is an appreciation for this way of being – existing within a complex web of relationships that permeates Indigenous worldviews and reaches beyond the physical world. To illustrate, Gardner (2000) describes how she first learned from a classmate about the meaning behind the term "S'óhl Téméxw" [S'óhl = Our, Respectful or Sacred; Téméxw = Country, Land, or World; mexw = Us, the People] (p. 9). The classmate also pointed out that "Us, the People, are included in our term for the Land" (p.9). Gardner explains her understanding of the interrelationships this way:

> I am discovering that S'óhl Téméxw is not just words, is not simply a representation of the physicality of the World. S'óhl Téméxw is a representation of a holistic concept that links the people spiritually to the physical world, to each other, and to all our ancestors and is expressed best through our Halq'eméylem language. These interrelationships define our culture, define who we are as Stó:lō people, and in fact define our world view. (p. 10)

Linking spirituality to the physical world "may be stretching the Western notion of science" (Hermes, 2000, p. 393). However, integrating Indigenous epistemology (e.g., intuition and spirituality) into science curriculum can prove useful especially

> if it makes connections – makes what students read in a textbook come to life with meaning, connects what they have lived to what they are learning, and connects to past traditions which are quickly being forgotten or abandon [sic] – then it is an act of deconstructing and appropriation that is in line with the mission of culture-based curriculum. (p. 393)

Developing a culture-based curriculum, therefore, is not simply about adding-on to curriculum (e.g., adding Indigenous course content or labelling different learning styles). Hermes (2000) suggests "that it is the relationships between teacher/students/curriculum/identity within the class that encourages and invites students to continually re-create who they are in that class, not the specific content" (p. 395). Thus, the context, as opposed to content, determines cultural relevance and appropriateness in curriculum. "Relationality" according to Orr et al. (2002) "affirms a collective Mi'kmaw cultural identity, rooted in family stories of language and values, as a first priority. It also demonstrates curricular values of how to live together respectfully and responsibly as part of their wider Mi'kmaw community" (p. 350). In terms of community development, it would be inspiring to see the Mi'gmaq language used not only in the local schools, but also increasingly present in a much wider context, heard and spoken everywhere in the community, as it was when my parents and grandparents were growing up. Back then, the language was a living community language – heard not just in a few homes on rare occasions, but throughout the entire community on a daily basis. When I was growing up, my parents did their part to maintain our language, encouraging my siblings and I to speak only Mi'gmaq at home, even though we were enrolled in French Immersion at school. Currently, my aunt Janice encourages people to return to our Mi'gmaq ways of knowing, being, and doing by speaking our language: "*'Lnui'sultinej te'sigisg'g*" ("Let's speak our people's language everyday").

EXPLORING ISSUES OF IDENTITY

Issues of cultural identity among Indigenous students (including those of mixed heritage) need to be considered in light of the messages they are getting from dominant society. Exploring Indigenous relationships and worldviews is also seen as

> one way to validate students' identity as Anishinabe [Ojibwe] while still recognizing there is a dominant discourse which is a little (sometimes a lot) different, and this is useful to learn too, but not without qualifying it first, recognizing where it comes from and not hiding, confusing or otherwise allowing it to replace the knowledge that has been home grown. (Hermes, 2000, p. 393)

As Gardner (2000) reflects upon her youth, she realizes how these messages can become internalized even at a young age:

> "What are you doing?" my older sister said to me one day when I was about six years old. "I am washing my hands," I said. "But you have been washing and washing and washing," she said, "why are you doing that?" "Because I want them to be nice and white like my mother's," I said. Well, my mother's hands were not white at all, but they sure were not as brown as my dark little suntanned hands. How soon we learned that "White is right." (p. 8)

Later in life, when Indigenous students contemplate whether or not they should further their formal education, there is often a perception that "they are forced to choose between a Native and an 'assimilated' identity. This dichotomy emerges as a result of a colonial structuring of the school curriculum that has been uncritically accepted" (Hermes, 2000, p. 389).

The classroom, therefore, should become a space where students can feel free to explore meanings and identities and how they are formed. In a classroom setting described by Hermes (2000), the teacher invites students to pose questions and make meanings within the class:

> The answer to the question, "who will we be as Anishinabe [Ojibwe] in this classroom?" is not a closed question. Participation and trust make the curriculum culture based; in this particular context it is the students themselves who tailor their questions to their identity needs. (Hermes, 2000, p. 395)

Hermes (2000) further explains that in this type of approach to curriculum, students become aware of the dynamic nature of identity formation since they are allowed

> to explore meanings and identities, that is, they are supported to bring all of their experiences into the room. A teacher who says 'this is Ojibwe culture class,' or 'today we are doing Indian art,' could easily preempt this. Categories that separate academics from culture tend to narrow the identity of 'Indian' and could be misleading for a Native American student who likes to draw both eagle feathers and Nintendo images. (p. 395)

EXPLORING INDIGENOUS LANGUAGES

Meanings can also be explored through Indigenous languages, providing insight into culture, identity, and worldviews. Gardner (2000) recalls hearing and reading that the Elders said, "The language is central to our identity … the land is the culture … and our world view is embedded in our language" (p. 9).

I believe teachers should promote Indigenous language use whenever it is feasible. Orr et al. (2002), for example, write about a teacher who "knows her students' use of their Mi'kmaw language is closely related to their identity as Aboriginal peoples and she encourages even the most fledgling speakers to use their ancestral language as part of their classroom experiences" (p. 341). Using both English and Indigenous languages can transform the learning environment into one where students feel safe. One teacher recounts how using two languages in the classroom "makes a big difference with the kids. It makes it friendlier and they aren't as intimidated. They can give the answer in Mi'kmaq if they want to, or maybe the concept is easier to understand in our language" (Orr et al., 2002, p. 341). Orr et al. (2002) further explain how, with this teacher,

> Using both Mi'kmaw and English languages in her pedagogy allows her to teach concepts more clearly and deeply. Analogies to Mi'kmaw concepts serve as bridges to English scientific ones and affirm her students' confidence in their own linguistic knowledge. (p. 342)

I see teachers encouraging students and parents to use their heritage language in the home as a powerful example of a decolonizing activity. Educational and collective responsibility for language are evident when teachers assert, "It has to be encouraged in the home. The residential schools beat the Mi'kmaq out of us, and it's about time that someone put it back" (Orr et al., 2002, p. 338). Revitalizing Indigenous languages helps to restore balance in mind, body, heart, and spirit. As expressed by one of the teachers, "You have to feel the language in your heart: what good is it for me to do something that I don't want to do?" (Orr et al., 2002, p. 338). My mother, Mary Ann, told me how one day a young man in one of her language classes described how learning the language was filling a hole in his heart. This notion of feeling the language in your heart makes me think of the implications in my own ways of doing – not just doing something I want to do because I am told to do it, but doing something because I want to – because I have internalized the cultural teachings, things that I have learned from my family, relatives, and other community members.

As expressed by one teacher, cultural teachings can also be connected to learning about science:

> My upbringing showed me culturally relevant science. I've seen science, I've seen culture, and I've seen the two of them connect. My father introduced science to me ... When I was growing up there were a lot of things I learned from my father. It wasn't pointed out as science, it was pointed out as a way of living, and it was a way I had to learn. (Orr et al., 2002, p. 340)

HONORING SPIRIT

Some educators may question the role of spiritual ideology in the classroom, particularly in a science classroom. For Indigenous students, however, honoring their languages, traditions, and worldviews also means honoring the spirits of everything surrounding them; as seen in an earlier section, everything is interrelated and interconnected. In some cases, the school setting can be used to re-establish cultural values that may have been lost or forgotten as a result of colonization. Orr et al. (2002) describe a teacher who

> knows the importance of Mi'kmaw values of sharing, respect, and helping and works to demonstrate these for her students. She recognizes that in some homes, children are not getting cultural and spiritual guidance and she uses opportunities within her classroom to teach these values. (pp. 347-348)

As Gardner (2000) explains, exploring Indigenous languages can provide insight into the concept of spirit:

> The Katzie, a Downriver Halkomelem-speaking people, believed that animals and plants, and perhaps even rocks, possessed power and smestí:yexw, a word that means vitality and thought combined, for there was no conception of one without the other. The water, wind, the sun, the moon and the stars also possessed power, vitality, and thought, and people could share in these powers of nature. (p. 10)

In the language classes taught in my home community, one of the first things students learn is that nouns in our language are categorized as being either animate or inanimate. This type of gender classification (animate/inanimate) is unique to certain Indigenous languages and not present in the English language. Therefore, it may surprise some to learn that certain objects such as feathers, shirts, potatoes, and containers are considered animate entities in Mi'gmaq.

Listening to elders and other fluent community members, and reflecting on the words they use, is helping me to better understand that in traditional Mi'gmaq ways of knowing, animate entities were referred to as such because of some perceived or assigned spiritual essence or quality. What I am realizing by exploring Mi'gmaq ways of knowing through language is that by revitalizing Mi'gmaq language use, reclaiming it as a community language, we honor the spirit of our community. Community development happens when we collectively (re)discover and honor our traditional Indigenous knowledge and science in our local contexts. There is no better classroom for learning about Indigenous knowledge and science than in our natural world, our own environment, or *gm'tginu*, our land.

THINKING DIFFERENTLY, THINKING CRITICALLY

Aikenhead (1997) notes that crossing cultural borders, or shifting cognitive patterns, can be described as "thinking differently" (p. 225). Aikenhead also notes that while the "capacity and motivation to participate in diverse subcultures are well-known human phenomena" (p. 225) the ability to navigate transitions and move between settings differs among individuals. If Indigenous students are to cross cultural borders and learn different ways of knowing, they should also learn to think critically. Snively and Corsiglia (2001) further comment on the need for critical thinking:

> This kind of critical thinking is necessary to enable students to understand how WMS [Western modern science] is a particular way of thinking about the natural world, rooted in Western culture, and how the purposes of WMS could be changed to create future sciences that better meet the needs of diverse societies. (pp. 22-23)

In terms of cross-cultural science education, Snively and Corsiglia (2001) ask, "Should we develop a teaching approach that merely develops an appreciation for TEK [Traditional Ecological Knowledge] and IK [Indigenous Knowledge], or one that goes further into the implications of racism, history, and definitions, and attempts to deconstruct old prejudices" (p. 24). Delving deeper into some of these areas can be challenging and even controversial. For example, it may not always be appropriate to apply curriculum theories such as critical theory or resistance in an Indigenous context. As Martin (2003) expresses,

> My belief as an Aboriginal researcher is that I actively use the strength of my Aboriginal heritage and do not position myself in a reactive stance of resisting or opposing western research frameworks and ideologies. Therefore, I research from the strength and position of being Aboriginal and viewing anything western as 'other', alongside and among western worldviews and realities. (p. 205)

On the other hand, Brown (2003) insists that "Resistance is a strength, and nurturing resistance can strengthen a community" (n.p.). She further explains that she offers "the idea of resistance in order to dispel the myth that a community has to 'get along' or 'pull together' in order to be strong" (n.p.).

Whether or not my actions are labelled as critical or resistant, as a Mi'gmaq, it may be easy for me to state that there is a need to move beyond the borders of Western science in order to promote understanding and respect for other cultures and other ways of knowing. Nonetheless, as someone who has experienced a formal training in Western science and research, I can appreciate that "a cultural perspective for science education represents a radical shift in thinking for some educators" (Snively & Corsiglia, 2001, p. 26). As a starting point, I would suggest that educators begin by exploring some of the differences and similarities between Western science and Indigenous science – to view science through two different lenses – what Elder Albert Marshall refers to as "two-eyed seeing" (www.migmaqresource.org/vid.html).

UNDERSTANDING DIFFERENCES AND SIMILARITIES

In creating culturally relevant science education curriculum, educators need not worry about having to radically change the content of science courses. What I suggest, however, is that educators be open to understanding differences and similarities between Western science and Indigenous science. As Snively and Corsiglia (2001) recommend,

> the focus of instruction should not be on presenting information so that children of ethnic minorities will *accept* the scientifically accepted notion of the concept, but on helping students *understand* science concepts and exploring the differences and similarities between their own beliefs and Western science concepts. (p. 26)

Teachers can encourage students to consider Western science and Indigenous science as two different ways of knowing. "Although the two perspectives may interpret the world differently, students should also see that the two overlap and can reinforce one another" (Snively & Corsiglia, 2001, p. 28). Hermes (2000) posits "that instead of continuing to sort out cultural differences, an approach that assumes culture is relational and constantly created anew would open up possibilities for culture-based curriculum" (p. 396). By understanding our traditional custom and practices, and situating these within a modern context, Indigenous language instructors can play an important role in helping to develop these types of cross-cultural curricula.

LIVING COMFORTABLY IN TWO WORLDS

In recognizing differences and similarities between Western science and Indigenous science, educators may better appreciate the challenges that face Indigenous students. Aikenhead (1997) maintains that "school science should encourage students to learn science in a way that empowers them to make everyday choices about participating in either a First Nations cultural setting or the dominant Canadian cultural setting" (p. 224). In other words, students "should develop the facility to cross cultural borders from the everyday subcultures of their peers, family, and tribe, into the subcultures of school science, and science and technology" (p. 224). Aikenhead adds that these "border crossings are essential to the success of cross-cultural education for First Nations students" (p. 224). I would add that educators, too, should strive for such "cultural competence" – so as to "help students live bi-culturally between home and school cultures, by developing a greater understanding of, and respect for, their culture of origin" (Orr et al., 2002, p. 334).

Indigenous teachers may be well suited for promoting bi-cultural education. For example, Orr et al. (2002) describe how "Nicole, after the teaching of her father, has found ways to honor both Aboriginal and European knowledge alongside each other and validate Mi'kmaw knowledge by showing it to be science" (p. 342). In fact, Orr et al. (2002) report that the Mi'gmaq teachers they interviewed "are able to live comfortably between ways of the past that are less known to their students, and their students' experiences with contemporary cultural ways" (p. 343). Moreover, the teachers' pedagogy prepares their students to live comfortably in two worlds, that is, "to live in a society which is in-between ancient Aboriginal linguistic and cultural ways and the competing realities and pressures of the dominant society (p. 343).

I would add that non-Indigenous teachers play an equally important role in promoting a bi-cultural education. Cultural differences should not be used as a justification for dismissing Indigenous students' poor performance in schools. Rather, educators can learn to recognize institutional structures as cultural boundaries so as to help students better navigate between two worlds. As Hermes (2000) explains:

> The theory of cultural discontinuity and the subsequent recognition of differences in learning has been effective in explaining failure, but recognizing that cultural boundaries are constantly changing may encourage an expansion of the notion of culture-based curriculum, and promote success. (p. 397)

CONCLUSION

Attempts to make studies in science a viable option for Indigenous students involve more than just adding Indigenous course content to an existing curriculum and assuming that it is culturally relevant. There is a need for educators and students to recognize that there are different ways of knowing about science, based on different worldviews. One of the best ways to explore these different ways of knowing is through language.

Decolonizing education may involve having to challenge colonial epistemologies – most of which are rarely questioned because of their dominant place in society. At the very least, there is a need for greater understanding of Indigenous ways of knowing, being, and doing, so that these can be valued and respected in schools and classroom settings. Ideally, we would also encourage learning in traditional contexts, outside of classrooms, within Indigenous families, communities, and Nations.

Educators play an important role in fostering a learning environment that allows for sharing of stories, using Indigenous languages, and enacting cultural values, not only in schools but in home and community environments as well. Using Indigenous languages represents one strategy for understanding different worldviews.

As discussed, becoming aware of different worldviews does not mean having to accept or embrace these views as one's own, but it allows for greater understanding of differences and similarities and promotes critical thinking. Understanding Indigenous ways of knowing, being, and doing is important for developing cross-cultural science education curriculum; it is essential for recognizing and appreciating ever-changing cultural and community boundaries, which Indigenous students must constantly negotiate and navigate in order to live comfortably in various cultural landscapes.

REFERENCES/BIBLIOGRAPHY

Aikenhead, G. S. (1997). Toward a first nations cross-cultural science and technology curriculum. *Science Education, 81*, 217–238.

Brown, L. (2003). *All my relations: Community building in difficult times*. Notes for remarks to the studies in policy and practice forum "Mid-Term crisis: Exposing the impact of provincial government decisions." Centre for Innovative Teaching, University of Victoria.

Gardner, E. B. (2000). Where there are always wild strawberries. *Canadian Journal of Native Education, 24*(1), 7–13.

Hermes, M. (2000). The scientific method, Nintendo, and Eagle feathers: Rethinking the meaning of "culture-based" curriculum at an Ojibwe tribal school. *International Journal of Qualitative Studies in Education, 13*(4), 387–400.

Martin, K. (2003). Ways of knowing, being and doing: A theoretical framework and methods for Indigenous and indigenist re-search. *Journal of Australian Studies, 76*, 203–214.

Munro, P. (1996). Resisting "resistance:" Stories women teachers tell. In W. Pinar (Ed.), *Contemporary curriculum discourses: Twenty years of JCT* (pp. 425–457). New York: Peter Lang.

Orr, J., Paul, J. J., Paul, S. (2002). Decolonizing Mi'kmaw education through cultural practical knowledge. *McGill Journal of Education, 37*(3), 331–354.

Snively, G., & Corsiglia, J. (2001). Discovering Indigenous science: Implications for science education. *Science Education, 85*(1), 6–34.

MELA SARKAR

7. GETTING INTO MED SCHOOL OR BECOMING A HEALER? WESTERN MEDICAL EDUCATION AND INDIGENOUS KNOWLEDGES

INTRODUCTION

A mother speaks

In this narrative I tell the story of the way my daughter, a young woman living in Montreal, embarked on her formal medical education at a well-known and conventionally "Western" M.D. program at one of Canada's larger universities. I thought her story was worth telling, not only because I am her mother, but also because of the role played in Nina's[1] decision and subsequent adventures by Indigenous knowledges as they were apprehended and interpreted by one non-Indigenous white Canadian teenager. We might normally think of a young person who applies to medical school and trains to be a doctor as someone with a fairly "mainstream" Western majority society approach to the profession of medicine, and more generally to health and illness. Through the story of this one applicant to med school who I know so well, I will discuss ways in which Indigenous knowledges of several kinds can come into the life of a young person living in a large North American city in the early 21st century and thereby radically affect her vision of the world and her life choices. The need to integrate Indigenous "ways of being, knowing and doing" (Martin & Mirraboopa, 2003) into "traditional Western" epistemologies and lifestyles is seen by many to be increasingly urgent in a world where the consequences of *not* being cognizant of non-Western approaches is proving to have disastrous effects on our planet and the species with whom we share it, as well as on our own species. I hope to show that one need not necessarily have Indigenous roots oneself nor spend long stretches of time in remote communities to profit from what Indigenous knowledges have to offer all peoples – Indigenous and non.

By vocation and training I am an applied linguist. My initial interest in the field, rooted in my parents' past, was in the ways in which immigrant integration into a majority society is mediated through language, with a focus on the ways children from minority, immigrant-origin communities learn the majority language through schooling (Sarkar, 2002, 2005a). I spend a lot of time thinking, researching and writing about issues related to the way people teach, learn and use second languages. Although in some ways I write as an academic whose professional life is lived wholly within academia – for example, I would not otherwise have met and been inspired by the colleagues whose original set of contributions to this volume were the nexus of this collection, nor chosen to write an academic piece in the ethnographic tradition rather than some other kind of essay – in a very important way I write this not as an academic but as a mother. I write with love and pride in my daughter and what she has accomplished in her 21 years. Her decision to enter the healing profession has taken her, and now me, far from my own field of applied linguistics. I do not claim expertise in fields outside my own fairly narrow one, the discourse of medical or development education, for example, and my grasp of relevant theory – whether in those domains or around the dauntingly large set of issues related to indigeneity – is recently acquired and incomplete. What I feel I can offer is a parent's insider perspective on the process of watching a child grow into a woman who is passionately engaged with some of the most fundamental questions now confronting all of us. As Nina herself tells me from her recent experience, the Cree people of northern Canada don't have a word that precisely translates the English word "health"; the word they use means literally "being alive well" (Adelson, 2000). My linguistic training in etymology tells me that "health" at bottom means "wholeness". To be healthy, to be alive well, is to be hale and to be whole. Because questions of language use are so important to me, the other way I come to this story is through the study of language.

FROM APPLIED LINGUIST TO CRITICAL APPLIED LINGUIST

The field of applied linguistics has been undergoing major upheaval over the past decade or two. Barely had this scholarly offshoot, by Linguistics out of Foreign/Second Language Teaching (if I may approximate a pedigree) attained something approaching respectability in the Academy around the mid-1980s (Lightbown, 1985) than uncontrollable internal forces began working to break it down. Linguistics as a *discipline* is a product of nineteenth- and twentieth-century efforts to do precisely that, to discipline human communicative activity in all its unruly and wayward variety and to reduce it to a manageable "object of study". Despite half a century of efforts by Departments of Linguistics worldwide, the putative object is not an object at all; not any kind of noun, except in our reified imaginings, but some-"thing" that could more appropriately be referred to using only verbs, and possibly would be if the controlling hand of Greek- and Latin-derived categories did not still lie so heavy over Western science (Harris, 1990; Janicki, 2006; Makoni & Pennycook, 2007; Pennycook, 2007). Many Indigenous languages have no word to refer to the "language" itself, other than a form or forms meaning "how we speak", "how the people speak" (Abley, 2003).

Indigenous languages as main carriers of Indigenous knowledges

Applied linguists attempt, at least ideally, to put the structural knowledge posited by theoretical linguists and the practical insights garnered by language teachers, planners, translators, ethnographers and so on to work in the service of language learners and users. This has too often meant a preoccupation with English, as spoken by first and/or second language users, as taught (Lightbown & Spada, 2006), as imposed from above (Phillipson, 1992), as reached for from below

(Niranjana, 1991; Ramanathan, 2005; Rajagopalan, 1999), and as developing new varieties (Kachru, 1986; 1992). There is an underlying assumption that one accepts that the label "English" in fact corresponds to something with a recognizable shape. One need not (Pennycook, 2007) and for my purposes here I will not take a position one way or the other.

However, a substantial amount of work has also been done exploring other languages, some of them non-European, and some of those Indigenous (Dixon, 1997; Nettle & Romaine, 2000). The insights brought back to mainstream, Western applied linguistics by people working in Indigenous contexts – more and more of whom are themselves Indigenous, although this was not formerly the case – have created a new awareness that bodies of knowledge reside in the structure and vocabulary of languages themselves, and cannot readily be translated (Dixon, 1997; Elgin, 2000). To grow up as a fluent user of a language is to inherit a way of seeing the world and of breaking it down into categories that is particular to that language. This idea, first introduced to Western linguistics by Whorf in the 1930s (Lee, 1996; Whorf, 1956) and usually called the Sapir-Whorf or "Linguistic Relativity" hypothesis (Wayne State University, n.d.), was viewed with extreme skepticism by linguists for many decades. Recent work by Indigenous language scholars has done a great deal to bolster scholarly recognition of that fact (Battiste, 1998; Reedy, 2000; Tolenoa & Hough, 2005). When no fluent speakers of a language remain, a mode of perception, as central for its users as English-based modes are for most readers of the words I write here, has been irretrievably lost.

This understanding came to me only very gradually and after conventional Western training in the applied linguistics subfield of Second Language Acquisition. Because of my family background – one parent from South Asia (Bangladesh) and the other from a long line of prairie Ukrainians in Canada – I had many opportunities to hear about and witness first hand the struggles of newly arrived immigrants – people from populous and independent areas abroad – to adjust to their sudden linguistic marginalization and minoritization when they landed in North America. It was a revelation to me when, through reading about different kinds of minority-language speakers and communities, I realized how many of these were not the immigrant-origin people I had grown up with. For speakers of Indigenous languages, the experience of colonization and its attendant brutalization went far beyond even anything the British Raj had perpetrated in my father's horror stories.

Recent work on linguistic human rights by Skutnabb-Kangas (2000), and others, although necessarily enumerative and essentializing in its attitude to languages and their speakers (Makoni & Pennycook, 2007), has performed a crucial service in raising awareness about threatened languages and encouraging both professional applied linguists and lay native speakers to think about ways of revitalizing them. This means giving them new life, so they may continue to be windows onto the world for new generations of speakers. From the "purification" approach described by Fishman (2006) in almost caricatural terms as a wishful return to a wholly constructed past Golden Age of linguistic perfection, to the modern urban Indigenous vernaculars described and theorized for Africa (Ferrari, 2005; Higgins,

2004; Makoni & Meinhof, 2003), Australia (Mitchell 2004), and even including Europe (Urla, 1999, on Basque) there has been an upsurge of interest in Indigenous language revitalization. The "traditional", "classical" older forms of the disciplines of linguistic anthropology and anthropological linguistics are being held up to increasing scrutiny by modern scholars. The peoples who came under the inquisitive lens of Western scientific inquiry have mostly realized, hopefully not too late, that the missionary-linguists, well-meaning literacy educators, participant-observer anthropologists and their ilk who came in droves to study and "help" them may have done far more harm than good over the last century and a half. However noble the intentions of the colonizers – to give them a rather large benefit of the doubt – the energy driving the whole huge colonial enterprise was and remains tainted (Tuhuwai Smith, 1999).

At the same time, the "ELT industry"[2] in all its many forms has also been re-theorized, beginning with Phillipson's landmark study of English linguistic imperialism in 1992 and continuing into a rapidly growing body of scholarship that extends and refines Phillipson's analysis of fifteen years ago (Canagarajah, 1999; Pennycook, 1994; Block & Cameron, 2002). On many fronts, re-analysis of formerly taken-for-granted principles and practices has resulted in a new, critical applied linguistics (e.g. Pennycook, 2001). Owing much to critical pedagogy (Auerbach, 1995; Freire, 1970/2000), and critical discourse analysis (Fairclough, 2001), this emerging set of writings on how humans communicate through language has, in my view, given the field a new lease on life.

Invitation and validation

In the spring of 2006 I was invited to join a research team in my department (which specializes in teacher training within the field of education generally). The team was working on grant proposals to fund a joint community-university project with a First Nations community in rural Quebec. The proposed project centered on an Indigenous language teaching initiative currently under way in the community, in which literacy-based teaching approaches take second place to oral pedagogies with key visual support (Metallic, this volume; Wilmot, 2006). Alphabetic-literacy based language teaching, which is rooted in the colonizing past, has often not been successful where many Indigenous languages are concerned (Bielenberg, 1999; Donaldson, 1998). As an applied linguist in our department with a history of being interested in what happens when minority language speakers have to negotiate the linguistic impositions on their community by the dominant majority-language culture that surrounds them (Sarkar, 2002; 2005a&b; Park & Sarkar, 2008), it seemed logical for me to be involved; I also felt very flattered by the invitation. Years of reading about Indigenous languages, most of which face overwhelming odds against long-term survival, had made me realize how inappropriate it is for a non-Indigenous researcher on language – or any other topic – to assume she can just walk into an Indigenous community and expect to be welcomed as an expert (Tuhiwai Smith, 1999). It was therefore a significant moment in my life when the Indigenous educators concerned agreed that I should be on the team. A year later, in spring 2007, we received the funding we needed to link up to the community of Indigenous learners and teachers, and the intense involvement afforded by this new research initiative gave me the opportunity to deepen my understanding of Indigenous issues outside as well as inside the language domain. The profound reorganization of our common Western scholarly heritage that becomes necessary when we start to consider the notion and the contribution of Indigenous epistemologies is one that I consider I have barely embarked on. New reading (e.g. Canagarajah, 2002; Makoni & Pennycook, 2007) and new ideas continue to unsettle a lifetime's worth of preconceptions about knowledge and where it comes from that I have acquired while being schooled in, by, and ultimately for the "Academy".

Also in early 2006, serendipitously, my 20-year-old daughter came back from a three-week stay in Guatemala in the context of a special development work program that was built into her final pre-university year. As a direct result of the effect this experience had on her, she decided that some of the university applications she would send off would be to pre-med programs. Quebec is the only Canadian province to allow entry into the four-year M.D. program to be speeded up through the option of a pre-med year (other provinces require a bachelor-level degree as entry requirement). Quebec is also the only remaining province to require 13 years of schooling before university entry instead of 12. Six years of primary school are followed by five of secondary and then two of CEGEP (Collège d'éducation générale et professionnelle or "junior college"). Nina in fact did a three-year CEGEP program that offered extra features, such as the three-week stay abroad that took her to Guatemala.

As part of her ethnographic school assignment in a Mayan village in Guatemala, Nina met an Indigenous healer-midwife-shaman (curandera, comadrone, sacerdote). It was the unanticipated recognition she got from Magdalena, as a future fellow healer, that confirmed her intention to apply to M.D. programs, although she did not see herself as having the typical profile of such an applicant. Somewhat to her surprise, she got into one of them, got through her pre-med year, and is in her first year of med school proper as I write this. During our discussions at home around where she should apply, I was impressed by the links Nina made between her experiences in a Mayan village in Guatemala and her decision to apply to pre-med.

Shortly before our research team learned that we had been granted funding to research the Indigenous revitalization initiative, the graduate students' society of our department (EGSS, for Education Graduate Students' Society) held its annual conference. One of the panels was entitled "Critical Reflections on the Convergence of Education and Development with Indigenous Knowledges" and included participation by several doctoral students (see contributions by Harvey, Metallic, Stocek and Langdon, this volume); the panel was in fact the genesis of the present volume. Listening to these presentations was profoundly inspiring. The new paths being trodden by younger scholars with the will and the expertise to make links between their years of experience in Indigenous communities – from the Canadian North to Africa – and topics in mainstream academia were like a confirmation for me that the new directions I was myself pursuing were the right ones. Getting the grant funding was further validation and opened up a whole new series of research vistas.

These developments in my life as a university-based academic and as a parent were happening at a time when I felt I needed a new way to situate myself. It was a time of transition between the kind of research I had been doing previously (much of it rooted in my children's experiences with language and/or schooling) and the new, to me, area of research with Indigenous peoples, while also making links with my new status as a mother of adult children pursuing careers of their own. Listening to Janine, Christine, Jonathan and Blane talk about living in Indigenous communities for years at a time caused a new penny to drop, an inner voice to make itself heard, saying, "But it needn't be years on end. Maybe you don't need to spend time there for so long, maybe you can mostly be HERE and still change, maybe it can happen before you reach Ph.D. level. Maybe Indigenous knowledges can reach lots of young people who actually stay right here. Look at Nina and the Mayan curandera – that was less than three weeks!"

So I offered this piece to the editor of this volume, and he graciously accepted it. As a mentor of graduate students in a mainstream institution and also as a mother of children on very specific educational paths[3], I was privileged to be able to see the "education for development" piece and the "Indigenous knowledges" piece fitting together in a very special way. By telling my daughter's story, I hope to show here that – given openness and willingness on the part of the adults in their lives – Indigenous knowledges of several kinds can affect the life and life choices of non-Indigenous urban youth in very positive ways.

Method and unconventional ethnography: "Can I interview you, dear?"

Although I had a vivid memory of Nina telling me, shortly after her return from the three-week stay in Guatemala, that she was going to apply to med school as a direct result of her meeting with a traditional Mayan healer, I didn't want to tell my story but to find a way for her to tell hers. Nina agreed to participate in an ethnographic interview so that I would have something more solid to go on than memory, something we could both refer to. The 80-minute audiorecorded and transcribed (by me) conversation we had on May 22, 2007 – abstracted from the rest of our lives together, much of which has also been an ongoing conversation and which is necessarily part of the data as well – constitutes the main database on which this paper is built.[4] As much as possible I will use Nina's own words to tell her story.

Reading Indigenous research has taught me that my own perspective cannot, must not, be kept out of the reporting. This is true for any research reporting; how much more true must it be when a researcher is collaborating with her own child to tell that child's story (Mehra, 2001)? I make no pretense of objectivity here. Nina's own critical reading and comments on the present text have been the subjectivity that counterbalanced my own.

At the time of this interview, Nina was heading into yet another round of exams as part of her pre-med year. We had our conversation after a family supper in a quiet room at home. I did not work from a prescripted interview protocol, but let the conversation develop naturally as much as possible. For me as a mother, this meant a somewhat unnatural desisting from putting my oar in and giving unsolicited opinions on what my daughter was saying. My goal was for the majority of the conversation to be produced by Nina, either in response to my questions or in her own pursuit of a train of thought set off by our discussion with minimal intervention from me. I am not sure how successful I was.

NINA TELLS HER STORY

The following pages take the reader through my interview with Nina in thematic rather than chronological fashion. As natural conversations tend to, our discussion dipped and soared and zig-zagged back and forth over space and time. I have broken it down here according to three main themes. The first could be called "origins"; I needed to sort out for myself how Nina's experience in Guatemala was grounded in her earlier years. Like most parents, I thought I knew what it meant to have grown up being this person, my child, when what I actually knew was what it meant to me to have watched her grow up. The second section goes into Nina's stay in Guatemala in detail, with special emphasis on her encounter with the Mayan *curandera*. The third steps back a bit from this experience and puts it into the context of classical Western medical training. In the third section I also tried to get a sense of how Nina saw that training unfolding in an as-yet-unrealized future, especially in light of her interest in Indigenous and other non-Western ways of knowing about and doing healing. So: past, present, future.

"Witches are healers": uncles, aunts and unexpected influences on childhood

When Nina declared her intention to apply to med school, I assumed there must be a connection to her childhood experiences as a member of an alternative-medicine-embracing family. Since early childhood, Nina and her brother had spent part of every holiday with my sister Tia, her partner Chris and Tia and Chris's children in Toronto. Tia has been a practicing midwife under Ontario law since shortly after provincial regulation of midwifery in 1991. Nina is the eldest in her age group and was for a long time the only girl. From an early age she was an eager listener to Tia's stories about her work. Tia's partner Chris, a naturopath and homeopath, is our family's *de facto* in-house, unpaid, on-call health care practitioner. All five of the children in this extended family are thus far more familiar with alternative medicine than with the usual Western ("allopathic") kind. I thought surely this was the beginning of Nina's interest, and asked her about her early memories of those childhood visits, but it turned out that she remembered very little; only the following:[5]

Nina: ... Tia being dressed funny.

Mela: And how about Chris?

Nina: [laughs] I don't know.

Mela: Okay, never mind. Okay.

Nina: Giving me remedies, I guess. 'Cause when we were sick, we had a cut, and then I had to call him [i.e. from Montreal], and tell him the story, if I was more feeling bad about turning or falling, and things [laughs]. I know all this about homeopathy, from a long time, because of Chris.

A full explanation of why it is that, when treating an apparently unrelated problem, homeopathic practitioners may ask patients questions like "Are you more afraid of turning, or of falling?" – often in relation to dreams as well as to waking life – would require a separate paper. Homeopaths treat the patient, not the disease. A wide spectrum of symptoms and characteristics typically comes into their diagnosis. Nina has known this from her earliest childhood. However, I realized after talking to her that any link between that childhood knowledge and her attraction to healing as a profession was in my mind, not hers.

Nina did, however, go on to make a link between her desire to have children of her own, her aunt Tia's calling and her own interest in the healing professions:

Nina: Plus, I always knew I wanted to have kids, too. Always. Since I was so little. I always knew. And I think I might be going into midwifery or something. That's very linked, I find. Having kids. People who enjoy the idea of having kids, right, would go into midwifery. More than the general population.

Nina, however, considered that the root of her interest in becoming a healer lay elsewhere. Until she reminded me during this conversation, I had quite forgotten, but from the age of ten to about twelve she was very interested in Wicca, the ancient nature religion that is considered by many to be a tenacious survival form of pre-Christian European religious traditions (Jones, 1998; Pearson, Roberts & Samuel, 1998). Wicca predates the patriarchal mindset imposed on European cultures by Christianity, following in the wake of other, more ancient and less Semitically derived Indo-European sky-father-god based religions (Gimbutas, 1991). Females and feminine principles are paramount in Wicca; goddesses are generally more important than gods. For this reason, following its modern revival in mid-twentieth-century Britain (Hutton, 1998), Wicca has been joyfully embraced and enthusiastically developed by many European and North American feminists who had no other Indigenous female-centred spiritual traditions to turn to (Starhawk, 1979). Popular introductions and manuals about Wicca in its late-twentieth-century incarnation abound (e.g., Starhawk, 1979, and all her subsequent work; Tultéan & Daniels, 1998).

Nina: I was interested in Wicca when I was eleven. That's exactly that ... You bought me a pentacle for my eleventh birthday. Because I was in a witch circle, Mom...You bought me a book of witches ... about witch potions, and ...white magic stuff.

Mela: And what was all that about for you at that time?

Nina: Well, white magic is botany, cures and stuff. It's about healers. Witches are healers ... historically. You bought me 'Burning Time'... the book. And then after I was interested in massotherapy and acupuncture.

I was interested in Wicca when I was eleven too. For young girls growing up in a culture that is still essentially patriarchal, it offers powerful models for what female and feminine strength might look like – girl power, woman power (Puttick, 1998). Although at this ten-year distance in time I can't be sure, I think it might have been my idea to buy Nina that eleventh-birthday pentacle. In that year, 1997, the National Film Board of Canada's 1990 documentary "The Burning Times" and the spinoff book were well-known to Canadian feminists. The thousands of witches (practitioners of Wicca) who were persecuted, and the "white magic" they practiced, are now recognized as being what remains of the ancient healing traditions of Europe that were driven underground, by the spread of patriarchal Christianity coupled with the rise of Renaissance learning and male-dominated modern science. Historically, witches have been, in fact, not just healers but Indigenous healers.

Nina continued to make links between the decision to enter med school and the alternative therapies in which she had for so long been interested, from quite a different point of view:

Mela: Med school is such a classic Western approach. It's not midwifery school. It's not massotherapy school. It's very rigid and disciplined and high-status and high-tech. So that was a decision you made ... Can you tell me about why you made that decision?

Nina: You have access to everybody. Massotherapy or all the other things, it's only people that can pay for them that can have that service, you see? Because they're not government-covered. You are only interacting with people from a certain elite class. So that's limited.

Mela: That's not true for Tia because midwifery in Ontario ...

Nina: Yeah, but not in Quebec.

Mela: Oh. If midwifery in Quebec had been like midwifery in Ontario ...[6]

Nina: Maybe, but I have to see how much I like midwifery when I'm gonna be with her this summer [for four weeks of the summer between her pre-med year and her first year of med school proper, Nina arranged to "shadow" her aunt's Toronto midwifery practice as a special student]. But medicine's even more interesting, because it's more broad. It's even more complete. It's not just one part of life. You're with people at all times.

As one of her retrospective contributions to this piece as I wrote it, Nina emailed me that she was "getting an MD diploma because it gives you more credibility, more access to more people (especially more disadvantaged people) and also a good background knowledge of anatomy and pharmaceutical stuff (good to know when so many people are on a shitload of meds) as compared to other alternative medicines." Classic Western medical training can therefore be perceived by young people embarking on the seven-year process as, not necessarily the best way into this vocation, but the most credible one for Western youth. Comments by Nina later in the interview made it clear that she sees herself as part of a growing number of medical professionals who are trying to change medical training and practice from within:

> Nina: What's encouraging me is that I'm not the only one ... Tons of other people are trying to do this. So that's good.
>
> Mela: In your program?
>
> Nina: No. In the world. I think more and more in the world ... There's more and more conferences and stuff ... And more and more interchanges, exchanges ... cliniques of *médecine intégrée*, whether it's different professionals working together, *interdisciplinarité* ... it's the whole thing of the systems.

INDIGENOUS KNOWLEDGE FROM GUATEMALA: INTERCULTURAL EXCHANGE FEEDS A NEW LIFE PLAN

As I now see more clearly in retrospect, through her adolescent years Nina continued to develop her interest in the healing arts and alternative medical traditions. She grew very close to her aunt and uncle in Toronto and learned a great deal about their work. In her mid-teens she undertook a short training course in massage therapy. But when she was finishing secondary school and deciding on a post-secondary program, I don't recall her talking to her parents about medicine as a potential post-CEGEP choice. The decision seems to have arisen directly from her experiences in the particular program she was in – one which she chose partly because of the opportunity to participate in development work as an integral part of the program. It was this program which took her to Guatemala and to her life-changing encounter with an Indigenous healer.

The cultural exchange program

Like many other North American educational programs (in Canada, for example, Canada World Youth; Katimavik), Nina's CEGEP (pre-university college) offers interested students in their late teens the opportunity to find out first hand what development work is like. For three weeks in late December and early January of the final year in a three-year program, forty 18- or 19-year-olds are placed with families in two villages where the population is mainly Indigenous in either Mexico or Guatemala. Ethnic Mayans make up the majority of Guatemala's population and have had a long and bloody relationship with the Spanish-speaking colonizers of this part of the world (Menchú, 1984; Wright, 2003). After centuries of war and blatant anti-Indigenous racism and oppression, the need to build or rebuild infrastructure for the rural population is intense. Spanish-speaking humanities teachers at the Montreal CEGEP Nina attended have developed a relationship with rural school boards that allows them to send young Québécois to stay with local families where there is a student their age to connect with. Although a local Mayan language is the home language for these families, schooling is mainly in Spanish, the colonial language and language of power in Central America. The Quebec students must develop a certain minimal fluency in Spanish before they leave, as part of their required coursework preparation.

> Nina: It's a cultural exchange. In the sense that ... they see how we are, and we see how they are, because we're living together. That's why it's called échange. Even though they don't come. Because we're exchanging things ...when we're there, we do a presentation on Quebec, and stuff like that.

> Mela: What is it you were supposed to do when you were down there? All I remember was how you made four hundred tortillas.

> Nina: There's an aspect of it that's *humanitaire* ...we give them money to build a second floor for the school. We helped paint it. We installed computers, and stuff like that. And people cleaned some environmental [waste] cleaning. Other people did other things ...We formed committees on each of the things we wanted to do ...You have to be on one of the committees. I was on the *informatique* committee. So I was in charge of installing the computers we brought. There was the health committee, that was actually for us, because it was if one of us falls sick ... But, they did bring stuff that they gave there. So they tried to do stuff, they tried to go get pharmacies to donate stuff we could bring there. And they brought them ...toothbrushes. And vitamins ...

The young Quebec students received a mark for the stay in Central America, a credit course in their program, based on three things:

> Nina: One aspect was how we did on our committee, the other aspect was how we did on our *problématique* [research project], and the third aspect was how we did in integration.

It was this *problématique* that led to Nina and her research partner's encounter with the Mayan *curandera*, as part of their research project on the theme of Health:

> Nina: Each person had to be in a team of two on a *problématique*, and you had to conduct interviews, it was in [an] anthropological frame ... Because our teachers are anthropologists. And because it's *sciences humaines*, also. And it's *échange culturelle*. So. And there was ... fifteen themes, and you got to choose a theme with your partner, and ... I was in Health ... Indigenous struggle is another theme. It's themes, you have to collect interviews, collect anthropological data, find informants ... And then you have to write a big paper, thirty-page ... term paper and ...we presented them all a big thing with all the things we collected. With everybody's thing.

Doing anthropology

The fledgling anthropologists[7] decided themselves who to interview, and devised their own interview protocols:

> Nina: The theme of health, you have to find out about health there. I just interviewed people, and then you find out what you find out.
>
> Mela: How did you do that, interviewing people?
>
> Nina: The question we figured we would ask was, 'Which is the most efficient, the traditional system, or the Western medicine system?' But of course the answer was, the mix, right? But we weren't very on the ball about that ... What we did, we interviewed of both systems, so the private doctor – there was only one private doctor and there's only one government doctor because they didn't come all the time, the government health post, I don't know what it's called in English, *posta de salud*. So we interviewed the private doctor ...There were NGO clinics, but there was only nurses working there, so we interviewed two nurses. We interviewed the bone-setter. We interviewed two *comadronas*, midwives ... one of them was also *sacerdote*, which is 'priest', and also *curandera*, which is 'healer'. And we interviewed a herbalist, in a shop ... I remember nine or ten interviews. We also interviewed two mothers of families ... general people. Of course we didn't interview only health professionals.
>
> Mela: I'm interested in knowing how you decided what questions to ask your interview participants.
>
> Nina: Well, that was before we went. It was so difficult, eh? We had to make a *schéma d'entrevue* [interview protocol], but it changed so much when we were there, because we we figured out some questions and then our teacher helped us, you know, [by saying] 'Maybe you should think more of these questions'. And when we were there we found out that some questions, it just didn't make sense to ask them. And some other questions were recommended by one of the brothers of the family where Annie [Nina's class research partner for the Health theme] lived ... He was the one that introduced us to the bonesetter. And he says, 'But, you know, you have to ask these questions, because these are the most important questions. It's polite, you know, you can't not ask these questions.' So we asked questions we wouldn't have asked otherwise. So important!
>
> Mela: What were those questions?
>
> Nina: 'How did you know you were a bonesetter?' And 'When did you know you were a bonesetter?' And 'How did you learn to do it?' And 'How do you do it?' Those were basically the basic questions. 'How did you know you were supposed to do this?' 'How did you *learn* to do it?' and 'How do you *do* it?' And 'With what?'

Mela: And the person who was helping Annie, did he explain why those were the most important questions?

Nina: No. It's just the most important questions. Because you *figure* why. It's because they know by a dream or something. It's always these big affairs, of knowing. Because they have the *donne*, they have the gift, you know?

The idea that one can and in fact should come to understand something as important as one's whole future life path "by a dream or something", through revelation of a *donne* or gift, is one that runs all through Nina's recounting of her experience. It was, I think, the single most significant piece of knowledge she brought back with her. In retrospect, it is clear to me that many of the important adults in Nina's life – both her parents, and Tia and Chris – came to an understanding of their intended life's work in this way. We all felt a very strong, often inexplicable, call (this is the real meaning of the word "vocation", from the Latin verb "to call") and we followed the call. Chris has, in fact, made the study of dreams a central part of his own vocation as an alternative psychotherapist; he is gaining increasing recognition in the field of dream interpretation (Sowton, 2007). My own call led me into an area of scholarship which, ironically, does not readily acknowledge the importance of this kind of intuitive process. Nina seems to be achieving an enviable balance. The "basic questions, 'How did you *know* you were supposed to do this?', 'How did you *learn* to do it?' and 'How do you *do* it?' And 'With what?'" reflect a deep awareness that the "knowing" and the "supposed to" are linked to a very specific epistemological stance about a person's place in the universe. In telling me about this part of her experience and what it taught her about her gift, Nina gave me the gift of a part of myself I had not previously been able to allow a public voice.

A life-changing encounter: Magdalena – curandera, comadrona, sacerdote

During our talk, Nina explored this idea of healing as a gift the healer has been born with from various angles. It became more concrete as we moved into a discussion of the interview that was to prove so significant for the choices she would make after returning from Guatemala. The interview was set up for Nina and her partner by the school principal, partly because:

Nina: … it's a school board that's not like a regular school board. It's a school board of revitalization of Mayan culture. So he knows lots of stuff about Mayan culture that other people don't know, because it was put down a lot …

Mela: So he was more specialized than other school directors.

Nina: He knew lots of stuff about traditional culture, so he was talking to us about the way of curing and the way of conceiving health and stuff, and the traditional cosmological vision… and he said, 'You know, the best one here, you should really go talk to this one, she's the most elder, the most respected, of all of the healers here, I can put you in contact with her.' So we went with him, he introduced [us and] left, you know. And we stayed to do the interview. We only knew that she was a midwife, actually. But then when we asked her 'What are you?' – because we also asked that, 'What do you call yourself?', you know.

"Magdalena" (a pseudonym) called herself three things: *curandera* (traditional healer), *comadrona* (midwife) and *sacerdote* (priest or shaman):

> Nina: *Curandera* is more than a *comadrona*. But all *curanderas* can become *comadronas*. Because all doctors, all healers can be midwives ... The difference is that *comadronas* will only be called for births, whereas *curanderas*, you can go if you have any illness, you know? If you just don't feel well. *Curanderas* will, a healer will, mainly use herbs, or other things, but mainly herbs. Whereas the aspect of being a *sacerdote* is that they know how to do the prayers, know how to do all the more psychic work ... all these things connected with spirituality.

Being a midwife was something Magdalena was destined to do from birth. When Nina and Annie asked how she knew she would do this, she explained in detail:

> Nina: She said that it was ... she just always knew ... Because she's a very experienced midwife too, eh? And she explained to us that how depending of how the baby is in the position when he's born, they know what he'll do, sometimes, you know? Not all positions, but certain characteristic positions — this is a baby that's meant to be *that*, later. And so she had the characteristic thing, they knew that she was going to be a healer. She was fated. She had two things. I don't remember, something in the head, and something in the hand position.

Two things stood out for me in Nina's recounting of this one interview among several, not just immediately after she returned but also during my recorded talk with her over a year later. First, there was the extraordinary hospitality Magdalena showed to the two visiting students. She made time for them in the middle of her busy day (she was over eighty and had numerous domestic responsibilities for her family, including cooking for her grandchildren and great-grandchildren); not only that, but she was more than generous with her knowledge:

> Nina: ... she was a really strange woman. Because she was ... [had] very much energy, you know? She had also been doing it for I don't remember how many years, like forty years. And she had started doing it when she was already thirty. I don't remember... We didn't calculate how old she was. I know she told us. She was eighty-something ... She didn't look super old. She was super smiling and you felt very reassured when you were with her...She was giving us so many things ... She was giving us, you know, when we asked how you cure things, she was giving us lots of details. She was even going to get each ... When she would talk about one way of curing one thing with this tea, whatever, she would go and she had all the plants in her back of her house ... She had hundreds of plants in her house. And she

would go get the plant and she would give us some, she would show us, 'This is this plant, and you can keep this plant'.

Second, as Nina and I retrospectively talked our way back with Nina and Annie back through the interview with Magdalena, it became clear that this generosity stemmed from Magdalena's perception that Nina herself had a gift:

> Nina: We were saying, 'Thank you, thank you so much' … you know, 'This is so kind of you', we said something like that. And then as a reply she said, 'Well, I'm saying all this, you know why I'm saying this … It's because *you're* going to be a midwife, a *comadrona* too.' In a smiley, a nice way. And I was, like, 'What?' … And she says, 'Yes'. But she was talking to me directly. And so I found it very strange that she said that. She said it like it was something that she *knew*. You know, she was very nice to be with … So it was funny that she would say something directly to you like that. She was really saying it, like … not that she was informing us. But she said, 'That's why I'm doing it. That's why *you* can know these things.'

Magdalena's conviction about Nina's fated life path made a deep and lasting impression on her. At the time, she felt an unusual and emotionally powerful resonance:

> Nina: When she said that, I got as if I was … resonating on some … it's cheesy to say. You know like you feel when you have some, how Chris says it, that there's a charge of energy you get, like … what's the word he uses for interpreting dreams? As if you've hit the mark, you know? He says, you know, making associations, and then one as if there's more energy there. You don't even know why you feel it's more that one. He said that's the surest clue to say that that's actually the right association … Even that I cried. Not very much, I was shy … But it was strange. Because there was no reason to.

> Mela: When she said that, you cried?

> Nina: Yeah, but not, like *Boo-hoo-hoo*! Just because you're overwhelmed. When we came out, me and Annie, we were like, 'Oh my god, that was so crazy'. She was a very special person.

A couple of months after coming back, Nina applied to med school. When she explained this plan to me shortly after she returned from Guatemala, it was clear that there was a strong connection to the interview with Magdalena and what Nina had learned about herself from this Indigenous Mayan healer and shaman. Without ever having met her before, Magdalena looked deep into the heart of this young woman from far away and told her exactly what she needed to know at that point in her life. The editor of this volume commented in his feedback on an earlier draft of this chapter that, "Magdalena is not generous with her knowledge with everyone, but is with Nina because of her future, her gift. This logic is similar to the story of learning that Coleman's chapter on the bonesetter will tell, where the bonesetter does not entrust his teaching to anyone, but rather picks someone who has the gift.

This underscores a very different understanding of knowledge production and sharing. As a result, we need to pause to analyze not only the way that knowledge is produced in Indigenous communities, but the way it is shared. The primacy of relationships is key here, and a deep recognition that people must not expect this knowledge to come easily. Sharing is a choice, and as such knowledge is to be cherished and not sold" (J. Langdon, personal communication, December, 2007). In her recounting of this interview, Nina says that Magdalena's decision to share a very special kind of knowledge with her "made her think" about what kind of a person she is, what she's interested in, and why. As I read over her words, I see Nina making an intuitive leap of precisely the kind that the practice of medicine requires. The kind of education we give people might, in the usual run of things, make them think about whether they would make a "good doctor" – not whether they have a "power to heal". Magdalena's words enabled Nina to make the needed connection between those two:

> Mela: I remember that when you came back from Guatemala, you spoke about that particular interview. I don't remember you speaking about other interviews. You spoke about that one.
>
> Nina: She was the most impressive, that's why.
>
> Mela: And you made a direct link to your decision to apply to med school.
>
> Nina: Well, it's just that it made me think, yes, this makes sense, what I've been interested in and all that. Also in how I am. That I'm interested in the human aspect of things but also the scientific aspect of things and also the artistic, you know, art stuff, I'm also very interested in. And it made sense that in fact medicine was like a combination of all these things. Medicine is not a very precise science. It's intuition and things ... It's not precise. Of course I'm not a practiced clinician or whatever. But in my interests and what I would think, I would feel [I] accomplished doing ... and that makes sense with what would be helpful to society ... So maybe this would be something that would make sense. I don't have any conception that I will be necessarily a good doctor. But I think there's something, I feel that there's something that's like a power to heal ... But I don't know if I have [it]. But maybe I do. I don't know ... I would never have had the pretension of thinking I would be able to be a good doctor ... But since she said that, maybe I should try. To see if I am. You see?

Since she said that ... If it were possible to go back and thank her, we would. I suspect that such a person may have other ways of knowing how grateful our family is to her, regardless.

Nina in Guatemala, January 2006

SURVIVING THE PRE-MED YEAR: FIGHTING ASSIMILATION INTO THE
DOMINANT CULTURE OF MEDICINE

In the twelve months that elapsed between acceptance to med school and doing the interview with me shortly after the end of her pre-med year, Nina learned a great deal about the ways med students are acculturated into the discipline of Western medicine:

> Nina: The fact of medical school, it makes you assimilate things, and it becomes unconscious, you know? You integrate the whole system. Because you have to work with it, you have to pass the exams, and all these things ... because always the teachers are talking to you, right? So you integrate the whole system ... Our classes are very incomplete, but then you have no time to learn the stuff you're not learning. Because we barely have time to learn what we are learning. So that's the problem ... We're already going to have *Introduction à la pratique clinique* [Introduction to clinical practice] next year. The class where we're with patients. There's so much pressure because of the competition, because of performance you have to always do in front of other people, *Apprentissage par projets* [Project-based learning], you're with eight people, you can't just say anything. You have to say stuff that then you don't look stupid ... you *have* to say stuff. Because you're marked on participation.

Nina found the first few months of pre-med rather alienating. However, after she found a few other people in her cohort who also felt that the classes were "incomplete", she had a supportive peer group with whom she discussed the need to explore "other systems" besides the one they were being indoctrinated into. Given the intensity of the med school year, this turned out to be something that can only be undertaken in any depth during the summer work-study stints (called *stages* in French) that med students typically find for themselves. As previously mentioned, during the summer between her pre-med year and the first year of the M.D. program proper, Nina arranged to spend time with her midwife aunt's Toronto practice as a special student. She also managed to get a job as a research assistant in a Cree community in northern Quebec for two months, a learning experience that she saw as having a direct link to her trip to Guatemala a year and a half previously. Like Mayan traditional healing, midwifery, and Wicca, Cree traditional medicine is "another system". Clearly some medical students see resisting assimilation into classical Western medical thinking as one of their main tasks:

Nina: So you integrate[8] the whole [med school] system, and ... that's why it's important for me to have another one. So that I can integrate it with care. I don't want to integrate everything. If there's bad things, of course there's bad things because the system is not working right now, in Quebec. And everybody knows that. It's just that they don't know how to change it because it's so integrated in all the health care professionals. The hierarchies and all these things, it's all integrated. You learn that it's normal, and nobody questions it. So if I want to be able to be critical, I have to know other ways, to give me a critical perspective. And to be able to see, oh, this is a flaw, maybe, but in fact there is a solution. It's not like it has to be like that. And to think of solutions, to think of, to be much more careful of what I do, you know?

Mela: Do you know other people who are thinking like this?

Nina: Ahhh ...Yasmine ... But she doesn't see it like that ... she's more in the natural medicine perspective. She's learning a lot about herboristerie, and about... naturopathy and stuff. But that also gives you another system ... You have to do it fast, because the more it goes, the more you have to integrate it [med school] ... I think we should think about what we're saying, but it's difficult because you don't have the time. So that's why I try to do it otherwise.

Doing medical school "otherwise" is important because, as Nina pointed out in our interview, the best way to develop a critical perspective on the system one has grown up in is to become familiar with other systems:

Nina: Whenever you find an alternate way of doing something, it makes you question ... If you only know one thing you cannot question it because you think that's how it is. If you know that there's other ways of it being, you know this ... It's like if you travel, you'll notice how we are, *here* ... Or if you learn another language, you notice about *our* language, in fact, what's particular, that you wouldn't have ever thought was particular. Well, it's the same thing. If you learn of a different system, you see what's in fact the characteristics of *our* system. Which you would never have known otherwise, because you assimilate it. And that's why I'm going now ... the soonest I can. That's why I want to do the midwifery thing, because midwifery is also a different kind of system, of seeing things.

Cree traditional medicine and other sources of alternative knowledge about health and healing

It was this richness of alterity in one particular Cree community that motivated Nina's decision to seek work there during the summer; she found out about the work they do there through the documentation they have already produced:

Nina: This is ... one of the only places where there has been research about Indigenous traditional medicine. So they have a library with all the information ... in the pamphlets and stuff, they even advertise it. Maybe there has been research other places, but not as much. Because the Cree is really different from the other Indigenous nations of Quebec ... they're more autonomous. They're the most politically emancipated. So it's not surprising that they're the ones that would put in the pamphlet, that that's what exists ... So it's probably easier to access, and that's why I know about it. They teach in Cree ... Traditional pursuits are more valued than in other places ... It's still more the old way of seeing things.

Mela: So it seems like you're saying that the Cree are, in effect, less colonized, or they've resisted colonization more.

Nina: No. They're further in the process of decolonization. They're not less colonized ... It's because of the *barrage électrique* [hydroelectric dam] thing, they've had to organize political resistance. So I know because in the pamphlets, because I looked on the Internet and stuff.

Indigenous knowledges are one among several kinds of alternate knowledge that medical students can draw on, but they are a special kind of different perspective:

Mela: What are you hoping to find out?

Nina: Different perspectives on how people conceive health, how people conceive everything to do with healing. Or childbirth ... with the Cree, it's such a different perspective, what I have learned so far, is that their definition of the word 'health' translates as 'being alive well', so it's everything to do with health, everything to do with how you *live*, what you eat, what you, if you can hunt, if the animals are there to be hunted, because that's what you eat, so it's so broad. How can I find out? ... In Guatemala, what did I decide to find out? I didn't decide before I got there. When I was there I was there, and my perspective, well, what I told myself, is, I'm there to learn.

My conversation with Nina took place shortly before she left for her summer job working for a Cree doctor in a remote northern community, so her actual experiences there are not part of the material I am drawing upon as I write this; perhaps the current piece is the first of several instalments on Indigenous and other alternate knowledges as a counterbalance to classic Western medical education.

When we spoke about future summer plans, Nina was thinking of spending her next summer studying acupuncture in China (where the World Health Organization has set up a recognized program for foreign medical students). Like Mayan or Cree traditional Indigenous healing:

> Nina: Acupuncture has ways of curing things that there's nothing that Western medicine can do for these conditions … it's the whole thing of the systems … like in psychology, [the] systemic school of thinking is coming to be more and more popular … The best way of saying it is that the relation between two things is as important as the two things.
>
> Mela: That's very much Chinese traditional medicine.
>
> Nina: Well, exactly. It's very much all other medicines than Western medicine … That's why there's people that don't want to recognize it. Because they don't understand why it works … It's concepts that are not recognized. And there's no scientific explanation … In fact, that doesn't change anything. Because in medicine there's tons of stuff that we don't know [understand] anyways, but that we still do.

As Nina said in her retrospective comment on the interview, "I think I will have to end up getting other trainings".

RELEVANCE TO THE HERE AND NOW – AND BEYOND THE HERE AND NOW

Nina and her story may or may not be typical of beginning medical students; this is not my specialized area as an educator and I have no way of knowing. But a close connection with this particular student's experience makes me wonder, as an educator (professionally) and as a patient of many different doctors over five decades (privately), whether it would not be possible and practical to considerably enlarge the usual path budding M.D.s travel. Most of all, though, it makes me wonder, as a mother, whether it might not be simpler than we think to make some small structural changes in the way we set up our children's routes into adulthood that would nonetheless ultimately have far-reaching effects. Medicine is only one of many "Western" vocations in which an enlargement and expansion of knowledge of the kind I have written about here would be possible, perhaps inevitable, if it were made easier for young Westerners to have frequent, significant (even if not sustained) contact with peoples and bodies of knowledge outside the usual purview of the discipline. The preparation they would need for such encounters isn't at all difficult to imagine. It would take only goodwill and a little expenditure in the way of books and materials not presently in the curriculum. The greatest challenge that would be faced along the way would be, probably, not the physical, material aspects represented by classrooms and curricula and costs of air travel, but mental barriers – not in the minds of twenty-year-olds, rather on the part of the educators two and three times their age who would have to assent to such a change in how programs are conceived and executed.

Would it be possible to bring Indigenous knowledges into medical education more generally? When I asked Nina to comment on this chapter, she pointed out that there are a lot of bits and pieces that we could bring together: "at University of the North in Manitoba the midwifery program that is for natives has courses and stuff about aboriginal medicine integrated into it, also McGill [not where she is enrolled] is supposed to be changing its curriculum (you should check this) so as to include stuff about aboriginal health and perhaps Indigenous knowledge ... but I'm not sure if it really does". As the parent of a young person who has made the commitment to classic Western med school training, I feel that I am only at the beginning of my own exploration of this vast and complex field of interlocking knowledges.

As Nina and I wound up our conversation, our discussion of the impossibility of "translating" traditional Chinese medical concepts from acupuncture into Western scientific terms brought us back around to my own field of language study. Then it took us beyond:

Nina: That's what some people are doing. Mostly Chinese people that are here ... So as to make it recognized. They're trying to prove it [acupuncture] through Western recognized things.

Mela: That's not necessarily going to work all the time. Just like there are some things that you can't translate into another language.

Nina: That's what they say, that it's impossible to make it completely coherent. Like it's impossible to translate exactly a language ... But in fact if there is one truth then it should be.

Mela: I think there's no one truth. I think what you see depends on where you're standing.

Nina: But then that would be the truth of it, that what you see depends on where you're standing. It's a different kind of truth, but it's still truth. Of course.

This epistemological stance seems to me to be compatible with Indigenous knowledge systems as I am coming to learn about them. It is also the stance taken by the ancient Hindu philosophers whose wisdom my father tried to pass on. Surely there is a way to make it compatible with medical education in this new century — even in, especially in, "the West", where alternative perspectives are so sorely needed for all our sakes, of course.

ACKNOWLEDGEMENTS

First and foremost I want to thank my daughter Nina for being who she is and for sharing her life with me so unreservedly. Not all mothers are so privileged and I am deeply grateful. Nina also read this chapter in draft form and gave essential and critical feedback throughout. The idea for this piece came from a panel presented by doctoral students at McGill's Faculty of Education in March, 2007 (see contributions by Harvey, Langdon, Metallic, and Stocek, this volume). I have benefited immeasurably from hearing these extraordinary young scholars speak about their work, and have been able to have more extended discussions with several of them. Thank you, Christine, Jon and Janine (to whom, in particular, my debt goes deeper than I can adequately express here). My encounters with panel chair and book "discussant" Liz Meyer, around this piece as well as a multitude of other issues to which my eyes have recently been opened, continue to amaze and delight me. If the coming generation of intellectuals and activists has many more such as these, knowledge creation in the current century is in good hands. Finally, I will forever remain indebted to my former doctoral supervisor, Patsy Lightbown, whose rigorous and compassionate early training provided the foundation on which my work is built — as an applied linguist, then as a critical applied linguist, and now as somebody who is increasingly sceptical of disciplinary definitions and is trying to move beyond them.

NOTES

[1] Nina's real name and the names of other family members are used with permission. Other names from her story, whether of people connected with her schooling at both CEGEP and university level or of members of Indigenous nations and places with whom she came in contact, are pseudonyms.

[2] English Language Teaching. Also ESL/EFL, English as a Second/Foreign Language. The word "industry", commonly used in the field, accurately reflects the massive financial and resource investments in this area (textbook production, teacher training, professional and lay publications, private language schools, and other "ESL services").

[3] Nina's younger brother Kobir, a rapper, does not come into this particular story; but his involvement in Montreal Hip-Hop has shaped my research path for the past five years (Sarkar, Winer & Sarkar, 2005; Sarkar, 2006; Sarkar & Winer, 2006; Sarkar & Allen, 2007; Sarkar, Low & Winer, 2007; Sarkar, 2008).

[4] The transcription was done in two stages; the first, "raw" transcription includes overlaps, pauses, restarts, self-corrections, and discourse markers such as "like" and "you know". The interview extracts used here are taken from the second-stage version in which all those things were removed. This second and final version preserves the characteristics of spontaneous oral discourse while adhering to minimal standards of readability for a general academic audience (i.e. of non-linguists).

[5] All interview extracts are from the May 22, 2007 interview. Most have been shortened to eliminate repetitions and circumlocutions.

[6] In comparison to some other Canadian provinces, Quebec was very late in recognizing midwifery as a legitimate form of medical practice (2006, in contrast to Ontario, 1991; Alberta, 1994; British Columbia, 1995; Manitoba, 2000; however, in the Atlantic provinces midwifery is still unregulated). Birthing women in Toronto, whatever their backgrounds, have a wide variety of choices when it comes to home or hospital births with midwives in attendance rather than MDs (whether family doctors or obstetricians). This is not yet true in Quebec where the process of regulation and training of midwives is still under way and where public awareness of choices for birthing women has not yet caught up to the law.

[7] Space does not permit a discussion of the historical and much-criticized relationship between Western-trained anthropologists and Indigenous peoples, but see Tuhiwai Smith, 1999, for a full discussion of this relationship.

[8] Nina is using the verb *integrate* in its French sense of "absorb, make a part of oneself".

REFERENCES

Abley, M. (2003). *Spoken here: Travels among threatened languages.* Toronto: Random House Canada.

Adelson, N. (2000). *'Being alive well': Health and the politics of Cree well-being.* Toronto: University of Toronto Press.

Auerbach, E. (1993). The politics of the ESL classroom: Issues of power in pedagogical choices. In J. Tollefson (Ed.), *Power and inequality in language education* (pp. 9–33). New York, NY: Cambridge University Press.

Battiste, M. (1998). Enabling the autumn seed: Towards a decolonized approach to aboriginal knowledge, language, and education. *Canadian Journal of Native Education, 22*(1), 16–27.

Bielenberg, B. (1999). Indigenous language codification: Cultural effects. In Revitalizing Indigenous Languages. Paper presented at the annual stabilizing Indigenous language symposium (5th, Louisville, KY, May 15–16, 1998).

Block, D., & Cameron, D. (Eds.). (2002). *Globalization and language teaching.* London: Routledge.

Canada World Youth. (n.d.). Retrieved April 30, 2008, from http://www.cwy-jcm.org/

Canagarajah, S. (1999). *Resisting linguistic imperialism in English teaching.* Oxford, UK: Oxford University Press.

Canagarajah, S. (2002). Celebrating local knowledge on language and education. *Journal of Language, Identity and Education, 1*(4), 243–261.

Dixon, R.M.W. (1997). *The rise and fall of languages.* Cambridge, UK: Cambridge University Press.

Donaldson, L. E. (1998). Writing the talking stick: Alphabetic literacy as colonial technology and postcolonial appropriation. *American Indian Quarterly, 22*(1/2), 46–62.

Elgin, S. H. (2000). *The language imperative.* Cambridge, MA: Perseus Publishers.

Fairclough, N. (2001). *Language and power (2nd ed.).* Harlow, Essex, UK: Pearson.

Ferrari, A. (2005). Interférence entre swahili et sheng dans l'enseignement à Nairobi. Paper presented at the Association Internationale de Linguistique Appliquée triennial meeting, Madison, WI, July 24–29.

Fishman, J. (2006). *Do not leave your language alone: The hidden status agendas within corpus planning in language policy.* Mahwah, NJ: Lawrence Erlbaum Associates.

Freire, P. (1970/2000). *Pedagogy of the oppressed (30th anniversary edition), with an introduction by Donaldo Macedo.* New York: Continuum.

Gimbutas, M. (1991). *The civilization of the goddess: The world of old Europe.* San Francisco: HarperCollins.

Harris, R. (1990). On redefining linguistics. In H. Davis & T. Taylor (Eds.), *Redefining linguistics* (pp. 18–52). London: Routledge.

Higgins, C. (2004). AAVE returns to Africa: "Black English" among Tanzanian youth. Poster presented at the American Association of Applied Linguistics annual meeting, Portland, OR, May 1–4.

Hutton, R. (1998). The discovery of the modern goddess. In J. Pearson, R. H. Roberts, & G. Samuel (Eds.), *Nature religion today: Paganism in the modern world* (pp. 89–100). Edinburgh: Edinburgh University Press.

Janicki,. K. (2006). *Language misconceived: Arguing for applied cognitive sociolinguistics.* Mahwah, NJ: Erlbaum.

Jones, P. (1998). The European native tradition. In J. Pearson, R. H. Roberts, & G. Samuel (Eds.), *Nature religion today: Paganism in the modern world* (pp. 77–88). Edinburgh: Edinburgh University Press.

Kachru, B. (1986). *The alchemy of English: The spread, functions and models of non-native Englishes.* New York: Pergamon Institute of English.

Kachru, B. (1992). *The other tongue: English across cultures.* Urbana, IL: University of Illinois Press.

Katimavik. (n.d.). Retrieved April 30, 2008, from http://www.katimavik.org

Lee, P. (1996). *The Whorf theory complex: A critical reconstruction.* Philadelphia: John Benjamins.

Lightbown, P. (1985). Great expectations: Second-language acquisition research and classroom teaching. *Applied Linguistics*, 173–189.
Lightbown, P., & Spada, N. (2006). *How languages are learned (3rd ed.)*. Oxford, UK: Oxford University Press.
Makoni, S., & Meinhof, U. H. (2003). Introducing applied linguistics in Africa. *AILA Review, 16*(1), 1–12.
Makoni, S., & Pennycook, A. (2007). *Disinventing and reconstituting languages*. Clevedon, Avon, UK: Multilingual Matters.
Martin, K., & Mirraboopa, B. (2003). Ways of knowing, being and doing: A theoretical framework and mthods for Indigenous and indigenist re-search. *Journal of Australian Studies, 76*, 203–214.
Mehra, B. (2001). Research or personal quest? Dilemmas in studying my own kind. In B. M. Merchant & A. I. Willis (Eds.), *Multiple and intersecting identities in qualitative research* (pp. 69–82). Mahwah, NJ: Erlbaum.
Menchú, R. (1984). *I, Rigoberta Menchú* (A. Wright, Trans.). London: Verso.
Mitchell, T. (2004). Doin' damage in my native language: Resistance vernaculars in Hip Hop in Europe and Aotearoa/New Zealand. In S. Whiteley, A. Bennett, & S. Hawkins (Eds.), *Popular music, space and place* (pp. 108–123). London: Ashgate.
Nettle, D., & Romaine, S. (2000). *Vanishing voices: The extinction of the world's languages*. New York: Oxford University Press.
Niranjana, T. (1991). Translation, colonialism and the rise of English. In S. Joshi (Ed.), *Rethinking English: Essays in literature, language, history* (pp. 124–145). New Delhi, India: Trianka.
Park, S. M., & Sarkar, M. (2008). Parents' attitudes toward heritage language maintenance for their children and their efforts to help their children maintain the heritage language: A case study of Korean-Canadian immigrants. *Language, Culture and Curriculum, 20*(3), 223–235.
Pearson, J., Roberts, R. H., & Samuel, G. (Eds.). (1998). *Nature religion today: Paganism in the modern world*. Edinburgh: Edinburgh University Press.
Pennycook, A. (1994). *The cultural politics of English as an international language*. London: Longman.
Pennycook, A. (2001). *Critical applied linguistics: A critical introduction*. Mahwah, NJ: Erlbaum.
Pennycook, A. (2007). The myth of English as an International Language. In S. Makoni & A. Pennycook (Eds.), *Disinventing and reconstituting languages* (pp. 90–115). Clevedon, Avon, UK: Multilingual Matters.
Phillipson, R. (1992). *Linguistic imperialism*. Oxford, UK: Oxford University Press.
Puttick, E. (1998). Goddesses and gopis: In search of new models of female sexuality. In J. Pearson, R. H. Roberts, & G. Samuel (Eds.), *Nature religion today: Paganism in the modern world* (pp. 111–122). Edinburgh: Edinburgh University Press.
Rajagopalan, K. (1999). Of EFL teachers, conscience, and cowardice. *ELT Journal, 53*, 200–206.
Ramanathan, V. (2005). *The English-vernacular divide: Postcolonial language politics and practice*. Clevedon, Avon, UK: Multilingual Matters.
Reedy, T. (2000). Te Reo Maori: The past 20 years and looking forward. *Oceanic Linguistics, 39*(1), 157–169.
Sarkar, M. (2002). Saute ça/"Jump this!": The acquisition of the faire faire causative by first and second language learners of French. *Annual Review of Language Acquisition, 2*, 157–201.
Sarkar, M. (2005a). "à l'école on parle français": second language acquisition and the creation of community in a multiethnic Montreal kindergarten. In F. Salili & R. Hoosain (Eds.), *Language in multicultural education (Research in Multicultural Education and International Perspectives series)* (pp. 310–342). Greenwich, CT: Information Age Publishing.
Sarkar, M. (2005b). Language of education policy in Quebec: Access to which majority language and for whom? In S. May, M. Franken, & R. Barnard, (Eds.), *LED2003: Refereed Conference Proceedings of the 1st International Conference on Language, Education and Diversity* (n.p.). Hamilton, NZ: Wilf Malcolm Institute of Educational Research, University of Waikato.
Sarkar, M. (2006). "La vraie langue française [n']existe plus": Français parlé et pratiques multilingues comme stratégies identitaires dans le rap montréalais. *Grenzgänge, 13*(25), 30–51.

Sarkar, M. (2008). "Still reppin' por mi gente": The transformative power of language mixing in Quebec Hip-Hop. In H. S. Alim, A. Ibrahim, & A. Pennycook (Eds.), *Global linguistic flows: Hip Hop cultures, youth identities, and the politics of language* (pp. 139–157). New York, NY: Routledge.

Sarkar, M., & Allen, D. (2007). Identity in Quebec Hip-Hop: Language, territory and ethnicity in the mix. *Journal of Language, Identity and Education, 6*(2), 117–130.

Sarkar, M., Low, B., & Winer, L. (2007). "Pour connecter avec le Peeps": Québéquicité and the Quebec Hip-Hop community. In M. Mantero (Ed.), *Identity and second language learning: Culture, inquiry and dialogic activity in educational contexts*. Greenwich, CT: Information Age Publishing.

Sarkar, M., & Winer, L. (2006). Multilingual code-switching in Quebec rap: Poetry, pragmatics and performativity. *International Journal of Multilingualism, 3*(3), 173–192.

Sarkar, M., Winer, L., & Sarkar, K. (2005). Multilingual code-switching in Montreal Hip-Hop: Mayhem meets method, or, "Tout moune qui talk trash kiss mon black ass du nord". In J. Cohen, K. McAlister, K. Rolstad, & J. MacSwan (Eds.), *ISB4: Proceedings of the 4th International Symposium on Bilingualism* (pp. 2057–2074). Somerville, MA: Cascadilla Press.

Skutnabb-Kangas, T. (2000). *Linguistic genocide in education? Or worldwide diversity and human rights?* Mahwah, NJ: Lawrence Erlbaum Associates.

Sowton, C. (2007). *Dreamreading manual: A method of dreamwork*. Toronto: Christopher Sowton. Retrieved April 30, 2008, from http://www.dreamreading.ca/

Starhawk. (1979). *The spiral dance: A rebirth of the ancient religion of the Great Goddess*. San Francisco: Harper & Row.

Tolenoa, A., & Hough, D. (2005). Preserving our language and culture: A Micronesian Sram Sram. In S. May, M. Franken, & R. Barnard (Eds.), *LED2003: Refereed Conference Proceedings of the 1st International Conference on Language, Education and Diversity* (n.p.). Hamilton, NZ: Wilf Malcolm Institute of Educational Research, University of Waikato.

Tuhiwai Smith, L. (1999). *Decolonising methodologies: Research and Indigenous peoples*. Dunedin, NZ: University of Otago Press.

Tultéan, P., & Daniels, E. (1998). *Pocket guide to Wicca*. Freedom, CA: Crossing Press.

Urla, J. (1999). Basque language revival and popular culture. In W. A. Douglass, C. Urza, L. White, & J. Zulaika (Eds.), *Basque politics and nationalism on the eve of the millennium* (pp. 44–62). Reno: Basque Studies Program, University of Nevada.

Wayne State University. (n.d.). Glossary—Cultural Anthropology, from Introduction to Anthropology 2100. Retrieved April 27, 2008, from http://www.anthro.wayne.edu/ant2100/GlossaryCultAnt.htm

Whorf, B. L. (1956). *Language, thought and reality: Selected writings of Benjamin Lee Whorf (edited and with an introduction by J. B. Carroll)*. Cambridge, MA: MIT press.

Wilmot, J. (2006, November). Listuguj Mi'gmaw language program. Paper presented at the National First Nations Languages Conference, Winnipeg, Manitoba, November 14.

Wright, R. (2003). *Stolen continents: Conquest and resistance in the Americas*. Toronto: Penguin Canada.

COLEMAN AGYEYOMAH & JONATHAN LANGDON

8. BUILDING BRIDGES FROM BROKEN BONES

Traditional Bonesetters and Health Choices in Northern Ghana

INTRODUCTION

While development as a field of practice can be thought of as a deeply conflicted space of both theoretical and practical debates – something explored more fully in the Dei & Simmons chapter above – there are still two practical elements that most practitioners agree need to be improved in order for the elusive "development" to occur. These are the elements of a society's level of education and of its health/wellness. Billions of dollars are spent every year by development agencies to determine the level of education and health in a society, and then to implement interventions intended to improve both of these quantitatively determined levels. Elsewhere in this collection, Harvey elaborates on the ways in which agencies use supposedly expert knowledge to discredit and appropriate local ways of knowing and being. We will not repeat this argument here, except to note that this process of discrediting and appropriation is highly pronounced in both education and health practice.

This chapter focuses on providing a rich, detailed, and empirical instance of a local iteration of health and wellness in Northern Ghana. As a result of research we have been engaged in over the past four years, a complex picture of how residents in one district in Northern Ghana judge the range of health and wellness choices available to them is elaborated. What is critical in this evaluation is the qualitative difference residents find between the health care services provided through government services and those provided by a local traditional bonesetter. The chapter begins by exploring this differentiation, but then it connects the high regard residents have for the bonesetter to differences in epistemic approaches to wellness, patient care, and the formation of future bonesetters. What has become clear over the four years that we have been discussing health and wellness with people in this district, as well as with the bonesetter, Chief Isshaku Gumrana Mahamadu, and with district health practitioners, is that traditional and Indigenous health practices remain both highly esteemed and the first point of call for ailments. It has become clear that dialogue and respect between the two epistemic systems can actually improve the range of health care options available in a disadvantaged community such as the one at the center of this study, but that this dialogue needs to be based not on the assimilation of bonesetting into the government allopathic system, but rather on an epistemic dialectic that resists a final synthesis of either of the two ways of understanding wellness. In this sense, what this chapter proposes is a bridge between these different iterations, a bridge residents can cross and use in the ways they see will help them best.

"TO DIE IS HONEY AND TO LIVE IS SALT"

In the later part of 2004, we both contributed to a participatory qualitative assessment of health services in a number of localities throughout Ghana. This assessment, dubbed *Community Voices*, worked with communities to first determine the indicators they thought were suggestive of good health practices and then to evaluate their local health providers based on these indicators (Gariba & Langdon, 2005). While conducting this evaluation, we were struck by the low opinion many of those participating had of the government-run health systems. The above proverb – "to die is honey and to live is salt" – was spoken by an elder in a town called Wale Wale, in the West Mamprusi district of Northern Ghana. He explained that he felt the approach of the government medical system, based on the Western allopathic method, was so contrary to his way of understanding health and wellness that he would rather die than go into this medical system to live. In other words death would be a preferable honey if he needed this system to live.

While this elder's opinion was extreme, it captured the spirit we encountered in the assessment, especially what emerged in the West Mamprusi District (Gariba & Langdon, 2005). Across all the localities, the consensus from the stories gathered in the assessment was that the government allopathic medical system was not well perceived. This is perhaps not surprising given that the services available to local residents have been consistently underfunded and the local medical staff underpaid since the advent of structural adjustment (Hutchful, 2002). Yet what the overall assessment indicated was that the main concern of participants was not necessarily the success of the treatment process, nor the number of staff that attended to them, but rather how humane the treatment was. Across the board participants spoke of experiences where they had been yelled at by health staff, or where they had been refused treatment because it was the weekend. One participant from another community in Northern Ghana added that a nurse once told her she should have come early in the morning as she was now ready to go home. Adding insult to injury, the nurse then told the community member to "go home and come back tomorrow" (Gariba & Langdon, 2005, p. 13). In Wale Wale, this sentiment was even more extreme, as stories surfaced about traditional birth attendants who took a pregnant woman in need of medical attention to the district hospital and were told to take the woman home because she was too poor – this despite a national policy of free medical treatment for pregnant women (Gariba & Langdon, 2005). In the resulting discussion, many of the young women present spoke of how they would not want their children to be delivered in the local hospital – echoing the feelings of the elder described above. In this sense, what surfaced strongly in the review was the lack of confidence communities across Ghana have in government health services, and how this lack of confidence is centered on not only being well treated – as in the quality and success of the treatment – but also being treated well – as in being treated humanely, with dignity regardless of a person's level of wealth.

What is interesting in the story that emerged in Wale Wale is the way young women planning families would not consider having their children in the hospital, placing their trust in traditional birth attendants instead. This pervasive feeling is indicative that, at least in Wale Wale, there is a choice people could make about wellness treatment; there is a different path to wellness than that of the government allopathic system, and this different path is in fact preferable to the allopathic system. The elder whose quote began this section had a similar sentiment. When we asked him after the evaluation of the allopathic system if he felt similarly about the bonesetter operating just outside of town, he looked at us as if we were asking him an absurd question. His response was, "the two are not the same at all."

THE TWO ARE NOT THE SAME

As we begin this section, we would like to add one important caveat: even as the elder in Wale Wale tells us that these two paths to wellness are "not the same" it is important to resist the temptation to create a false dichotomy between them. Much criticism has been levelled against the facile dichotomies between tradition and modernity, or a simplistic reading of the complexity of Indigenous knowledge systems (Dei et al., 2000; Semali & Kincheloe, 1999). And, even as we may be tempted to place these two paths of wellness in two separate universes of existence – the one primordial and linked to the land, the other modern and linked to Westernization and globalization – it is key to recognize that even though they may not be the same in the eyes of this elder, they both live in the same geo-temporal space for residents of Wale Wale. And, in many ways, it is their mutual presence that also helps each to define itself, as the very things that are critiqued in the allopathic system – such as lack of humane treatment – are the things upheld as virtues in the bonesetter's practice (this is expanded on further below). However, while we recognize the dangers of a false dichotomy and also the way these two systems overlap, contradict, and influence each other in present day Northern Ghana, we feel it is important to pause here and reflect on these two epistemologies of wellness in order to show where they "are not the same" and where they may have some points of convergence.

As we launch into this discussion of these two epistemologies it is important to acknowledge more fully the reality of the locality that frames this discussion. Northern Ghana, considered the labour reserve for the rest of the country since colonial times, has been traditionally marginalized from much of the urbanization taking place in Ghana's south (Saaka, 2001). While this history has meant much hardship for the north, it has also meant that in some ways its Indigenous systems of governance as well as its epistemologies of wellness have been less impacted by urbanization and Westernization than those in the south. It is important to note this dual legacy in the discussion that follows as it helps to explain why residents in Wale Wale have been so adamant that they maintain their ability to choose paths to wellness and why the allopathic system has such a poor reputation in the north. Nonetheless, out of respect for those who live in this space and place, any comments made in this chapter are mediated by our deep sense that it is only residents of this locality that can and should determine which system of wellness works best for them at any given time. As such, in the comparison that follows, we will avoid creating a hierarchy of epistemologies, one way or another, and will instead look for ways that each epistemic system could gain from the other without being assimilated by it or subordinated to it. But before going into this further, we want to follow the example of the other contributors to this book and connect these discussions more fully to concepts of Indigenous knowledges.

As George Dei, Budd Hall and Dorothy Rosenberg (2000) have described, Indigenous knowledges can be defined as "a body of knowledge associated with the long term occupancy of a certain place" (6). Semali & Kincheloe (1999) use a similar definition, seeing Indigenous knowledges as "an everyday rationalization that rewards individuals that live in a given locality" (3). Finally, McCarty, Borgoiakova, Gilmore, Lomawaima & Romero (2005) use a definition derived from the ILO convention 169, which notes that Indigenous peoples:

> Are regarded as Indigenous on account of their descent from the populations which inhabited the country, or geographical region to which the country belongs, at the time of ... colonization or the establishment of present state boundaries and who, irrespective of their legal status, retain some or all of their own social, economic, cultural, and political institutions. (1)

The connection to the antecedent colonial history and its effects on Indigenous knowledges is also an important aspect of both Dei, Hall and Rosenburg (2000) and Semali and Kincheloe's (1999) understanding of Indigenous knowledges. For both of these sets of authors, the critical role colonialism played in establishing hierarchies of knowledge that discredited local ways of knowing and being needs to be recognized in order to begin to come to terms with contemporary Indigenous epistemologies. Without this genealogical work, one runs the risk of enacting the simplistic dichotomy discussed above, and also the risk of failing to see how each epistemic system has been influenced by the other.

In beginning to situate the effects of colonialism on contemporary health epistemologies in Northern Ghana, Walter Mignolo's (2000) theory of local history and global design provides an apt theoretical framework for discussing the effects of what he calls the "colonial difference" without descending into simplistic binaries. In essence, Mignolo's theory is relational in nature, and is grounded in a context-driven assessment of the ways in which one local history dominates another and imposes a "global design," while the subjugated local history is forced to "adapt, adopt, reject, integrate or ignore" the global design:

> The colonial difference is the space where coloniality of power is enacted. It is also the space where the restitution of subaltern knowledge is taking place ... The colonial difference is the space where local histories inventing and implementing global designs meet local histories, the space in which global designs have to be adapted, adopted, rejected, integrated or ignored. The colonial difference is, finally, the physical as well as imaginary location where the coloniality of power is at work in the confrontation of two kinds of local histories displayed in different spaces and times across the planet. (2000, p. ix)

The fluidity of these relations is key in this interpretation; yet this fluidity does not underplay the effects of power and dominance by one local history on another. At the same time, this type of interpretation, along with those advanced by Dei et al. and Semali and Kincheloe, provide room for a non-essentialized version of Indigenous knowledges, a version of Indigenous knowledges that is living, adapting, rejecting, and changing in the contemporary world, even as it contends with the continued presence of global designs that wish to subjugate it by discrediting its status. This ongoing cycle and "continuum of conflict and dialogue," as Maurial (1999, p. 59) calls it – where Indigenous epistemologies have had to engage in ongoing conflict and dialogue with Western epistemologies – is coming to a head, as "Indigenous knowledges are emerging again in the present day as a response to the growing awareness that the world's subordinated peoples and their values have been marginalized" (Dei et al., 2000, p. 6). For Maurial (1999), it is a mistake to imagine an end in this circularity, but she does see the potential for dialogue to emerge as the mechanism through which this circular process of engagement plays out, rather than conflict. This circular process of engagement is an important metaphor for how we have come to understand the relationship between the bonesetter and the allopathic system in Northern Ghana – an understanding that informs our vision of a dialectic without synthesis discussed further below.

The living nature of Chief Isshaku Gumrana Mahamadu's practice is illustrated by the changing nature of the types of bone-breakages he now sees on a regular basis. Instead of dealing with what in a previous time might have been the occasional compound fracture of an arm or leg, Chief Isshaku now deals with compound fractures on a regular basis. This is as a result of the sole north-south highway in the country, running from Burkina Faso to Ghana's capital Accra, being literally on his village's doorstep. His is not the only bonesetting practice found close to the main highway – the other major bonesetter in the North is located in Nanton, a community just off the main highway one and a half hours south of Wale Wale. This change in practice is only one example of the living knowledge system that Chief Isshaku imbibes, and his shifting practice – grounded in the knowledge of the past yet enacted in the realities of the present – is a dynamic testament to ways in which Indigenous knowledge systems are adapting to the painful realities of Ghana's integration into a global market.

Yet, even given this adaptability, it should not be assumed that Chief Isshaku's practice is accepted by that aspect of Ghanaian society that is most heavily influenced by the global design – not to mention in the wider global sphere. There are two ways in which this Indigenous knowledge is still subjugated and accorded a lesser rank in terms of wellness practice. The first is connected to the notion of progress. Mignolo, Semali and Kincheloe, and Dei et al. have all contested the manner in which enlightenment ideas have discounted other ways of knowing, or have absorbed their ways of knowing into the Western concept of "universality" of experiences. The enlightenment helped establish a linear sense of history with an end goal of constant improvement of material existence. Ronald Wright (2002) has documented and critiqued this process eloquently, while Rist (1997) has connected this Eurocentric desire to the notion of "development". Yet this linear concept of history ignores the way that for many Indigenous peoples, history has not turned into progress, but rather what Mahia Maurial (1999) calls a "continuum of conflict and dialogue" where Indigenous knowledge systems are constantly having to adapt, adopt, reject, or ignore the global design.

The second mechanism through which this subordinated position is maintained is connected to what Francis Rains (1999) calls "historical amnesia," whereby the global design of the Western epistemic tradition dismisses thousands of years of Indigenous knowledge production:

> It is an interesting system, this "Western" knowledge production – it is self contained, self-sustaining, handy, convenient, and even tinged with a sense of righteousness ... Hermetically sealed, the closed system of "Western" knowledge production has been institutionalized, in a matter of several hundred years, to such a degree as to dismiss Indigenous knowledges based on thousands of years of experience, analysis, and reflection as primitive (317).

And, even in ignoring these systems of knowledge, Western epistemes have also conveniently forgotten the knowledge that they appropriated from many of these systems in the first place. As Farah Shroff (2000) notes in her discussion of the history of ayurvedic Indian medicine, the Portuguese and British colonial systems in India at first valued the skill of the ayurvedic doctors, but later, under British rule, the two main ayurvedic universities were destroyed and many of the researchers put in jail. This history is conveniently forgotten when ayurvedic medicine is discredited in contemporary times by the Western medical system.

But, as Dei et al. (2000) note above, Indigenous knowledges are resurfacing, partly as a result of the growing critique of the global design of Western epistemologies. Many new practitioners of allopathic/Western medicine are looking towards and learning from different epistemologies of health and wellness. One such story is found in Sarkar's chapter in this collection. Even in Ghana, these transformations are taking place, with traditional birth attendants now being recognized by the Ministry of Health, and with a traditional health practitioners association having been established in order to better integrate traditional health practice into the allopathic government system. But even as these transitions are taking place, it is important to recognize the continued adjustments being forced on traditional/Indigenous health and wellness systems by the government-run allopathic system. The power relationship between these two systems is still clear, and it is only in locations like northern Ghana, where the allopathic system is miserably under-staffed and under-resourced, that the bonesetters are given room to practice their approach to health without interference – and indeed with a grudging sense of respect from the allopathic practitioners in the area (interview with district chief medical officer, 2006).

This power relationship needs to be further explored here as it is instrumental to the ways in which hierarchies of knowledge are maintained, despite the well educated choices of residents in Wale Wale. In a typically Western allopathic evaluation of bonesetting and its "effectiveness" in Mexico, a study showed that the techniques used by the Indigenous bonesetter at the center of the study were based on "rational" approaches to dealing with fractures (Anderson, 1987). Thus, this bonesetter's practice was "approved" – something the thousands of patients he has a year could have easily told the research team prior to their study. A more recent study of Mayan bonesetter practice notes that the Guatemalan medical establishment has consistently questioned the capabilities of these bonesetters, suggesting that their practice is potentially harmful to patients as the bonesetters have not been trained in "Western trauma techniques" (Hinajosa, 2002, p. 22). Both of these studies reveal the hierachies of health epistemologies, where a practice that has passed through generations of patient approval is being evaluated not on the basis of the opinions of these patients, but rather on whether the techniques and rationale used by bonesetters match the Western process of dealing with broken bones. In Ghana, however, a very recent study carried out in the Brong Ahafo Region examined the question of bonesetter effectiveness from the vantage point of patients rather than from that of Western trained clinicians (Aries et al., 2007). The study revealed much the same attitude that our investigations show: bonesetters are held in high esteem by local populations, not just for their affordability but also for their technical prowess. The study found that 29 out of 43 patients chose to have their broken bones treated by bonesetters rather than the by government medical hospitals or clinics. The article goes on to conclude that there is a real potential that "Fracture treatment can serve as a model for respectful and efficient co-existence of traditional and biomedical medicine" (Aries et al., 2007, p. 564). Despite this progressive stance, and the recognition the study accords bonesetters, there is still a flaw in the approach in that the treatment methods used by bonesetters are still reviewed from a biomedical perspective, and the epistemic underpinnings of this approach are largely ignored. Much as the allopathic method itself focuses largely on the ailment, rather than on a holistic engagement with the lifestyle and environment of the individual involved, this study largely focuses on the practice of bonesetters and on the opinion of patients rather than trying to see the root philosophy of wellness from which the practice springs. In terms of power relations, even from the perspective of this last more sympathetic article, it is still through the lens of allopathic and biomedical epistemology that other epistemes of wellness are judged.

As a final point before delving more fully into the practice and philosophy of wellness of the bonesetter near Wale Wale, it is appropriate to return to the cycle and continuum of conflict and dialogue Maurial (1999) discusses, and to pause and think through how a more balanced approach to dialogue, rather than conflict, between contending local histories might be enacted. In discussing the potential mutual benefit Indigenous knowledges and Western academic knowledges could gain from each other, Semali and Kincheloe (1999) suggest that there needs to be a dialogue without resolution. Similarly, Mignolo (2000) critiques Bhabha's notion of hybridity – one possible result of merging two epistemic traditions – as he believes this would be a synthesis that denies the separate nature of the two local histories. Thus, from a dialogical perspective, thesis and anti-thesis must be in constant dialogue, yet they must avoid the modernist desire for synthesis, because synthesis comes with the potential for absorption of ideas and influences coupled with modernist amnesia that forgets to accord due respect to the source of ideas, and instead uses hierarchies of knowledge to discredit them. From this perspective there cannot be a finality in this continuum, as finality where there continues to be a hierarchy of knowledge leads necessarily to appropriation and assimilation. This then lends greater weight to Maurial's emphasis that in situations faced by Indigenous epistemologies, what must be worked for is not the acceptance and absorption of these ways of knowing by Western informed epistemologies, but rather an ongoing cycle of dialogue between the epistemes that allows both to maintain their own processes of knowledge production, yet also remain open to influence from the other. Like Maurial, we are convinced this is the only way to avoid or reduce the other aspect of her continuum, conflict.

BONESETTING, A PHILOSOPHY OF WELLNESS

Chief Isshaku Gumrana Mahamadu is the leader of a small town called Loagri, just outside of Wale wale. His position as chief also makes him the head of his clan, from which his line of bonesetters come. Over the course of the past 4 years, we have established a strong relationship with him, and with the Loagri community. This relationship has been fundamental in establishing the necessary foundation for our conversations. Through this process of dialogue both of us have learned a great deal about how to approach the notion of wellness, even as we have been privileged to develop a growing understanding of elements of Chief Isshaku's practice. There are four aspects of what we learned from Isshaku that we wish to share here in order to a) contribute to dialogue concerning Indigenous ways of knowing, and b) confront the global design that has attempted to place Isshaku's knowledge on a lower level than allopathic methods of dealing with ailments. These four elements include: 1) the historical background of Loagri bonesetting; 2) the philosophy of holistic wellness that informs Chief Isshaku's practice; 3) the core elements of his practice; and 4) the principles of formation of future bonesetters.

Chief Isshaku's clan has been practicing bonesetting in Loagri for six generations. The bonesetter operates in a web of other traditional wellness practitioners, including soothsayers who help diagnose the source of a problem, and herbalists who use generations of local environmental knowledge to create medications to help address ailments. These are not strict specialist boundaries, however, as in some cases – such as in Isshaku's clan – bonesetters serve as both herbalists and bonesetters. Their generations of knowledge of the local environment have afforded Loagri bonesetters a vast knowledge of different herbs that can be used to assist in the healing of broken bones. Isshaku has, however, noted that with the changing environment, and with the growing pressure on the land for food production due to population growth and land degradation, it is becoming more and more difficult to locate the herbs he needs to practice. As such he is forced to send his apprentices further and further afield to find the necessary herbs (interview with Chief Isshaku, 2007).

This recognition of the changing nature of the landscape is something Chief Isshaku has had to contend with as a result of the changing nature of Northern Ghana. Not only has a major highway cut his community in half, but the growing number of people who seek out his help has meant he has had to seek assistance from the district level government to build local-style hostels to accomodate the number of patients. Because of his close proximity to the highway, his practice has also had to contend with the curiosity of foreigners, as well as those travelling up and down the highway. For example, a group of Canadian students have made both physical and fundraising contributions towards building these hostels – a wonderful and needed helping hand, but also a source of strain as these students often need much hands-on guidance. These changes, added to the environmental changes, have meant that Chief Isshaku has had to show flexibility in adapting his practice to contemporary times (interview with Chief Isshaku, 2007).

But, despite these changes, Chief Isshaku has not changed his underlying philosophy of patient care. Unlike the allopathic method, which aims to diagnose an ailment based on the logic of deduction derived from the symptoms at hand, Isshaku believes that treating a broken bone is only one element of patient care. The most important aspect of his treatment is connected to understanding the larger issues in a patient's life that led him or her to break his/her bone. This philosophic approach is demonstrated by the manner in which Isshaku describes the various conditions of the patients in his care. He will usually begin far before the event that led to them breaking a bone, and he may even connect it to issues embedded in the ancestral past, if he knows enough of the patient's history. The event that led to the break will be put in context, even as it becomes part of the patient's story of recovery as well. In this way, a broken bone is seen as only one episode in a full life. This holistic view of patients as humans is also evident in his approach to keeping track of those who have come under his care. When asked for an estimate of the number of patients his village sees in a month, Isshaku describes the stories of those who have come, seeing each as a unique human interconnected with the world, rather than merely quoting the number of patients he has treated (interview with Chief Isshaku, 2007).

Similarly, the breaking of a bone is interlinked with the wider world outside the purview of the individual. A practice common to all bonesetters in Ghana is the use of a chicken as a symbolic connection between the patient and the wider environment. The chicken is given a broken appendage to match that of the patient's, and then is treated along side the patient. It is believed that if the chicken recovers, so too will the patient. This same technique is documented in the study mentioned above (Aires et al., 2007).

The other major features of Chief Isshaku's approach to wellness are also at variance with the contemporary manifestation of the allopathic method (though the Hippocratic oath may emulate some aspects of it). For instance, it goes fundamentally against Chief Isshaku's practice to ask for any payment for his treatment. The only cost associated with his attention is the cost of the chicken. It is his belief that the moment he asks for payment or reward for any treatment he gives will be the moment he loses his power to heal. In this sense, he sees his abilities as being bigger than himself, grounded in the generations of people who have gone before who give him the ability to help people. The patients in Loagri are treated as welcome guests, with many staying for long periods in homes throughout the community. This strikes at the core principle of never turning away people who need help. This is the main reason Chief Isshaku has asked for help to build the hostels; their presence will allow the families of patients some privacy so that they can stay longer and help care for their family members (interview with Chief Isshaku, 2007).

Added to this, one cannot overlook the importance of pain in the philosophy of wellness. Unlike the contemporary allopathic practice of sedation, pain is central to healing according to Chief Isshaku. It is a necessary part of the healing process. Isshaku demands the active engagement of his patients in their treatment, asking them to hold parts of their broken bone, or to help hold a bandage in place while it is tightened. This makes patients active agents in their own recovery, even as it forces them to live in the middle of the pain of their treatment (interview with Chief Isshaku, 2007).

In terms of the practice of bonesetting in Loagri, much is still shrouded in mystery. Although the role of the chicken is understood, the type and amount of herbs used for healing are a close kept secret. Additionally, the exact process through which a compound fracture is dealt with – using massage and rebuilding the structure of a bone piece by piece – is something which cannot be visibly observed. Broken bones that have not mended properly often need to be rebroken, something that is again done based on feeling the bone in question. Unlike his contemporaries decribed in the Aires et al. (2007) study of bonesetters in Ghana, Isshaku does not request a x-ray in order to determine the nature of a fracture. His practice is based on decades of training, and his sense of the health of a particular bone cannot be removed from his sense of the person, nor of the life s/he leads, nor the world s/he is a part of. All of this information assists Isshaku in helping patients – aspects which are completely ignored in common allopathic practice (interview with Chief Isshaku, 2007).

Finally, Chief Isshaku's description of the formation of the next generation of bonesetters also signals a vast difference from the allopathic method. The common joke told about what to call a medical school graduate who finishes last in his or her class is apt here: if this person also retains the title doctor, then doesn't one get worried about the quality of the care one might receive in his or her hands? In the case of bonesetting education, the period of formation is decades long, and is rarely complete until the day the current bonesetter passes on. All of Chief Isshaku's sons and nephews are potential bonesetters, but are under his constant watch; he waits to see which of them will show the true talent of connecting all the different qualities necessary to become a bonesetter: a meticulous approach to work and excellent retentive memory; a deep understanding of the necessity of never charging for care; a fundamental sense of the dignity and humanity of every patient; and, a high level of tolerance and respect. When one considers how much time most allopathic medical schools spend on these matters as compared to classes in anatomy and diagnostics, it is easy to see a glaringly different underlying approach to education.

In the allopathic tradition it is hoped that a doctor will behave ethically. In the bonesetter's tradition, this is the very foundation of practice (interview with Chief Isshaku, 2007).

CONCLUSION

In this last section, we wish to return to the statement of the elder in Wale Wale, who said that the bonesetter and the allopathic government hospital were "not the same at all." As mentioned above, the anecdotal evidence we have collected over the last four years suggests that the bonesetter features prominently in the wellness thinking of the people of the West Mamprusi district, as well as in the lives of those who have accidents along the length and breath of the highway that transects the district. We feel it is important to share some of these stories as they reveal much about the place of this system of care in the social imaginary of the people in the area.

Despite the fact that the bonesetter is often associated with those who cannot afford to pay for the expensive health services at government hospitals, there are many cases that we both know about where people with means, and with a Western-style education, have left the government hospital to seek out the bonesetter. One friend who had been working very hard, going from community to community, to monitor a major infrastructure project in the north, had a bad car accident as a result of his tiredness. In his subsequent recovery period, his broken leg mended badly and he was told he may never walk normally again. And then he was brought the huge bill for this terrible news. Luckily, he was told of one of the bonesetters operating in the north, and after going to him and having his leg re-broken and re-set, he is now able to walk again. He still speaks fondly of the time he spent living in the bonesetter's household. In this sense, bonesetters serve a wide community of people the allopathic system fails. Also, the bonesetters never discriminate based on wealth – a striking difference with contemporary allopathic practice.

But it must be recognized that bonesetters have their limits, even as the allopathic centers in Wale Wale have recognized they cannot treat fractures nearly as well as Chief Isshaku (interview with district chief medical officer, 2006). Patients know this too. In another story told to us, a young man who had been living in Japan for many years returned to Ghana and was on his way to Wale Wale to visit his parents when he had a car accident. After he had been stabilized for his internal wounds at the district hospital, he informed the staff there that he was leaving to have his broken leg and arm treated by Chief Isshaku. Isshaku still tells of the scene where this young man showed up still wearing the hospital's gown and holding his IV bag in his good arm.

The fluidity of bonesetter's practice is also something we have both observed. A patient we knew well had been abandoned in the Tamale regional hospital in the capital of the north, and begged to be taken to the bonesetter. Once there, the bonesetter realized the patient in question was depleted – something referred to as anaemia in the allopathic tradition – and instead of breaking the chicken's bone to become a symbolic twin to the patient's compound fracture, the bonesetter added the chicken to a medicinal soup that fortified the patient for the procedure to come.

All of these stories and many more are evidence that bonesetting is a critical component of the wellness of people from Wale Wale and beyond. It is critical that this role be properly recognized for respectful co-existence to not only continue, but also to deepen into a much stronger sense of the epistemic value both of these practices offer. In many ways the people of West Mamprusi are lucky to have access to such a rich and deeply rooted path to wellness. What is of great concern to us is the way in which current efforts to integrate Indigenous health knowledge into the allopathic method are stripping the knowledge of its philosophy and respect for those who have gone before, those still living and those who have yet to come, and selling off the practices and approaches for profit. Thankfully, Wale Wale is far enough from the country's capital to forestall this integration for now, and the relationship between the bonesetter and the chief medical officer is both appreciative and respectful. Yet these realities cannot last for ever, and some better arrangement must be found whereby the depth of bonesetting as a practice is recognized and given its own space to exist, even as it recognizes some of the inherent benefits of the allopathic method. This dialogue without synthesis or resolution is the best way to guarantee the continued choice for residents in Wale Wale of two paths to wellness that "are not the same".

REFERENCES/BIBLIOGRAPHY

Anderson, R. (1987). The treatment of musculoskeletal disorders by a Mexican bonesetter (sobador). *Social Science & Medicine, 24*(1), 43–46.
Ariës, M. J. H., Joosten, H., Wegdam, H. H. J., & van der Geest, S. (2007). Fracture treatment by bonesetters in central Ghana: patients explain their choices and experiences. *Tropical Medicine and International Health, 12*(4), 564–574.
Dei, G. J. S., Hall, B. L., & Rosenberg, D. G. (Eds.). (2000). *Indigenous knowledges in global contexts: Multiple readings of our world*. Toronto: University of Toronto Press.
Gariba, S., & Langdon, J. (Eds.). (2005). *Community voices: A civil society assessment of the pro-poor policies and programmes of Ghana's Poverty Reduction Strategy (GPRS) from 2004–2005*. Accra, Ghana: Institute for Policy Alternatives.
Hinojosa, S. Z. (2002). "The hands know": Bodily engagement and medical impasse in highland Maya bonesetting. *Medical Anthropology Quarterly, 16*(1), 22–40.
Hutchful, E. (2002). *Ghana's adjustment experience: The paradox of reform*. Geneva: UNRI.
Maurial, M. (1999). Indigenous knowledge in schooling: a continuum between conflict and dialogue. In L. Semali & J. Kincheloe (Eds.), *What is Indigenous knowledge: Voices from the academy*. New York: Falmer Press.
McCarty, T., Borgoiakova, T., Gilmore, P., Lomawaima, T., & Romero, M. (2005). Editors' introduction: Indigenous epistemologies and education – self-determination, anthropology, and human rights. *Anthropology and Education Quarterly, 36*(1), 1–7.
Mignolo, W. (2000). *Local histories/global designs: Coloniality, subaltern knowledges and border thinking*. New Jersey, NJ: Princeton UP.
Rains, F. (1999). Indigenous knowledge, historical amnesia and intellectual authority: Deconstructing hegemony and the social and political implications of the curricular "other". In L. Semali & J. Kincheloe (Eds.), *What is Indigenous knowledge: Voices from the academy*. New York: Falmer Press.

Rist, G. (1997). *The history of development: From western origin to global faith.* London: Zed.

Saaka, Y. (Ed.). (2001). *Regionalism and public policy in northern Ghana.* New York: Peter Lang.

Semali, L., & Kincheloe, J. (1999). Introduction: What is Indigenous knowledge and why should we study it. In L. Semali & J. Kincheloe (Eds.), *What is Indigenous knowledge: Voices from the academy.* New York: Falmer Press.

Shroff, F. (2000). Ayurveda: Mother of Indigenous health knowledge. In G. J. S. Dei, B. L. Hall, & D. G. Rosenberg (Eds.), *Indigenous knowledges in global contexts: Multiple readings of our world.* Toronto: University of Toronto Press.

Wright, R. (2004). *A short history of progress.* Toronto: Anansi Press.

LIST OF CONTRIBUTORS

Coleman Agyeyomah is the Executive Director of Venceramos Consulting, with over 20 years of experience in community and local development. He also recently completed a Masters degree at Leeds University in the UK, where he critically examined conventional notions of local development, especially from the perspective of Indigenous epistemologies. Although this Masters was an important opportunity to reflect on the current state of the development industry, from his perspective, the only education that has ever mattered has been what he garnered through years of working with communities throughout Northern Ghana.

Janine Metallic, a Mi'gmaq from the Listuguj First Nation, is a doctoral student in the Department of Integrated Studies in Education, McGill University. Her research interests include Indigenous knowledge, language revitalization, and science education.

Blane Harvey has been working for the last several years between international organizations and small Southern organizations coping with the consequences of climate change and ecological degradation. These experiences have been key inspirations to his research. His most recent work has been with peasant groups in eastern Senegal who have both benefited from and struggled with repeated development interventions in their communities. He is currently working with the Institute of Development Studies, University of Sussex, helping to build networks to address climate change.

Christine Stocek has been involved living and working in Wemindji, in Northern Quebec, on a number of culturally sensitive projects as a non-native employee, and volunteer. She is now engaged in a Participatory Action Research (PAR) project in Wemindji involving collaboration with a group of local artists. She is also a PhD candidate and researcher at McGill University.

Jonathan Langdon has been engaged in working with local organizations and movements in Ghana for the last 10 years. This work has always been grounded in privileging local notions of development, learning and knowledge over those determined by outside agencies – be they at the national or international level. In the Ghanaian context, the majority of his work has been based in Northern Ghana – the most underprivileged section of the country. This work has consisted of, amongst others, an assessment of health, education and local government services from community perspectives, and a study of the ways in which Indigenous forms of justice are accessed by the poor. He is currently in the final stages of completing a PhD at McGill University, where his dissertation is grounded in a participatory assessment of social movement learning in Ghana.

CONTRIBUTORS

Rodney Mark began to work for the Cree Nation of Wemindji, in Northern Quebec, as Youth Chief, then became Deputy Chief and is now the Chief of Wemindji's Band Council. He has been engaged in questioning received notions of governance, asking instead how to conceive of governance from a Cree perspective.

Marlon Simmons is a PhD Candidate in the Department of Sociology and Equity Studies at the Ontario Institute for Studies in Education, University of Toronto. His current research interests include anti-colonial thought, issues of governance and self in the context of schooling, Indigenous ways of knowing and educational reform. The focus of his thesis is on modernity and colonialism, with a particular attention to Diasporic experiences and the interplay in Canada. His concern with Diasporic experiences grew from a lived experience with Indigenous Caribbean languages.

Mela Sarkar is based in Montreal, Quebec, Canada, where she teaches and does applied linguistics research at McGill University's Faculty of Education. Her research focus is the linguistic empowerment of marginalized minority-language speakers within majority societies. Originally from Toronto, she has roots in Canada's South Asian (Bengali) and Ukrainian communities. Her research projects have included the French language learning of South Asians in Montreal, the creatively mixed language of rap that is emerging from Montreal's multiethnic hip-hop community, and, most recently, revitalization initiatives for endangered First Nations languages in Canada. With teachers at Listuguj First Nation (QC), she has worked on how to best teach the Mi'gmaq language to adults in the community, using an approach that respects Indigenous learning styles.

George Sefa Dei is currently Professor of Sociology and Equity Studies, Ontario Institute for Studies in Education of the University of Toronto (OISE/UT). His teaching and research interests are in the areas of Anti-Racism, Minority Schooling, International Development, Indigenous Knowledges, and Anti-Colonial Thought. Between 1996 and 2000 he served as the first Director of the Centre for Integrative Anti-Racism Studies at OISE/UT. For the 2007 – 2008 school year he has been a Visiting Professor at the Centre for School and Community Science and Technology Studies (SACOST), University of Education, Winneba, Ghana. In June 2007, he was installed as a traditional chief, specifically, as the Adumakwaahene of the town of Asokore, near Koforidua in the New Juaben Traditional Area of Ghana.